The United States and the Genocide Convention

The United States and the Genocide Convention

Lawrence J. LeBlanc

Duke University Press *Durham and London 1991*

Printed in the United States of America
on acid-free paper ∞
Library of Congress Cataloging-in-Publication Data
appear on the last printed page of this book.

For Mary, Liz, and David

Contents

Tables

Acknowledgments

The research and writing of this book have taken up a good part of my time over the last several years, and I am grateful to many persons who helped to bring the project to a close. Among these, I am especially indebted to Vernon Van Dyke, David Forsythe, Howard Tolley, Jr., Robert Beck, Natalie Kaufman, James Allison, and anonymous reviewers for Duke University Press, all of whom read the entire manuscript and made many helpful suggestions that improved the final product. In addition, Michael Switalski, James Marlin, Jeanne Bruns, Arthur Blaser, Tom Cunningham, Benedict Kingsbury, Daniel Turack, Margaret Courtright, Karen Greenstreet, and Ken Farmer read parts of the manuscript and shared with me their suggestions and encouragement. Despite the good help I have received from all of these persons, the usual disclaimer applies: I alone am responsible for any errors of fact or interpretation that remain.

I am also grateful to several persons on U.S. Senator William Proxmire's staff. In particular, I wish to thank Fred Duperrault for cheerfully attending with great efficiency to all my requests for information and documentation; and Larry Patton, an acknowledged key player in the ratification debate in the Senate, for sharing with me his insight into the politics of the ratification process.

Thaddeus J. Burch, S.J., Dean of the Marquette University Graduate School and Chair of its Committee on Research, generously provided me with faculty development grants in 1989 and 1990 that facilitated the final preparation of the manuscript. Reynolds Smith, my editor at Duke University Press, gave generously of his time and energy in seeing the manuscript through to publication.

Previous versions of chapters 3, 4, and 9 were published in *The American Journal of International Law* (vol. 78, 1984), the *Yale Journal of International Law* (vol. 13, 1988), and *Wisconsin International Law Journal* (vol. 6, 1987), respectively. The passage of time since the publication of these articles necessitated substantial revision of the arguments I had made. Nonetheless,

I was able to use some passages from the articles, and I wish to thank the editors of these journals for granting me permission to include those passages in this book.

Finally, my special thanks go to my wife, Mary, who read and provided friendly criticism of different drafts of the manuscript through the years. I could not have completed the book without her help and support.

Chapter 1 Introduction

And, who opposes the Genocide Treaty? The John Birch Society, Phyllis Schlafly's Eagle Forum, the Liberty Lobby, and a few other far-out, extreme fringe groups. The groups that oppose the Genocide Treaty constitute a politician's dream of what each of us dearly wish we could identify with our opponent. . . . —Senator William Proxmire, Senate floor debate, February 1986

This book examines issues and problems related to the ratification of the Genocide Convention by the United States. The systematic annihilation of millions of Jews and members of other groups by the Nazis during World War II provided the impetus for the adoption of this convention. The word "genocide" was, in fact, coined to apply to situations in which individuals become the object of destruction not for any reason peculiar to them but simply because they are members of an identifiable group. The United Nations General Assembly discussed the subject in 1946 and decided to sponsor an international legal instrument concerning it. Work on the draft convention was completed about two years later, and it was adopted by the General Assembly on December 9, 1948, unanimously and without abstentions.[1] Although the convention was adopted amid substantial skepticism regarding its potential effectiveness, enough countries ratified it to bring it into effect on January 12, 1951. It has since been ratified by many other countries, including the Western powers who are allies of the United States, bringing the total number of parties to 102.[2]

In the United States, however, the question of whether or not the convention should be ratified became the subject of sporadic, acrimonious debate for almost forty years, extending from June 1949, when President Harry S Truman requested the Senate's advice and consent to ratification of the convention, to February 1986, when the Senate adopted a resolution of ratification. The Senate vote on the resolution was overwhelming: eighty-three in favor, eleven against, and six not voting[3] — a margin well beyond the two-thirds present and voting required to approve a treaty. Even then the United States did not immediately become a party to the convention because the Senate resolution, otherwise known as the Lugar-Helms-Hatch Sovereignty Package, consented to ratification conditionally—subject to two "reservations," five "understandings," and a "declaration" that the United States would not deposit its instrument of ratification at the United Nations until Congress enacted domestic legislation to implement the convention.[4] This legislation itself became controversial, though a bill, the Genocide Convention Implementation Act, was passed in October 1988.[5] In November 1988 President Ronald Reagan deposited the U.S. instrument of ratification at the United Nations. The instrument included all of the conditions specified in the Sovereignty Package, except, of course, the declaration regarding the implementing legislation.[6] According to Article XIII of the Genocide Convention, the convention became binding on the United States ninety days later, in February 1989.

Given the nature of the crime of genocide, why should proposals to ratify the Genocide Convention have engendered such protracted debate? The widespread ratification of the convention by other states does not, of course, necessarily lead to the conclusion that the United States, too, should have ratified it long ago, but it raises the question of why it did not. The extended, if sporadic, debate, the conditional nature of the resolution of ratification that was adopted in 1986, and the controversy over the passage of the implementing legislation in 1988 all suggest that proposals to ratify the Genocide Convention raised serious issues in the minds of opponents. But what were those issues? What arguments were advanced, and how cogent were they? What solutions were put forth to resolve the issues, and what are their possible or probable implications? These are among the questions dealt with in this book.

My concern with the controversy over ratification of the Genocide Convention should not be understood to mean that I attach undue importance to the act of ratification itself.[7] In fact, there are reasons for pessimism about what the formality of ratification alone achieves. After all, broad acceptance of the convention has not resulted in the achievement of its two principal objectives—the prevention and punishment of the crime of genocide. Since World War II, genocide is alleged to have occurred in various regions of the world: in Africa, against tribal groups in various countries, including Burundi, Rwanda, and Uganda; in Latin America, against primitive Indian tribes in Paraguay and Brazil; in Asia, during the breakup of India in the late 1940s, the creation of Bangladesh in the early

1970s, the struggle for control of Cambodia (formerly Democratic Kampuchea) by the Khmer Rouge in the 1970s, and the suppression of Tamil separatists in Sri Lanka during the 1980s.

Case studies of these and other episodes provide persuasive evidence that the crime of genocide has occurred. In fact, the evidence suggests that some of the parties to the Genocide Convention have violated it with impunity, with no serious effort being made at the international level to hold them accountable. It is therefore not surprising that some scholars and human rights activists have expressed skepticism and even cynicism regarding the potential effects that ratification of the Genocide Convention would have. These skeptics, including some who have endorsed ratification, have emphasized the need to develop techniques and strategies that could be employed to prevent the occurrence of genocide, not just outlaw it. In this connection, some have called upon individuals and international nongovernmental organizations to exercise vigilance in combating genocide. Some have promoted the development of a genocide "early warning system" that could monitor, report, and predict the trends and factors leading to genocide and other basic human rights violations.[8] Some have suggested the creation of a committee on genocide consisting of experts who would function like the committees established under other international human rights instruments.[9]

Undoubtedly, the persistence of genocide calls for action by individuals and nongovernmental organizations. But this would not obviate the need for action by states, and agreeing to an internationally recognized and accepted rule on genocide, and insisting on compliance with it, are ways in which states can act. Despite the difficulties that might attend the enforcement of the Genocide Convention, we should not assume that it is pointless to endorse the rule on genocide affirmed in it simply because it may be difficult to enforce.

Moreover, practical benefits could accompany ratification of the convention. Genocide is a crime under customary international law. The International Court of Justice (ICJ) said as much in an advisory opinion it issued in 1951 in connection with reservations some states had made upon ratifying the convention;[10] and the United States apparently agrees, as indicated in the authoritative *Restatement of the Foreign Relations Law of the United States.*[11] Precisely what the content of that customary law is, and whether or not it differs in any meaningful way from the law established by the convention, remain unclear. Ratification of the convention could help to clarify this issue so far as the United States is concerned. It could also strengthen the hand of the United States in international forums in dealing with allegations of genocide. Many diplomats who have represented the United States at international conferences have testified that by not ratifying the Genocide Convention the United States effectively deprived itself of any basis for speaking out, even for demanding that an investigation be carried out, in instances of alleged genocide. Any attempt to raise the issue would, understandably, lead others to charge that the United States was being hypocritical: how could it profess to be concerned about genocide if it refused to ratify the one international legal instrument that pertains to it? Some have argued that the failure to ratify has undermined U.S. efforts on behalf of human rights generally.[12]

The disagreements over the merits of ratifying the Genocide Convention are so profound and long-standing that they are likely to persist into the future, even though the United States has at last become a party. A study of the controversy over its ratification is important for two main reasons. In the first place, the question of whether or not the convention should be ratified was an issue in U.S. foreign policy for many years. Yet, apart from a few studies that have dealt with specific aspects of the controversy over its ratification, we know relatively little about the issues and problems that arose in the debate and how they were resolved. Nor do we know very much about the main participants in the debate and their strategies and tactics. Second, despite the adoption of a resolution of ratification in February 1986, the convention could remain an issue in foreign policy in years to come because of the conditional nature of the resolution.

Ratification as a Foreign Policy Issue

The question of whether or not any treaty should be ratified by the United States is fundamentally a matter of foreign policy. In other words, it is a political issue whose resolution can be characterized by conflict as much as by cooperation. In fact, in the realm of foreign policy, the U.S. Constitution invites both conflict and cooperation between the executive and legislative branches of the government.[13] As we shall see, the U.S. experience in dealing with the Genocide Convention amply demonstrates this point in regard to the exercise of the treaty-making power.

The treaty-making power, broadly conceived, is a shared power. According to Article II, section 2, of the U.S. Constitution, presidents have the power, "by and with the Advice and Consent of the Senate, to make treaties, provided two-thirds of the Senators present concur." Historically, problems have arisen in interpreting various aspects of this clause. How do presidents "make" treaties? What does it mean to say that the Senate gives "advice and consent" to treaties? Does the Senate have a role to play in the negotiation of treaties, or is its role limited to the approval of treaties? These questions have been answered in practice. Presidents or their designated representatives have dominated the negotiating process, so the making of treaties has come to be understood as an executive function. On some occasions presidents have included members of the legislative branch in the negotiation process, as occurred, for example, when the United Nations Charter was drafted, but by and large the Senate's role in the treaty-making process has been to give or withhold its approval. Should it give its approval, the president then proclaims (ratifies) the treaty.[14]

The potential for conflict in the treaty-making process is therefore quite great. A president may or may not choose to seek the Senate's advice and consent to the ratification of a treaty, and his decision will probably depend at least in part on what he perceives the national interest of the United States to be. The Senate may or may not decide to give its consent, and its decision may reflect a different conception of the national interest. Most presidents since World War II have perceived ratification of the Genocide Convention as being in the interest of the United States. In fact, with the exception of President Dwight D. Eisenhower, for reasons discussed later, all presidents since Truman have endorsed ratification, though some, notably Richard Nixon, Jimmy Carter, and Ronald Reagan, pushed harder for ratification than others. But the presidents faced formidable opposition in the Senate.

It is ironic that the issue should ever have become so controversial. The U.S. delegation to the United Nations participated actively in the negotiations that led to the convention's adoption, and, whatever misgivings they might have had about any of its provisions, they shared in the broad consensus on the instrument as a whole. A representative of the United States signed the convention, indicating agreement in principle with what it provides. Therefore, President Truman might have believed that the Senate would treat his request for advice and consent to ratification of the convention in June 1949 as a routine matter. Instead, it was then that the long and bitter struggle over ratification began.

A subcommittee of the Senate Committee on Foreign Relations held hearings on the Genocide Convention in 1950. It recommended ratification, but in the face of vigorous opposition from some senators and from powerful and influential organizations such as the American Bar Association (ABA) the full committee failed to report the convention to the Senate. During the 1970s Presidents Nixon and Carter urged the Senate to reconsider the convention. Their efforts produced somewhat different results from those of President Truman, but not ratification. The Committee on Foreign Relations or subcommittees thereof held hearings on the convention in 1970, 1971, and 1977, and favorably reported it to the Senate in 1970, 1971, 1973, and 1976.[15] Throughout all these years, however, the Senate actually debated the possibility of adopting a resolution of ratification only once, in 1973–74, and it fell victim to a filibuster. The committee held hearings again during the Reagan administration in 1981, 1984, and 1985. In 1984 another filibuster prevented the adoption of a resolution of ratification. Instead, the Senate adopted a nonbinding sense of the Senate resolution in which it endorsed the principles affirmed in the convention and pledged to act expeditiously on it when the new Congress convened in 1985.[16] The Senate did not actually adopt a resolution of ratification, however, until February 1986.

Throughout these years the Genocide Convention was the subject of intensely emotional debate that stimulated extraordinary action. Senator William Proxmire (D., Wisconsin), for example, unquestionably the leading proponent of ratification, spoke in its favor every day the Senate was in session from 1967 until the resolution of ratification was adopted in 1986—over three thousand speeches. In recognition of his important contributions to the ratification effort, the Senate Committee on the Judiciary decided that the Genocide Convention Implementation Act of 1988 would also be known as the Proxmire Act. On the other side, the most outspoken opponents of ratification were Senators Sam Ervin, Jr. (D., North Carolina), and Jesse Helms (R., North Carolina). They either engaged in, or threatened to engage in, filibusters to prevent ratification. Prominent individuals and organizations of various kinds also became involved in the controversy that surrounded the ratification effort. The debate, as we shall see in this book, was oftentimes characterized by profound concern among the most outspoken critics of the convention that it could be applied to race relations within the United States; that is, the convention could become a tool in the civil rights struggle. There was concern that the United States could be held accountable for genocide against groups like blacks and Native Americans. Although the resolution of ratification that was eventually adopted was supported by an overwhelming margin that cut across party and ideological lines, all eleven senators who voted against it were extremely conservative Republicans: Jeremiah Denton (Alabama), John East (North Carolina), Jake Garn (Utah), Barry Goldwater (Arizona), Charles Grassley (Iowa), Jesse Helms (North Carolina), James McClure (Idaho), William Roth (Delaware), Steven Symms (Idaho), Strom Thurmond (South Carolina), and Malcolm Wallop (Wyoming).[17]

By the time the Senate adopted the resolution of ratification in February 1986, the Genocide Convention had been pending Senate action longer than any other treaty. Nonetheless, apart from a few studies that have focused on specific aspects of the controversy, we know relatively little about the issues and problems that arose in the debate over ratification of the convention, or how they were resolved. A study that provides a comprehensive analysis of these issues and problems, as this book aims to do, could be of broader interest and significance than for the insight and knowledge it would contribute regarding the struggle over the ratification of the Genocide Convention alone. It may also throw light on what we might expect should the Senate ever turn its attention to other international instruments of a similar nature. The Genocide Convention is, technically, an international criminal law convention, though it is commonly perceived to belong to the larger category of human rights instruments that have been adopted by the United Nations and other international organizations since World War II. A number of such instruments await Senate action, including the International Covenant on Civil and Political Rights, the Covenant on Economic, Social, and Cultural Rights, the Convention on the Elimination of All Forms of Racial Discrimination, and the American Convention on Human Rights. President Carter signed these instruments when he visited the United Nations and the Organization of American States in 1977, and he then transmitted them to the Senate and requested its advice and consent to their ratification.[18] If experience with the Genocide Convention provides any insight into the likely fate of these instruments, and it probably does, they will remain in committee for many years to come.

The Conditions of Ratification

The second reason why the controversy over the ratification of the Genocide Convention by the United States is important concerns the resolution of ratification. As we have seen, the resolution, the so-called Lugar-Helms-Hatch Sovereignty Package, consented to ratification conditionally. The fact that these conditions came to be regarded as constituting a "sovereignty package" itself suggests that, collectively, they were intended to seriously qualify the nature of the international obligation the United States was proposing to assume by ratifying the convention. Would such suspicions of the United States's intentions have any merit? Put another way, do the terms of the Sovereignty Package suggest that U.S. ratification of the Genocide Convention was only of symbolic significance? The question is important in view of the fact that the convention has already been ratified by over one hundred states, and under the international rules of treaty law these states have a say in determining whether or not the U.S. conditions are acceptable. Moreover, even if the other parties to the convention raise no objections to the conditions spelled out by the United States, under the doctrine of reciprocity they could invoke the U.S. conditions in their own defense. Thus, even a party that ratified the convention without a reservation to the role of the International Court of Justice in interpreting and applying the convention could invoke the U.S. reservation to this effect if ever the United States attempted to lodge a complaint against that state before the court. Hence, it is arguable that by insisting on the adoption of the Sovereignty Package, the Senate effectively gutted the U.S. ratification of the convention.

It should be emphasized that the Sovereignty Package was developed pursuant to the Senate's constitutional role in giving advice and consent to the ratification of treaties. Theoretically, when a president requests advice and consent to the ratification of a treaty, the Senate has three options. First, it can reject the treaty, in which case the president cannot ratify it. But the rejection of a treaty, though not unprecedented, is not always a politically viable option. The subject matter of a treaty could be considered so important that its rejection might be perceived as an affront to a president that could undermine his credibility and have adverse international consequences for the country. Or, as appears to have been the case regarding the Genocide Convention, a treaty could be perceived to have a moral quality that rules out action as extreme as rejection. For Senator Proxmire in particular, ratification of the convention was a moral imperative; he also believed it was good foreign policy because the failure of the United States to ratify undermined its leadership role in the field of international action on human rights. Even though eleven senators voted against ratification, most senators seemed to agree with Proxmire that it was a moral imperative and symbolically important.

But what if the Senate, for whatever reasons, cannot approve a treaty as submitted? In such a situation it has no alternative but to delay the treaty's ratification or to consent to its ratification conditionally. In the case of the Genocide Convention, the Senate exercised both of these options: as discussed earlier, it delayed ratification by engaging in sporadic debate on the merits of the convention for almost forty years; and throughout this time it always intended that if ratification were to occur, it would be conditional. In fact, it is noteworthy that the initiative in connection with virtually all of the conditions stipulated in the Lugar-Helms-Hatch Sovereignty Package came from the Senate. It is perhaps more noteworthy that the terms of the package were dictated by the *opponents* of ratification. The chief architect was Senator Jesse Helms, the arch-critic of the convention during the 1980s. Senator Richard Lugar (R., Indiana) played a more passive role in its formulation. At the time the Senate consented to ratification of the convention, Lugar was chairman of the Committee on Foreign Relations, and he ushered the Sovereignty Package through the floor debate. Although he aggressively supported the package, most of the substantive ideas embodied in it came from Senator Helms and, to a lesser extent, from Senator Orrin Hatch (R., Utah), then chairman of the Subcommittee on the Constitution of the Committee on the Judiciary. Hatch chaired hearings of his subcommittee in 1985 that provided much of the rationale for the so-called constitutional reservation in the Sovereignty Package, and he vigorously defended the entire package in Senate floor debate.[19]

The Sovereignty Package covers almost the full range of conditions that the Senate can stipulate when approving the ratification of a treaty. Generally, the Senate can choose among "amendments," "reservations," "understandings," and "declarations." The choice of any of these conditions depends upon the Senate's objectives. Like the basic question of whether or not to consent to the ratification of a treaty, the question of whether or not to consent conditionally is fundamentally a matter of policy. If the Senate decides to consent conditionally, the terms it can stipulate vary in their effects or consequences. The condition with the most far-reaching consequences is an amendment, because it requires that a treaty be renegotiated before it can take effect. The Sovereignty Package contains no amendment, although, as we shall see in chapter 4, the Senate discussed the possibility of amending Article II of the Genocide Convention to expand its coverage to political groups. Declarations, in contrast, are usually less consequential and generally proclaim conditions that must be fulfilled, sometimes prior to actual ratification. A declaration in the Lugar-Helms-Hatch Sovereignty Package stated that the United States would not deposit its instrument of ratification at the United Nations until the Congress passed implementing legislation. That declaration had the effect of postponing the date on which the United States actually became a party to the Genocide Convention by almost three years, until the passage of the Proxmire Act in October 1988.

Reservations and understandings are more commonly stipulated, and potentially more troublesome, conditions. The Lugar-Helms-Hatch Sovereignty Package contains two reservations and five understandings. One reservation is the so-called constitutional reservation mentioned earlier. In effect, it asserts the primacy of the U.S. Constitution over the Genocide Convention. The other reservation pertains to Article IX of the convention, which deals with the role of the International Court of Justice in resolving disputes regarding the interpretation, application, and fulfillment of the convention. The five understandings address a number of matters involving Article II of the convention, which sets forth the basic definition of the crime of genocide, and other articles of the convention that pertain to its enforcement. These reservations and understandings are discussed in later chapters of this book. What is important for the moment is that the difference between these two types of conditions is quite significant and was explained in a 1971 State Department memorandum to the Committee on Foreign Relations. The memorandum was consistent with the terms of the Vienna Convention on the Law of Treaties of 1969, which is generally recognized as the authoritative statement on the law of treaties; it is recognized as such even by the United States, which is not a party.[20]

According to the State Department memorandum, a *reservation* excludes or varies the legal effect of one or more provisions of a treaty in their application to the reserving state; an *understanding* merely explains or clarifies the meaning of one or more provisions of a treaty but does not exclude or vary their legal effect.[21] From a purely legal point of view, therefore, a reservation is more important than an understanding. The memorandum stressed, however, that the matter of distinguishing between reservations and understandings is more complicated than merely looking at the labels affixed to them. Whether or not a "statement modifies the legal effect of [a] treaty or merely expresses its true intent depends on the substance of the statement and is not solely within the judgment of the State making the statement."[22] The other parties to a treaty have a voice in determining whether or not the conditions of ratification that a new party wishes to impose are acceptable. They even have a voice in determining whether or not the conditions are appropriately labeled.

Other parties to the Genocide Convention are therefore entitled to object to the labels used in the Lugar-Helms-Hatch Sovereignty Package. They could argue, for example, that statements labeled as understandings do not merely clarify provisions of the convention but actually modify or exclude their legal effects and constitute reservations. They could then also object to the reservations on the ground that they are incompatible with the object and purpose of the convention. The consequences of any such objections, according to the relevant provisions of the Vienna Convention on the Law of Treaties, would depend upon the intentions of the states making them, and range from the relatively inconsequential (they could simply register an objection) to the severe (they could indicate that they do not consider the United States a party to the convention).

Since the other parties to the Genocide Convention could object to the terms of the Sovereignty Package, and their objections could vary in their consequences, one of my most important objectives in this book is to examine the content and rationale of the U.S. reservations and understandings with a view to determining whether or not objections that might be raised by other parties would have merit. The issue for other parties in deciding whether or not to object to the U.S. conditions is, of course, at least partly—and perhaps mainly—a political issue. In other words, apart from the question of whether or not an objection has any merit, the objecting states would have to determine if it would be politically wise or unwise to mount an objection to a U.S. condition. One might suppose that the answer to this question would depend upon whether or not the objecting state is an ally of the United States or is in some other way dependent upon the United States. But the issue is also in part legal; that is, would an objection actually have merit given what the convention says in light of its object and purpose? It is obvious that legitimate disputes regarding these matters could arise among the parties, and the convention itself prescribes procedures for resolving them should they occur. Article IX states that any disputes regarding the interpretation, application, or fulfillment of the convention can be brought to the ICJ upon the request of any of the parties to the dispute.

The matter is not simply one of academic disputation. The Genocide Convention is a United Nations treaty, and the instruments of ratification to it are deposited with the secretary general; as a matter of course he circulates among all the parties to the convention any instruments of ratification that are deposited with him. This provides the parties an opportunity to examine the content and implications of any conditions specified in such instruments. The United States deposited its instrument of ratification in November 1988. By December 1989, nine European countries (Denmark, Finland, Ireland, Italy, the Netherlands, Norway, Spain, Sweden, and the United Kingdom) had formally filed objections to certain conditions specified in the Sovereignty Package, demonstrating that there are limits to what even allies will accept when important principles of international law are at stake.[23] All nine countries objected to the terms of the constitutional reservation. The objecting states expressed concern that the U.S. reservation either violated international treaty law, inasmuch as a country cannot invoke the provisions of its domestic law as justification for failure to live up to an international legal obligation, or at least created uncertainty about the extent of the legal obligation the United States was assuming by ratifying the convention. Three of the nine states also objected to the U.S. reservation to Article IX of the convention—the article that prescribes a role for the International Court of Justice in interpreting and applying the convention. Only one of the nine, the Netherlands, indicated in its objection that it did not consider the United States a party to the convention; the others remained silent on this issue. Other parties may yet raise additional objections to the U.S. conditions. Of course, the other parties will decide for themselves, at least initially, whether or not such objections have any merit, and precisely what effects they expect their objections to have. In fact, such determinations properly belong to the other parties and to formally recognized institutions such as the International Court of Justice. Nonetheless, we should examine the content and rationale of the U.S. conditions with a view toward appraising their effectiveness in addressing the issues they purport to deal with. Why were they believed necessary? What arguments were advanced for and against their inclusion in the Sovereignty Package, and how cogent were they? Do other parties to the convention have reasonable grounds for objecting to them?

Organization of the Book

Since most of the articles of the Genocide Convention have at one time or another been scrutinized in Senate hearings and debates on the floor as proponents and opponents of ratification fought over the meaning of words and phrases, an article-by-article analysis of the convention and the issues and problems that each article gave rise to seemed feasible as an organizational scheme for this book. At the same time, such an approach seemed inappropriate and unnecessary for two reasons. First, some articles of the convention pertain to purely procedural matters, such as where instruments of ratification are to be deposited, and they have scarcely been the subject of discussion, let alone controversy, in the United States. Second, although this book is a case study, I wanted to use concepts and ideas that would fit the book into the larger body of relevant political science literature. In this connection I found concepts in the framework employed by Harold Jacobson in *Networks of Interdependence* most useful.[24]

Jacobson approaches the study of international organizations in terms of the functions they perform. These functions fall into five major categories: informational, norm creating, rule creating, rule supervisory, and operational. The informational and operational functions are irrelevant to our concerns in this book. The former includes the gathering, analysis, and dissemination of data and viewpoints; the latter includes such things as the use of the resources that international organizations have at their disposal.[25] But the norm-creation, rule-creation, and rule-supervisory functions are relevant to our analysis, especially the latter two.

"Norm-creation," as Jacobson defines it, involves the "definition and declaration of standards" in instruments such as declarations and resolutions that do not have legally binding effect, but rather "are designed to affect the milieu in which domestic and world politics are conducted."[26] The United Nations and other international organizations have adopted many such norm-creating instruments. Perhaps the best example in the field of human rights is the Universal Declaration of Human Rights, which was adopted by the UN General Assembly in 1948. The General Assembly also adopted a norm-creating instrument relating to genocide in 1946 in the form of a resolution. But since this resolution was superseded by the more important Genocide Convention, and, indeed, was really a building block on the way to the adoption of the convention, I have discussed its background, terms, and significance in chapter 2 as an important step in the process of rule-creation on genocide.

"Rule-creation," according to Jacobson, also involves the definition and declaration of standards, but, unlike norms, rules are framed in instruments that can have legally binding effect. Rule-creating instruments normally must be properly ratified by states to become binding; the mere fact of their adoption by any international organization does not make them legally binding upon all its member states.[27] Examples of such rule-creating instruments are the many treaties, conventions, and covenants that international organizations have adopted in the field of human rights. The Genocide Convention is a rule-creating instrument in that it elaborates a definition of the crime of genocide in an instrument that can become legally binding upon states. That rule is now the authoritative rule for all the states that are parties to the convention. It is probably authoritative for other states as well, because, as noted earlier, genocide is a crime under customary international law, and the Genocide Convention provides what is arguably the most widely accepted definition of the crime.

But the Genocide Convention does more than create a rule on genocide. It also contains provisions that relate to what Jacobson calls "rule-supervision." The function of rule supervision involves the measures that can be taken "to ensure compliance with the rules that are in force by those subject to them," and "could entail several steps, ranging from detection of evidence that a violation had occurred, through verification of that evidence, to the imposition of sanctions."[28] These functions are performed by various types of international mechanisms, although domestic enforcement of international obligations is also quite common. The General Assembly relied on a combination of domestic and international measures in the case of the Genocide Convention. It is to be enforced by the individual parties through the domestic legislation that they adopt on genocide. So far as the international measures are concerned, the convention prescribes roles for the ICJ and the political organs of the United Nations. It also contemplates the creation of an international criminal court, but that has not yet come into existence.

Since the U.S. debate over the ratification of the Genocide Convention focused on various aspects of the rule and the rule-supervisory measures that are elaborated in it, I found it very useful to organize this book into two main parts corresponding to these two functions. Part 1 (chapters 2–5) deals with several issues of general importance regarding the application of the convention, and with various specific issues that arose in connection with Article II, the principal article of the convention that sets forth the rule on genocide. A number of provisions of the Lugar-Helms-Hatch Sovereignty Package that pertain to the rule are also analyzed in those chapters. Part 2 (chapters 6–9) examines the issues that arose in connection with the need to develop domestic implementing legislation and the respective roles of the ICJ and the proposed international criminal court. These chapters also address various provisions of the Sovereignty Package that are relevant to the rule-supervisory measures.

In dealing with the many issues discussed in parts 1 and 2 of this book, I found it necessary to delve into the drafting history of the convention and other UN documents in order to appraise the cogency of the arguments advanced on them in the United States. In addition, I have drawn on a number of case studies of genocide, and historical and specialized works on the subject to provide illustrations that give meaning to the convention's provisions. The book is thus as much about the strengths and weaknesses of the Genocide Convention as it is about the issues raised in the debate over its ratification by the United States.

Part I The Rule: What Is Genocide?

Chapter 2 Development of the Rule on Genocide

> *[I]t is clear that the Genocide Convention is a moral document. It is a call for a higher standard of human conduct. It is not a panacea for injustice, [but it will] make an important step toward civilizing the affairs of nations.*
> *—Senator William Proxmire, 1977 Senate hearings*

What is genocide? For most people, the word calls to mind the atrocities committed against the Jews, Poles, Gypsies, and other groups before and during World War II. For some, the word also calls to mind the Turks' slaughter of hundreds of thousands of Armenians during World War I. In fact, these two cases are generally regarded as constituting the modern historical paradigms of genocide. But there is also substantial confusion regarding the meaning of the term. It is often perceived of simply as mass murder, though the Genocide Convention makes it clear that genocide is more than that, or as a crime against humanity, though it is not, strange as it may seem, regarded as such under the terms of the convention. It has been applied, or alleged to apply, to circumstances so different from one another that it is clear that those who make the accusations have different conceptions of the crime. As the Senate Committee on Foreign Relations has often indicated in its reports, the word "genocide" has been loosely bandied about in recent years. Let us look, then, at how the author of the word "genocide" defined it and how it came to be defined the way it is in the Genocide Convention.

Raphael Lemkin's Definition of Genocide

Raphael Lemkin, a Polish jurist of Jewish origin, coined the word "genocide" in *Axis Rule in Occupied Europe* (1944). He derived the term from a combination of the Greek word *genos*, which means "race" or "tribe," and the Latin word *cide*, which means "killing."[1] He noted that the word "ethnocide," a combination of the Greek word *ethnos*, which means "nation," and the Latin word *cide*, would convey the same idea as genocide.[2] In fact, it is noteworthy that Lemkin did not adopt "ethnocide" rather than "genocide" to identify the crime he had in mind, because, as we shall see, he liberally used the words "nations" and "national groups" in his definition. Be that as it may, the important point is that Lemkin conceived of genocide in broader terms than simply killing members of groups; rather, he thought of it as the *destruction* of groups which could be brought about by a variety of means including, but not limited to, outright killing of their members.

> Generally speaking, genocide does not necessarily mean the immediate destruction of a nation, except when accomplished by mass killing of all members of a nation. It is intended rather to signify a coordinated plan of different actions aiming at the destruction of essential foundations of the life of national groups, with the aim of annihilating the groups themselves. The objective of such a plan would be disintegration of the political and social institutions, of culture, language, national feelings, religion, and the economic existence of national groups, and the destruction of the personal security, liberty, health, dignity, and the lives of the individuals belonging to such groups. Genocide is directed against the national group as an entity, and the actions involved are directed against individuals, not in their individual capacity but as members of the national group.[3]

According to Lemkin, there are two main stages in this genocidal process: in the first stage, the oppressor seeks to destroy the "national pattern" of the oppressed group; in the second stage, the oppressor seeks to impose its own national pattern on the oppressed group.[4]

The passages quoted above suggest that Lemkin was concerned solely with the destruction of national groups. At another point in his work, however, he tells of his concern as early as 1933 over actions aimed at the "destruction and oppression of populations," and that he had proposed then that two offenses, which he called "barbarity" and "vandalism," be made crimes under international law. He defined the crime of barbarity as "oppressive and destructive actions directed against individuals as members of a national, religious, or racial group," and the crime of vandalism as "malicious destruction of works of art and culture because they represent the specific creation of the genius of such groups."[5] Since Lemkin believed that these two crimes, taken together, amounted to what he would later call genocide, it would seem that he had in mind groups other than national groups as possible victims of genocide.[6] While he failed to provide a clear and consistent definition, his work provides insight into the nature of the crime.

Lemkin and the Genocide Convention

Lemkin fled Poland in the wake of the Nazi invasion in 1939. By 1941 he had emigrated to the United States, and subsequently he served on the faculties of several law schools, including Duke and Yale. During World War II he served the government of the United States in various capacities, including a stint as a staff member at the Nuremberg War Crimes Trials. He had begun to collect evidence of Nazi atrocities against the Jews, Poles, Gypsies, and other groups while he was still in Europe, and this documentary evidence later formed part of his major work on the subject of genocide, *Axis Rule in Occupied Europe*.[7]

After World War II Lemkin became an outspoken advocate of the conclusion and adoption of a convention on genocide by the United Nations. By then, according to some accounts, he displayed such devotion to the cause that he had become known as a "dreamer" and "fanatic."[8] Still, he was able to persuade enough UN delegates to support the idea of drafting a convention that the General Assembly adopted a resolution in 1946 (to which we shall return shortly) that set in motion the work on what eventually became the Genocide Convention. Lemkin served as a consultant to the UN Secretariat when it prepared the first draft of the convention. Many of his ideas were incorporated into that draft, but it proved unacceptable to many states for various reasons, and the definition of genocide eventually adopted for the convention fell short of what Lemkin seemed to have in mind in his work.[9]

Lemkin and the Ratification Effort in the United States

Whatever shortcomings Lemkin might have thought the Genocide Convention possessed, he became an indefatigable champion of it, and he lobbied aggressively for its ratification by the United States in the late 1940s and early 1950s. In the process he became something of an issue himself. He had apparently lobbied too aggressively, annoying a number of prominent and influential senators. Consequently, despite his prominence in the field, Lemkin was not called to testify when a subcommittee of the Senate Committee on Foreign Relations held the first hearings on the convention in 1950. When he died in 1959, the question of whether or not the United States should ratify the Genocide Convention was not even under active consideration in the Senate.

Remarks made during the 1950 hearings revealed the extent of some senators' displeasure with Lemkin's lobbying tactics. The remarks were so critical of him personally that it is not surprising that their publication was suppressed for nearly twenty-five years, finally being released in a compilation of executive sessions of the Senate Committee on Foreign Relations in 1976. In 1950 one committee member, Senator H. Alexander Smith (R., New Jersey), observed that he and others were troubled by the definition of the "new idea" of genocide. Moreover, he could not understand why the "biggest propagandist" for the Genocide Convention should be "a man who comes from a foreign country who . . . speaks broken English."[10] Smith claimed that he knew of "many people who have been irritated no end by this fellow running around." Although he was "sympathetic with the Jewish people," Smith believed that "they ought not to be the ones who are propagandizing [the convention], and they are."[11] Adrian Fisher, legal adviser to the State Department at the time, pointed out that Lemkin was a private citizen doing what he thought he should do. But Smith still believed that "having a man talking broken English in the forefront" of the ratification movement was a "mistake psychologically," and that many other senators were irritated by Lemkin's lobbying activities.

Even senators who supported ratification in 1950 had mixed emotions about Lemkin. Senator Henry Cabot Lodge, Jr. (R., Massachusetts), for example, suggested during the hearings that Lemkin had "done his own cause a great deal of harm" and that he should be notified of that fact.[12] Even the strongest supporters of ratification, such as Senators Brien McMahon (D., Connecticut) and Theodore Francis Green (D., Rhode Island), felt that if Lemkin was not the "biggest minus quantity" in the struggle over ratification, he was the "least plus quantity."[13]

The remarks at the 1950 hearings suggest that Lemkin had become regarded as a dreamer and fanatic on the subject of genocide as much by senators as he was by UN diplomats and personnel. Different life experiences and the "realities" of politics undoubtedly had much to do with the different perspectives of Lemkin and his detractors. Lemkin had lost all of his family in the Holocaust, and he had come to believe deeply in the utility of international law in the prevention and punishment of genocide.[14] In fact, as noted earlier, Lemkin had agitated for the development of international legal standards in this field as far back as the early 1930s. But the senators had no similar life experiences. Moreover, as we shall see, some of them were profoundly skeptical about, and even hostile to, the notion of assuming an international legal obligation on genocide. The subcommittee of the Committee on Foreign Relations that held the hearings in 1950 recommended ratification, but the full committee failed to report the convention to the Senate. As a result, it languished in committee until President Nixon resurrected it in 1970.

There is nothing on the subsequent record that approaches the criticisms of Lemkin made during the 1950 hearings, at least not by senators. On occasion, however, such criticisms were made by representatives of extremely conservative fringe groups. At the 1985 hearings of the Committee on Foreign Relations, for example, Trisha Katson, legislative director of Liberty Lobby, an organization that never found any redeeming features in the Genocide Convention, got Senator Jesse Helms to agree to have printed in the hearings the conclusion of a book by James Martin titled *The Man Who Invented "Genocide": The Public Career and Consequences of Raphael Lemkin.*[15] Martin attacked Lemkin on many grounds, including his failure to display "the faintest concern for majorities anywhere."[16] He also criticized *Axis Rule in Occupied Europe* as a flimsy effort to document Nazi atrocities: "Since he did not witness anything he included in his book, Lemkin essentially is passing on the substance of sources hostile to the Germans, much of it inflammatory rhetoric from various conduits of anti-Axis opinion-making, incapable of confirmation then and little of it since, with more than a dollop of ordinary mendacity."[17]

In essence, Martin's book seems to be a diatribe against Jews, Zionists, and Communists, and it undoubtedly appeals only to fringe groups such as Liberty Lobby. Katson herself evidently thinks highly of the book and agrees with its central line of reasoning, as she indicated at the 1985 hearings:

> As a believer in our constitutional republic, I am opposed to any alien political philosophy that would undermine it, be it Marxism, communism, socialism, national socialism or Nazism, or Zionism.
>
> For the purposes of my testimony, it is important that I point out that Zionism is not synonymous with Judaism. Zionism is a political movement while Judaism is a religion. I know Jews who are anti-Zionist. Also I know Zionist Christians.
>
> I am concerned with how pro-Zionist forces have aided in America's having a one-sided foreign policy in the Middle East. I would like to at this point note that every witness that spoke here today and also at Senator Hatch's Subcommittee on the Constitution last week mentioned different horrendous acts of genocide and holocausts that have occurred in the past, and while it was alluded to that Israel might be accused by the Arabs of committing genocide, there has never been a word said on the record that they possibly might be guilty of it.
>
> I would like to take this time to speak on behalf of the Palestinian people who have been victimized by acts of genocide on the part of the Zionist-controlled government of Israel.[18]

During the 1970s and 1980s Lemkin was sometimes recognized and praised for his work on genocide and the Genocide Convention. Nonetheless, the attacks against him during the 1950 Senate hearings, and Trisha Katson's testimony at the 1985 hearings, provide some insight into the pettiness that has sometimes characterized the ratification debate. They also provide some insight into the thinly veiled, and not-so-thinly veiled, anti-Semitism that has sometimes been expressed. For very obvious reasons Jews have had a deep and long-standing interest in the ratification movement. As one might expect, organized Jewish groups repeatedly endorsed ratification of the convention, and prominent Jewish individuals such as Arthur Goldberg, and Jewish senators such as Jacob Javits (R., New York), worked hard to secure ratification. At the same time, these individuals and groups, as well as tireless proponents of ratification such as Senator William Proxmire, always took pains to rebut the notion that the issue of ratification was a "Jewish issue." For Proxmire, in particular, ratification of the convention was a moral imperative and therefore an issue for everyone. Moreover, he saw ratification as good foreign policy because the failure of the United States to ratify undermined its leadership role in the field of international action on human rights. Yet, as we shall see throughout this book, critics of the convention have been all too willing to use any argument, however base or petty, to defeat the ratification movement.

The Role of the United Nations in Defining Genocide

Although Raphael Lemkin coined the word "genocide," it was up to the United Nations to adopt the official "rule," or definition of the crime. The organization was involved in this process of rule creation for about two years, from 1946 to 1948. Its work began when the delegations from Cuba, India, and Panama took the initiative and proposed that the subject of genocide be placed on the agenda of the first regular session of the General Assembly in 1946. After some discussion of a draft resolution in committee, the assembly unanimously and without debate adopted Resolution 96 (I) on genocide on December 11, 1946. That resolution created the "norm" on genocide. Specifically, it elaborated basic standards that were to be incorporated into the more important convention on genocide that the General Assembly resolved to conclude. As such, it was a necessary first step on the way to the adoption of the Genocide Convention. For this reason it is quoted in full.

> Genocide is a denial of the right of existence of entire human groups, as homicide is the denial of the right to live of individual human beings; such

denial of the right of existence shocks the conscience of mankind, results in great losses to humanity in the form of cultural and other contributions represented by these groups, and is contrary to moral law and to the spirit and aims of the United Nations.

Many instances of such crimes of genocide have occurred when racial, religious, political and other groups have been destroyed, entirely or in part.

The punishment of the crime of genocide is a matter of international concern.

The General Assembly therefore,

Affirms that genocide is a crime under international law which the civilized world condemns, and for the commission of which principals and accomplices—whether private individuals, public officials or statesmen, and whether the crime is committed on religious, racial, political or any other grounds—are punishable;

Invites the Member States to enact the necessary legislation for the prevention and punishment of this crime;

Recommends that international cooperation be organized between States with a view to facilitating the speedy prevention and punishment of the crime of genocide, and, to this end,

Requests the Economic and Social Council to undertake the necessary studies, with a view to drawing up a draft convention on the crime of genocide to be submitted to the next regular session of the General Assembly.

Resolution 96 (I) addressed three important matters: first, it provided the essential rationale for a convention on genocide; second, it set in motion the process through which such a convention was to be drafted; and, third, it outlined in general terms the basic elements of the rule on genocide that would be affirmed in that convention. Let us consider each of these points.

Why a Convention on Genocide Was Believed Necessary

The origins of the Genocide Convention lie in the atrocities that were committed against the Jews, Poles, Gypsies, and other groups by the Nazis during World War II. However, Resolution 96 (I) does not refer to this particular episode of genocide. Rather, it refers to the crime in a broader historical perspective, which is arguably one of its main strengths. Clearly, the resolution is not grounded in any particular historical experience, which gives it a timeless quality. It refers to "many instances" of genocide that resulted in "great losses to humanity." It asserts that "punishment of the crime of genocide is a matter of international concern," and it goes on to affirm that the crime is a "crime under international law."

The reason why a convention on genocide was believed necessary is implied in these basic principles. Its instigators aimed to establish genocide as a crime whenever it occurs. A convention establishing genocide as a crime whenever it occurs would overcome a major problem that had arisen as a result of the Nuremberg War Crimes Tribunal's interpretation of its own charter. The tribunal, which was established by the Allied powers at the close of World War II to try high-ranking Nazi war criminals, was empowered by its charter to try persons for crimes against humanity such as murder, extermination, and deportation of civilian populations. As we will discuss in chapter 5, some of these acts later fell within the meaning of genocide as it is defined in Article II of the Genocide Convention.

But the tribunal had interpreted its charter as meaning that persons could be convicted of committing crimes against humanity only if they had committed those crimes in execution of or in connection with an aggressive war. This interpretation had important practical implications. It meant that any crimes against humanity that were committed prior to September 1, 1939, the date of the opening of the war against Poland, did not fall within the purview of the tribunal.[19] Many activists, including Raphael Lemkin, believed that this interpretation created an undesirable and dangerous loophole that could be closed only through the adoption of a convention that would make genocide a crime whenever it occurs. Article I of the Genocide Convention effectively does this by stating that genocide is a crime under international law "whether committed in time of peace or in time of war." In this respect, therefore, the convention not only reiterates what Resolution 96 (I) had to say about the issue but states it with greater clarity and force.

It is arguable that if the Genocide Convention had been made applicable only to crimes committed during times of war, there would have been no need for it. Such a narrow construction would have had devastating consequences regarding many of the allegations of genocide that have been made since World War II. Genocide is alleged to have occurred, for example, during periods of acute domestic strife in Rwanda in the late 1950s and early 1960s, and in Burundi in the early 1970s.[20] In other instances, genocide is alleged to have occurred during periods of no domestic strife, such as the atrocities committed against the Aché Indians in Paraguay.[21] In none of these instances could it be said that a state of war existed, yet it may very well be that genocide did occur.

Genocide is also alleged to have occurred during periods that might be reasonably characterized as wars; for example, during the struggle over the creation of Pakistan in the late 1940s and Bangladesh in the early 1970s.[22] In addition, as we will see in chapter 3, there were widespread charges that the United States was waging a genocidal war in Vietnam during the 1960s and 1970s, and the so-called Russell Tribunal found the United States and powers allied with it "guilty" of the charges. The charges, as well as the judgment of the tribunal, have been the subject of a great deal of debate. As far as many critics of the convention in the United States were concerned, it did not matter that the Russell Tribunal was an unofficial body. What mattered was simply that the charges were made and that they were fairly widespread. At one point the government of North Vietnam cited the massacre of civilians at My Lai as proof that the United States was waging a genocidal war.[23]

Without rendering a judgment on any of these episodes, since such judgments properly belong to courts, it is important to note that genocide is alleged to have occurred in a great variety of circumstances since World War II. Some scholars and human rights activists are concerned that minorities throughout the world remain exposed to genocide and genocide-like acts. In retrospect, therefore, the General Assembly very wisely aimed to conclude a convention that would apply whenever the crime of genocide occurred. The fact that the drafters followed through on this objective has made the Genocide Convention potentially applicable to many of the cases that have arisen in the post-World War II period.

The Process of Drafting the Convention

The last paragraph of Resolution 96 (I) indicates that the General Assembly expected to act on a convention on genocide at its second regular session in 1947. To this end, it charged the Economic and Social Council (ECOSOC) with undertaking the necessary studies that would culminate in the preparation of a draft convention. The ECOSOC turned to the UN Secretariat for assistance in this matter. Specifically, it asked the Secretariat to prepare a draft convention. The Secretariat, using experts in international and criminal law such as Raphael Lemkin as consultants, prepared a draft convention by June 1947. However, the process of preparing a final draft that the General Assembly could adopt began to slow down. The UN Secretariat submitted its draft to the Committee on the Progressive Development of International Law and Its Codification, but the committee declined to make any comments on it since the member states of the United Nations had not yet done so. The secretary general then requested the member states to submit such comments, but very few of them replied. Consequently, when the ECOSOC met in July 1947, it deemed any action on the draft convention inappropriate and referred the matter back to the General Assembly.[24]

Important philosophical disagreements arose in the General Assembly. Some delegates took the position that Resolution 96 (I) should be fundamentally altered; that is, that the ECOSOC should be charged with studying the question of whether or not a convention on genocide was desirable and necessary. Others insisted that the assembly had already decided that the conclusion of a convention was a worthy and important goal, and that instead of changing course it should reaffirm Resolution 96 (I). The assembly endorsed the latter viewpoint. It adopted another resolution, Resolution 180 (II), in which it reaffirmed Resolution 96 (I) and requested that the ECOSOC "continue the work" it had begun and "proceed with the completion of a convention" on genocide. The assembly now hoped to consider a draft convention at its third regular session in 1948. While Resolution 180 (II) brought about the desired result, it was not adopted with as much enthusiasm as Resolution 96 (I) had been. The vote on Resolution 180 (II) was thirty-eight in favor, none against, and fourteen abstentions.[25] Apparently no one could vote *against* a resolution on genocide (as no one would later vote against the adoption of the convention itself), but some were having second thoughts; a genocide convention was not an urgent matter on their agenda.

What explains the change in attitude? The official records indicate substantial displeasure among some representatives at the United Nations with the content of the Secretariat's draft convention. But their displeasure with the provisions of the draft reflected the deeper philosophical reservations they had begun to develop regarding the question of whether or not a convention was truly necessary or desirable. Undoubtedly these problems were made worse by the emergence of the cold war between the United States and the Soviet Union, which seemed to make many of the UN representatives considerably more cautious about the possibility of international cooperation in the further development and strengthening of international law.

These issues came to the forefront when the ECOSOC, in keeping with Resolution 180 (II), began to work on a draft convention at meetings in February and March 1948. It examined the Secretariat's draft, which reflected a very liberal construction of the guidelines laid down in Resolution 96 (I). The draft aimed to protect "racial, national, linguistic, religious, or political groups." In sweeping terms it branded as criminal many physical and biological acts aimed at the destruction of such groups in whole or in part, or of "preventing [their] preservation or development."[26] It specified acts that would be punishable, including attempt to commit genocide, participation in genocide, conspiracy to commit genocide, and engaging in a variety of "preparatory" acts such as developing techniques of genocide and setting up installations. It called for punishment of "all forms of public propaganda tending by their systematic and hateful character to provoke genocide, or tending to make it appear as a necessary, legitimate, or excusable act." It called for the creation of an international criminal court to try offenders in cases when states were unwilling either to try them or to extradite them to another country for trial.

The representatives of states with divergent political, economic, and social systems expressed dissatisfaction with the terms of the Secretariat's draft convention at meetings of the ECOSOC. The Venezuelan representative, for example, criticized the breadth of coverage of the draft, arguing that the ECOSOC was concerned with "a very delicate matter, which required careful, unhurried, and profound study. The question of the sovereignty of states was involved."[27] The Australian representative stressed that "while speed was essential, it was even more important to ensure that the convention . . . be based on solid legal and moral principles which would command universal respect and would be enforced" by all member states.[28] The Brazilian representative expressed the view that the convention had to "be considered in two aspects, the political and the legal."[29] A number of representatives, the French and Polish among them, stressed "political" aspects of the convention which they felt the ECOSOC should resolve before beginning work on drafting a convention.[30] The representative of the United Kingdom was perhaps the most pessimistic about the outcome. He argued that it was not clear that anything beyond what the General Assembly had already done in Resolution 96 (I) was either necessary or desirable. The resolution had branded genocide a crime under international law. What further sanctions could the proposed convention provide? He feared that, "on the contrary, it might have the reverse effect and only serve to weaken the force of international law."[31]

Although the comments varied in substance, most representatives on the ECOSOC seemed to be concerned about the same thing—the Secretariat's draft convention "lacked realism."[32] As the Soviet representative put it, the definition of genocide contained in the draft was "much too wide."[33] In brief, most representatives on the ECOSOC seemed to think that they were more attuned to "political realities" than were Secretariat personnel and experts such as Raphael Lemkin. The experts could concern themselves with developing the best possible rule on genocide, but the representatives of states had to consider what their governments would accept. The ECOSOC therefore resolved to create an ad hoc committee consisting of representatives of seven states (China, France, Lebanon, Poland, USA, USSR, and Venezuela). It met during April and May 1948 and took into account mainly the technical provisions of the Secretariat's draft in preparing its own.[34] The ad hoc committee's draft then became *the* draft convention that was discussed and revised by the Sixth (Legal) Committee of the General Assembly.

The Sixth Committee of the General Assembly debated the terms of the Genocide Convention during meetings it held from September through November 1948, and its final draft was adopted without alterations at a plenary meeting of the General Assembly in December 1948. The committee's deliberations were marked by sharp differences of opinion among the delegates on matters of principle as well as details of specific provisions of the convention. In fact, the attitudes expressed in the ECOSOC on the Secretariat's draft convention provided a good indication of the sort of debate that would occur again in the assembly. Many provisions of the Genocide Convention were heavily influenced by political and ideological considerations. This is not to say that the convention is flawed as a result; the drafters managed to produce a good instrument that was surely more acceptable to states than the Secretariat's draft would have been. Nor is it to say that there was anything unusual in the fact that political considerations influenced the outcome, for it is hard to imagine any law, domestic or international, that is not influenced by political considerations. Nonetheless, it is important to bear in mind that the drafters were diplomats who represented states, and these states had different interests so far as specific provisions of the convention were concerned. At the same time, as diplomats, the drafters had to find ways to produce an instrument that would be acceptable to a large number of states. In fact, the question of what would be acceptable to states was at all times a matter of great concern to the drafters. Achieving that goal meant that compromises of various sorts had to be reached, and these compromises did not always reflect the best possible choice among competing principles and ideas, but rather the most acceptable choice.

The Basic Elements of the Rule on Genocide

The political compromises that the drafters of the Genocide Convention had to make are apparent in many of its provisions, including those that pertain to the basic elements of the rule on genocide. Although Resolution 96 (I) provided the drafters with some guidance on what the General Assembly expected the convention to say with regard to the rule, in some crucial respects the resolution was vague and even contradictory. Consequently, while the drafters were able to adhere to the provisions of Resolution 96 (I) in some cases, in others they found it either necessary or desirable to exercise discretion.

One issue on which the drafters were able to adhere rather closely to Resolution 96 (I) was the question of who could be convicted of committing genocide. Significantly, the resolution does not say that the active backing or connivance of a government is necessary in the commission of genocide. Rather, it refers to the punishment of "principals and accomplices—whether private individuals, public officials or statesmen." The drafters of the Genocide Convention discussed this formula at length, especially in connection with Article IV of the convention. Some representatives on the Sixth Committee believed that Article IV should make it clear that genocide is "committed, encouraged, or tolerated by the rulers of a State."[35] This position was understandable in light of the historical context in which the convention was being drafted: it was obvious to everyone concerned that Hitler's government had committed, encouraged, and tolerated the commission of genocide. Nonetheless, a formal proposal to include a provision in Article IV to the effect that government complicity was necessary in cases of genocide was overwhelmingly rejected by a vote of forty against, two in favor, and one abstention.[36] Those who argued against the proposal maintained that genocide could be committed without the active backing of a government—for example, by terrorist organizations or even private individuals—and that in some instances governments might be unable to prevent the commission of genocide.[37]

While the drafters of the convention took the same position as the General Assembly on the issue of government complicity, they had more difficulty endorsing the precise categories of persons who could be punished for committing the crime. Resolution 96 (I) refers to "principals and accomplices—whether private individuals, public officials, or statesmen." The drafters of the convention had some difficulty with these categories. Those most concerned about them were the representatives of states with monarchies, such as the United Kingdom, Thailand, Sweden, and the Netherlands. They pointed out that their kings could not be brought to trial, and that the words "heads of State," which some drafters wanted to use in Article IV, could not be used without creating serious constitutional problems for them. Various alternative combinations of words and phrases that were proposed—"agents of State," "rulers," and so on—were also deemed inappropriate by most drafters because they created, or seemed to create, undesirable exemptions, depending on the language into which they were being translated. Therefore, after extensive negotiations the drafters settled on the words "constitutionally responsible rulers, public officials, or private individuals" for Article IV.[38] The clause "constitutionally responsible rulers" was intended to create an exemption for monarchs who cannot be brought to trial.

Critics of the convention in the United States have never expressed any serious concern about the exemption that Article IV creates. But they have often criticized the convention's failure to require government involvement or connivance in the commission of genocide. These critics usually cited the Nazi case, and, of course, Stalinism, and insisted that genocide was inconceivable without at least the connivance of a government. The issue was repeatedly raised, especially during the 1970s and 1980s. At the 1971 hearings of the Senate Committee on Foreign Relations, for example, Eberhard Deutsch, testifying on behalf of the American Bar Association, which at the time opposed ratification of the convention, maintained that "for genocide to be an international crime, and accordingly a matter of international concern appropriately the subject of a treaty with other nations under the Constitution of the United States, it must, by definition, be committed with the complicity of the government concerned—not merely by individuals."[39] During the 1980s Senator Jesse Helms, ever prepared with statements intended to clarify—or confuse, as the case might be—provisions of the convention, proposed that if the United States should ratify the convention, it should be with an understanding that "complicity of government" is an "essential element" of the crime of genocide.[40]

The problem with Senator Helms's proposal, as with Eberhard Deutsch's earlier argument, was that it would have rewritten the Genocide Convention in a very fundamental way. The understanding was therefore more on the order of an amendment, which would have required the renegotiation of the convention before the United States could become a party to it. The understanding would surely have made the convention inapplicable in all cases of, say, racially motivated lynchings that were not committed with the backing of the government, and probably was proposed precisely to eliminate charges of genocide in such cases. But the arguments involving this issue, carried to their logical conclusions, could have extremely undesirable consequences that one supposes—or hopes—even Senator Helms would not like. They would mean that no treaty could be concluded on, say, terrorism or hijacking if such a treaty aimed to punish individuals who act without the backing of a government. Presumably no one would want to reach this conclusion. In fact, one of the positive features of the Genocide Convention is that it recognizes the international responsibility of individuals for criminal acts, an issue that was dealt with at Nuremberg. In its judgment the Nuremberg Tribunal expressed the dictum: "Crimes against international law are committed by men, not by abstract entities, and only by punishing individuals who commit such crimes can the provisions of international law be enforced."[41]

Supporters of ratification successfully rebuffed attempts to rewrite the convention to require the complicity of government in the commission of genocide. Apart from the highly undesirable consequences of such proposals, those who defended the convention as written pointed out that it does deal with both individuals and states[42] inasmuch as it specifies that the parties may call upon the United Nations to take appropriate action under the UN Charter to prevent and suppress genocide (under Article VIII). Moreover, under Article IX, the parties can bring disputes concerning the interpretation, application, or fulfillment of the convention, including those relating to state responsibility for genocide, to the International Court of Justice.[43] (We shall return to this point in chapter 9.)

Although the drafters were able to follow through on the terms of Resolution 96 (I) regarding individual responsibility for genocide, other aspects of the rule on genocide were more problematic. The resolution is vague, even contradictory, regarding some key points that had to be addressed in the convention. For example, it states that genocide is "a denial of the right of existence of entire human groups, as homicide is the denial of the right to live of individual human beings"; it then refers to past instances of genocide when "racial, religious, political, and other groups" had been destroyed "entirely or in part." But by what acts or techniques could a denial of the right of existence be effected? Would only killing members of the groups constitute genocide? Or would other acts, such as Lemkin's "barbarity" and "vandalism" also constitute genocide? Was it necessary for entire groups to be destroyed, or could genocide be committed against parts of groups? To what groups should the convention extend protection? Religious, racial, and political groups are expressly mentioned in Resolution 96 (I): did this mean that the convention must cover all of them? What "other groups" did the General Assembly have in mind?

These questions illustrate in broad strokes the difficulties the drafters of the convention faced in elaborating the rule on genocide. Resolution 96 (I) could be invoked – and was invoked, especially during debates in the Sixth Committee – whenever its terms supported a particular position that one or another delegate wished to take. In fact, the drafters were able to exercise considerable discretion on key points. As a result, they inserted in Article II of the convention, the core article, some of the ideas and statements expressed in Resolution 96 (I); in other important instances they altered the resolution's terms.

In view of the importance of Article II, it is not surprising that it was the most controversial article when the convention was drafted. It subsequently became exceedingly controversial in the United States in the struggle over ratification. Article II is quoted in full below to facilitate discussion of the various issues involved.

> In the present Convention, genocide means any of the following acts committed with intent to destroy, in whole or in part, a national, ethnical, racial or religious group, as such:
> a. Killing members of the group;
> b. Causing serious bodily or mental harm to members of the group;
> c. Deliberately inflicting on the group conditions of life calculated to bring about its physical destruction in whole or in part;
> d. Imposing measures intended to prevent births within the group;
> e. Forcibly transferring children of the group to another group.

This article makes it clear that genocide is a crime committed against groups of human beings. Beyond that, it identifies certain elements crucial to the definition of the crime, including (1) the notion of the intent to destroy groups, (2) the types of groups to which the convention extends protection, and (3) the kinds of acts considered genocidal. All of these elements became major issues in their own right during the drafting stage and, later, in debates over ratification of the convention by the United States. In fact, specific aspects of some of these elements became so controversial in the United States that the opponents of ratification insisted on framing statements in the Lugar-Helms-Hatch Sovereignty Package indicating what the United States understands them to mean.

As understandings, the statements presumably were intended to explain or clarify the meaning of certain words and phrases in Article II, and not to exclude or vary their legal effect, as would reservations. But as we discussed in chapter 1, under the international rules of treaty law, other parties to the Genocide Convention have a voice in determining the appropriateness of the labels used by the United States in the Sovereignty Package; they could also object to the conditions if they should find them incompatible with the object and purpose of the convention. The other parties, of course, may be reluctant to raise objections to the U.S. conditions, especially if they are in some important way dependent upon the United States. Be that as it may, the possibility that objections could be raised exists. With this in mind, let us turn to the three main elements of the rule on genocide that are affirmed in Article II of the convention.

Chapter 3 The Intent to Destroy Groups

In my opinion, as I understand the sort of lynchings that have taken place in this country in past times, they have not been accompanied by the intent to destroy in whole or in part an ethnical, racial, or religious group. I think genocide, as defined in the treaty, does require that specific intent.—William Rehnquist, 1970 Senate hearings

Article II of the Genocide Convention defines the crime of genocide in terms of an intent to destroy human groups as such. More specifically, the article speaks of the "intent to destroy, in whole or in part," national, ethnic, racial, or religious groups. The problem is how to interpret the relationship between the two parts of this phrase. Must there be an intent to destroy an entire group for the actions taken against any part of it to be considered genocidal? Or could an intent to destroy only a part of a group be genocide? If the intent need be to destroy only part of a group, what constitutes a "part" of a group? Could, say, the murder of a single individual constitute genocide?

These questions are important from the standpoint of interpreting and enforcing the rule on genocide affirmed in the Genocide Convention, and they were among the most important ones raised during the drafting process. They were also the cause of great controversy in the struggle over ratification of the convention by the United States. Some critics of the convention argued that interpreting the phrase "intent to destroy, in whole or in part," is so problematic that the United States should not ratify the convention for that reason alone; but if it should ratify, it should do so only with an understanding of how it interprets the phrase. Among other things, these critics argued that the phrase would make the convention applicable to racially motivated lynchings, thus perhaps opening the way for it to become an important tool in the civil rights struggle within the United States. These issues were first raised at the 1950 Senate hearings on the convention, and it was assumed ever after that if the United States were to ratify the convention, it would do so with an understanding regarding the phrase. Thus, in this chapter we encounter the first understanding in the Lugar-Helms-Hatch Sovereignty Package.

The Intent to Destroy, in Whole or in Part

The reason for the controversy over the phrase "intent to destroy, in whole or in part," lies in the construction of the phrase, specifically in how to interpret the relationship between its two parts—"intent to destroy" and "in whole or in part." Does the phrase mean simply what the ordinary meaning of its words convey—that the intent could be to destroy a group *either* in whole or in part? Or did the drafters of the convention intend to say something different?

Opinions on the Meaning of the Phrase

Many commentators on the convention have examined the meaning of the phrase "intent to destroy, in whole or in part." The views of three are especially to the point and deserving of attention here. Bunyan Bryant observed:

> it is clear that syntactically, the "intent to destroy" refers either to the destruction of the whole group or destruction of a part of the group. Thus, an intent to destroy a part of the group (even without an intent to destroy the whole group) could presumably still be considered genocide. Unless the intent were express, however, the intent to destroy the group would be difficult to prove, except in those instances where the mere number of people of the group affected was significant. Practically speaking, then, the number of victims may be of evidentiary value with respect to proving the necessary intent.[1]

In a similar vein, Nehemiah Robinson, perhaps the best-known commentator on the convention, observed in 1960:

> According to the [wording of Article II], the aim need not be the total destruction of the group. Thus, *Genocide is not necessarily characterized by the intent to destroy a whole group;* it suffices if the purpose is to eliminate portions of the population marked by specific racial, religious, national, or ethnic features. The restriction to a "group," as an assemblage of persons regarded as a unit because of their comparative segregation from others, would have left open the question whether the aim must be the

> destruction of the group in the whole of a country, in a part of it, in a single town, etc. The addition of the words "in part" indicates that Genocide has been committed when acts of homicide are joined with a connecting purpose, i.e., directed against persons with specific characteristics (with intent to destroy the group or a segment thereof). Therefore, *the intent to destroy a multitude of persons of the same group because of their belonging to this group, must be classified as Genocide* even if these persons constitute only part of a group either within a country or within a region or within a single community, *provided the number is substantial;* the Convention is intended to deal with action against large numbers, not individuals even if they happen to possess the same group characteristics. It will be up to the courts to decide in each case whether the number was sufficiently large.[2]

Ben Whitaker, the rapporteur of a 1985 United Nations report on the convention, advanced similar arguments:

> Genocide need not involve the destruction of a whole group. Argument has occurred as to whether an attack affecting half of a small group more closely approximates to genocide than a massacre which affects only one tenth of a larger group of several million people. The relative proportionate scale of the actual or attempted destruction of a group, by any of the means listed in Articles II and III of the Convention, is certainly strong evidence to prove the necessary intent to destroy a group, in whole or in part. *"In part" would seem to imply a reasonably significant number, relative to the total of the group as a whole, or else a significant section of a group such as its leadership.* On the other hand, it has been urged that, given the *mens rea* of such intent, the Convention should be interpreted as applying to cases of "individual genocide," where a single person was a victim of any such acts, *though strictly even such a minimalist interpretation requires evidence of more than one victim, since the plural is used consistently throughout Article II (a) and (e).* In order that the gravity of the concept of genocide should not be devalued or diluted by the inflation of cases as a result of too broad an interpretation, the present Special Rapporteur suggests that considerations of both proportionate scale and of total numbers are relevant. Other attacks and killings do, of course, remain heinous crimes, even if they fall outside the definition of genocide.[3]

Each of these analyses focused mainly on the plain meaning of the language used in Article II, although the authors also speculated about the intentions of the drafters of the convention in their comments, for example, about the convention being intended to apply to a multiplicity of victims. But precisely what the drafters intended to say in various phrases of the convention, including the phrase "intent to destroy, in whole or in part," is not always clear. Since the issue became such an important one in the U.S. debate over ratification, we should explore what the drafters had to say about the phrase.

The Intentions of the Drafters

The drafters of the Genocide Convention distinguished between the crimes of homicide and genocide. As they saw it, homicide becomes genocide when the underlying intent relates to a group. Obviously, individuals are the victims in the commission of both crimes, but in genocide they become the victims because of their group identity, not because of anything peculiar to them as individuals. This was one of the main reasons why Raphael Lemkin coined the word "genocide" in the first place. It was necessary, of course, for the drafters to recognize that even the partial destruction of a group could constitute genocide, for otherwise the concept would not have been applicable until a very high proportion or all of its members had been killed. In fact, it was for this reason that a Norwegian delegate on the Sixth Committee of the General Assembly proposed that the words "in whole or in part" be included in Article II of the convention. His proposal was overwhelmingly adopted by a vote of forty-one in favor, eight against, and two abstentions.[4]

Whether or not the purpose of the Norwegian amendment was to say that the *intent* to destroy applied to *parts* of groups, however, is not as clear. There was substantial confusion in the United Nations on this matter. Some representatives in the Sixth Committee argued that the intent must be to destroy an entire group, but that genocide could be accomplished in stages initially affecting parts of groups.[5] Others were even concerned about the implications of the word "intent" in Article II. The representative of the Soviet Union, for example, proposed substituting the words "aimed at the physical destruction of" groups for "intent to destroy" groups.[6] In explaining his proposal he indicated that he had in mind acts *that resulted in the destruction of groups.* The proposal was supported by some representatives, most notably the French delegate, who argued that it would "guard against the possibility that the presence in the definition of the word 'intent' might be used as a pretext, in the future, for pleading not guilty on the ground of absence of intent."[7] This argument, as we shall see later, proved prophetic. For the moment, suffice it to say that the Soviet proposal received scant attention from the Sixth Committee despite its important implications. In any event, it was opposed by the U.S. representative, Ernest A. Gross, on the ground that it appeared to introduce a "fundamental modification" in the definition of genocide, because, in his view, intent was an essential element in the definition of a crime.[8] The Soviet proposal was rejected by a vote of thirty-six against, eleven in favor, and four abstentions.[9]

So far as the drafters' intentions were concerned, then, we can say that they decidedly took the view that the destruction of parts of groups, not only entire groups, could constitute genocide, and that the crime of genocide itself had to be defined in terms of an intent to destroy groups as such. Yet precisely how they saw the relationship between "intent to destroy" and "in whole or in part" is not clear.

Whatever the drafters intended to say, there seems no reason to quibble with the interpretations of Bryant, Robinson, and Whitaker that the ordinary meaning of the language in Article II is such that the intent could be to destroy one or more of the groups in question *either* in whole or in part. Moreover, Robinson's suggestion that a part of a group means a substantial part seems quite reasonable in light of the fact that the apparent aim of the convention is to deal with action against large numbers of people. In connection with this point it should be emphasized that Article IX provides that the parties to any dispute concerning the interpretation of the convention may request that the matter be taken up by the ICJ. As the representatives in the General Assembly were well aware, in any such dispute the court would look first to the language of the convention itself, and only if it were to find the language ambiguous would it look elsewhere for guidance in interpretation. Given the text of Article II, it would seem reasonable for the court to conclude—should it ever be called upon to resolve a dispute regarding the matter—that the intent could be to destroy a group *either* in whole or in part. Indeed, it would seem strange for the court to reach any other conclusion. It may be more difficult for the court to accept the proposition that a part of a group means a *substantial* part, as Robinson suggests, because the word "substantial" does not appear in the article, but this too would seem like a reasonable conclusion in view of the purpose of the convention.

The need for judicial interpretation of various phrases in the convention, including "intent to destroy, in whole or in part," is apparent, and there seems to be no reason why the ICJ could not be entrusted with the task. Nevertheless, profound distrust of the ICJ, and even objections in principle to any role for it in interpreting the convention, have figured prominently in debates over the phrase in the United States. In addition, arbitrary and erroneous interpretations of the meaning of the phrase, and the injection of cold war politics into the debates, have complicated matters.

Reaction to the Phrase in the United States

In the United States, confusion about the phrase "intent to destroy, in whole or in part," dates back to 1950, when a subcommittee of the Senate Committee on Foreign Relations held the first hearings on the convention. At the hearings, Dean Rusk, then deputy under secretary of state, testified on behalf of the Truman administration. He took quite a different position on Article II from that of the commentators discussed above. In response to questions put to him by Senator Brien McMahon, a strong proponent of ratification, Rusk argued that under Article II of the convention, the intention of the perpetrators of genocide must be to destroy an *entire* group:

> Genocide, as defined in article II of the convention, consists of the commission of certain specified acts, such as killing or causing serious bodily harm to individuals who are members of a national, ethnical, racial, or religious group, with the intent to destroy that group. *The legislative history of article II shows that the United Nations negotiators felt that it should not be necessary that an entire human group be destroyed to constitute the crime of genocide, but rather that genocide meant the partial destruction of such a group with the intent to destroy the entire group concerned.*
>
> SENATOR MCMAHON: That is important. They must have the intent to destroy the entire group.
>
> MR. RUSK: That is correct.
>
> SENATOR MCMAHON: In other words, an action leveled against one or two of a race or religion would not be, as I understand it, the crime of genocide. They must have the intent to go through and kill them all.
>
> MR. RUSK: That is correct. This convention does not aim at the violent expression of prejudice which is directed against individual members of groups.[10]

Rusk's testimony was evidently based on a report that the acting secretary of state, James Webb, had submitted to President Truman. That report, unfortunately, confused the issue by quoting a statement made by the U.S. representative in the Sixth Committee which seemed to say that the intent must be to destroy an entire group. At the same time, Webb's own analysis of the article suggests that he did not interpret it in that way. He stated that any of the acts specified in Article II, "if accompanied by the intent to destroy, in whole or in part, a national, ethnical, racial, or religious group," would constitute the crime of genocide.[11]

Webb's report and Rusk's testimony laid the foundation for confusion in the Senate that persisted for many years. Even during the 1970s and early 1980s, most senators who favored ratification of the convention seemed inclined to accept Rusk's 1950 testimony as authoritative. Many critics, on the other hand, argued that his testimony was not consistent with the ordinary meaning of the language in Article II.[12] The ABA's representatives were especially outspoken in this regard. The association opposed ratification of the convention from 1950 to 1976, and its representatives at the Senate hearings in 1950 and the early 1970s insisted that Article II meant that the intent could be to destroy a group either in whole or in part. This raised the question of what constituted a part of a group, and the ABA representatives insisted that it could mean a single individual, which could make the convention applicable even to racially motivated lynchings. Some proponents of ratification, including members of the ABA, argued that a part of a group meant a substantial part, but the official representatives of the ABA, such as Alfred Schweppe, insisted on adhering to the plain language of Article II. At the 1950 hearings Schweppe had this to say:

> The point is that [under Article II] the intent does not need to exist to destroy the whole group. It needs only to exist to destroy part of the group. Now whether we say part of the group could mean one person or whether we say a substantial part again requires us to inquire into the facts, as you often do in these cases, what is the group and how many were there?
>
> SENATOR MCMAHON: Part of the group—but because he is part of that group. Now, let's take a lynching case, for example. Let's assume that there is a lynching and a colored man is murdered in that fashion. Is it your contention that that could be construed as being within the confines of this definition; namely, with intent to destroy him as part of a group?
>
> MR. SCHWEPPE: Well, Mr. Chairman, I don't want to answer that categorically. Let me give you this illustration, though, and I will give you an opinion on it, just one man's opinion, and not that of the International Court, which will ultimately decide. Let's assume a little town where I live, where the colored groups are small, a very infinitesimal part of the population. Suppose . . . they have five colored people living in the town and, we'll say, that sometimes some crime of violence occurs, and as a result of it, some ill-meaning citizens in that

community—I wouldn't call them well-meaning—decide that they want to get rid of all of those people.

Well, are they proceeding against them because they want to get rid of them as a group, as a racial group? . . . I don't know. I say there is a question. . . . Now again, as I say, I don't want to put out these views as positive convictions. I can no more put them out as my opinions, but this whole concept of part of a group, which may be part of a group in a town, doesn't mean the whole group. Certainly it doesn't mean if I want to drive 5 Chinamen out of town, to use that invidious illustration, that I must have the intent to destroy all the 400,000,000 Chinese in the world or the 250,000 within the United States. It is part of a racial group, and if it is a group of 5, a group of 10, a group of 15, and I proceed after them with guns in some community to get rid of them solely because they belong to some racial group that the dictators don't like, I think you have got a serious question. That is what bothers me.[13]

Although Schweppe "took a back seat to no one in being opposed to genocide,"[14] it is clear that he as well as other ABA representatives who testified in opposition to ratification of the convention in 1950 were deeply concerned about its possible applications to race relations within the United States. As we shall see, especially in chapters 5 and 6, the issue came up again in connection with the meaning of various genocidal acts and the content of domestic implementing legislation. But the ABA's criticisms of the convention went far beyond mere technicalities like what constituted a part of a group. They were also concerned about the intentions and future prospects of the United Nations in the field of human rights, particularly about the drafting of treaties and conventions in this field, which they saw as threatening to national sovereignty. They voiced serious reservations about the role of the ICJ in interpreting the Genocide Convention, again for reasons of national sovereignty. And finally, they argued that while the terms of Article II of the convention might make it applicable to race relations within the United States, it would probably not be applicable to genocide against national and other groups behind the Iron Curtain. According to the ABA representatives, the Soviet Union would be able to evade charges of genocide by claiming that its suppression of, say, any national or ethnic group was not directed at the group as such but rather at political opponents of the regime. As we will see in chapter 4, the ABA representatives were among the leading critics of the drafters' decision not to extend protection to political groups under Article II of the convention.

Although they couched their arguments in legal terms, the preoccupation of the ABA representatives with Soviet policies suggests that their objections to the Genocide Convention were as much political as they were legal, and perhaps more so. In fact, as we shall have occasion to see in other chapters of this book as well, a pervasive anti-Soviet and prosovereignty attitude characterized the testimony of the ABA representatives. Moreover, they seemed extremely unwilling to trust courts to dismiss frivolous allegations of genocide if the United States ratified the convention, a curious attitude for persons who were considered titans of the legal profession.

The views of the ABA representatives were rather widely shared. They were endorsed by some senators, most notably Senator John Bricker (R., Ohio), who in the early 1950s introduced a controversial constitutional amendment (discussed more fully in chapter 6) that would have had an impact on the exercise of the treaty-making power. The ABA reversed its long-standing position and declared itself in favor of ratification of the convention in 1976, by implication, at least, disowning its earlier objections.[15] But this was not a decision easily reached, and many critics of the convention from within and without the ABA continued to voice objections to the phrase "intent to destroy, in whole or in part," insisting that it was either too difficult to interpret or would be interpreted in a way unfavorable to the United States.[16]

The U.S. Understanding Regarding "Intent to Destroy, in Whole or in Part"

In 1950 the differences of opinion among the opponents and proponents of ratification of the Genocide Convention regarding the phrase "intent to destroy, in whole or in part," gave rise to an understanding that was designed to clarify the meaning of the phrase. The subcommittee of the Committee on Foreign Relations that held the hearings in 1950 drafted the first version of the understanding. Nothing came of it, however, because the committee as a whole decided not to report the convention to the Senate. The committee drafted a somewhat different version of the understanding in the 1970s and included it in proposed resolutions of ratification during those years and in 1984. In retrospect, it is clear that there was never any doubt throughout all the years the convention was under consideration in the Senate that an understanding would be an essential condition of ratification—a price that would have to be paid by proponents of ratification if they wished to prevail. By the mid-1980s, then, it was a foregone conclusion that an understanding regarding the phrase would be included in the Lugar-Helms-Hatch Sovereignty Package; there remained only the question of precisely how the understanding would be framed.

The Development of the U.S. Understanding

The 1950 version of the understanding stated:

> That the United States Government understands and construes the crime of genocide, which it undertakes to punish in accordance with this convention, to mean the commission of any of the acts enumerated in article II of the convention, with the intent to destroy an *entire* national, ethnical, racial, or religious group within the territory of the United States, in such manner as to affect a substantial portion of the group concerned.[17]

The second version of the understanding, the one included in the resolutions of ratification proposed by the Committee on Foreign Relations during the 1970s and in 1984, stated:

> That the United States Government understands and construes the words "intent to destroy, in whole or in part, a national, ethnical, racial, or religious group as such" appearing in Article II, to mean the intent to destroy a national, ethnical, racial, or religious group by the acts specified in Article II in such manner as to affect a substantial part of the group concerned.[18]

The third version of the understanding—the one that appears in the Lugar-Helms-Hatch Sovereignty Package—states:

> That the term "intent to destroy, in whole or in part, a national, ethnical, racial, or religious group as such" appearing in Article II means the specific intent to destroy, in whole or in substantial part, a national, ethnical, racial, or religious group as such by the acts specified in Article II.[19]

It is noteworthy that the initiative in connection with all of these statements came from the Senate, not from the executive branch. The understandings were developed pursuant to the Senate's constitutional role in giving advice and consent to the ratification of treaties. As discussed earlier, when considering whether or not to give its advice and consent to the ratification of treaties, the Senate has several options, including giving its advice and consent conditionally. Under the doctrine of reciprocity, conditions stipulated by one state can be invoked against it by another state if a dispute should arise. As we have also seen, however, the validity of the labels attached to conditions of ratification by one party to a treaty are subject to question by other parties; the other parties can also question the compatibility of the conditions with the object and purpose of the treaty in question. The question therefore arises as to whether or not other parties to the Genocide Convention would have grounds for objecting to the U.S. understanding regarding the phrase "intent to destroy, in whole or in part."

Although the precise terms of the three different versions of the understanding quoted above vary, it seems that the United States has always been concerned about the two issues that the phrase "intent to destroy, in whole or in part," addresses: the problem of intent and the meaning of what constitutes a part of a group. Let us look at how each of these issues was addressed in the different versions of the understanding.

What Constitutes Part of a Group?

The drafters of the Genocide Convention decided to insert the words "in whole or in part" in Article II because they did not want to create the impression that an entire group must be destroyed before it could be said that genocide had been committed; they wanted it to be clear that the destruction of only a part of a group could amount to genocide. But what constitutes a part of a group? Commentators and others who have dealt with the issue, such as Bryant, Robinson, and Whitaker, have generally argued that a part of a group means a *substantial* part in view of the fact that the convention was intended to apply to actions against large numbers of people.

Raphael Lemkin argued along similar lines. Although he was not called to testify at the 1950 Senate hearings, Lemkin knew the specific criticisms of the convention, especially those expressed by the representatives of the ABA. In a letter to the Committee on Foreign Relations in April 1950, which was not published until 1976 (in a compilation of executive sessions of the Senate Foreign Relations Committee), Lemkin expressed dismay about the confusion surrounding the meaning of the phrase "intent to destroy, in whole or in part," particularly the meaning of what constitutes a part of a group.[20] He argued that the convention was intended to apply to large numbers of people, that the "destruction in part must be of a substantial nature . . . so as to affect the entirety."[21] This was quite a different interpretation from the one Dean Rusk and other Truman administration spokesmen had advanced in Senate testimony. Whereas Rusk had maintained that the intent must be to destroy an entire group, even if only a part of it is, in fact, destroyed, Lemkin was saying that the intent could be to destroy a group either in whole or in part, and that when only a part of a group is affected it must be a substantial part.

Given his interpretation of Article II, Lemkin could not understand why the convention should be ratified with "any special clauses of understanding."[22] If such clauses would expedite ratification, however, he thought they "might be considered"; and he recommended the following language: "On the understanding that the Convention applies only to actions undertaken on a mass scale and not to individual acts even if some of these acts are committed in the course of riots or local disturbances."[23] Lemkin's statement reflected his awareness of one of the most important bases of ABA opposition to ratification of the convention; namely, that under Article II, lynchings would be considered genocide. But he was skeptical that an understanding, even one such as he proposed, would resolve the issue. In fact, for one not directly involved in the political struggle over ratification of the convention in the Senate—indeed, for one who was deliberately excluded from that process—Lemkin was acutely aware of the politics inherent in the process. He observed: "At the meeting of the American Bar Association such 'understandings' were proposed and still the Bar Association fought the Convention and proceeded from time to time to find new reasons. If somebody does not like mustard, he will always find a reason why he doesn't like it, after you have convinced him that the previous reason has no validity."[24]

This is precisely what happened in the long and bitter debate over ratification of the Genocide Convention. As one argument was laid to rest, another rose to take its place. None of the concessions the proponents of ratification were willing to make to the opponents produced the desired results. The proponents of ratification have seemed always to be on the defensive, and the opponents on the offensive. As Lemkin realized, understandings, reservations, or any other conditions of ratification might effectively deal with legal technicalities, but they would not satisfy those whose basis for opposition to ratification was fundamentally political, or policy related, and who seemed to be profoundly distrustful of courts' ability to reach reasonable judgments.

Be that as it may, the 1950 version of the understanding was clearly drafted in a manner consistent with the testimony of Dean Rusk and other Truman administration spokesmen. It was also obviously designed to assuage the fears and concerns of the ABA critics who were preoccupied with the possibility that the convention would be applicable to lynchings and the like. It stated that the United States understood the controversial phrase "intent to destroy, in whole or in part," to mean that the *intent* must be to destroy an *entire* group and that the actions taken against the group had to affect a *substantial* portion of it.

The second version of the understanding should have been an improvement over the 1950 version. The word "entire" does not appear in the understanding from the 1970s, although it seems to say, along with the 1950 version, that a substantial part of a group would have to be affected by the genocidal acts committed against it. This second version of the understanding, however, suffered more from poor drafting than from anything else. Although the word "entire" does not appear in the statement, the Committee on Foreign Relations interpreted it as requiring such an intention. Throughout the 1970s and early 1980s the committee repeatedly explained: "[the understanding] serves to emphasize the importance which the committee attaches to the word 'intent.' Basic to any charge of genocide must be the *intent* to destroy an *entire* group because of the fact that it is a certain national, ethnical, racial, or religious group, in such manner as to affect a substantial part of the group."[25]

The committee defended its position by citing the 1950 testimony of Dean Rusk and other Truman administration spokesmen, but it was taken to task for its understanding when Alfred Schweppe reappeared at the 1971 hearings to denounce the ratification effort once more. Acknowledging that he was probably selected to testify because he had "a certain grandfather position" in the ABA—he was the "only person still alive" among those who had represented the association in 1950—Schweppe argued:

> This committee has undertaken in a gloss to say that basic to any charge of genocide must be the intent to destroy the entire group.
>
> Now that is an exact negation of the text which is to be construed not by this body but, under a later article [Article IX] to which the Genocide Convention refers, by the International Court of Justice.
>
> Now, the International Court of Justice is not going to say intent to destroy a group in whole or in part means only to destroy a whole group. . . .
>
> You say it means only that you must have the intent to destroy the whole group. The convention says you only need the intent to destroy part of a group; so there is a contradiction, gentlemen, in your report which I suggest that you very seriously consider.[26]

The committee did not take Schweppe's advice and reconsider its understanding. To the contrary, the committee continued to include the understanding in all resolutions of ratification it proposed during the 1970s and in 1984, perhaps because it was clear that neither Schweppe nor those who supported his point of view would be persuaded to support ratification of the convention no matter what conditions were spelled out in the resolution of ratification. In other words, perhaps the committee had come to the same conclusion Raphael Lemkin had reached in 1950: someone who does not like mustard will always find a reason why he doesn't like it. There is no doubt, however, that Schweppe was correct in his criticism of the committee's understanding.

Despite the somewhat different language, the first two versions of the U.S. understanding regarding the phrase "intent to destroy, in whole or in part," said the same thing. They were therefore both susceptible to objections by other parties to the Genocide Convention on one or both of the following grounds. In the first place, other parties could have claimed that the understandings were in reality reservations inasmuch as they modified the language of Article II rather than merely clarifying it. As Schweppe pointed out, according to Article II, the intent could be to destroy a group *either* in whole or in part; the U.S. understandings claimed that the intent must be to destroy an entire group. Second, other parties could have objected to the U.S. reservations on the ground that they were incompatible with the object and purpose of the convention. It is certainly arguable that the U.S. interpretations of "intent" in the understandings would have undermined any possibility of effective enforcement of the convention. As we shall see in a moment, the need to prove the intent to destroy a group, regardless of the number of victims, is already enough of a problem. The need to prove the intent to destroy an entire group would add to this problem, and perhaps even rule out the application of the convention to situations in which the drafters would most probably have expected it to apply. In short, there would have been much to commend objections to the first two versions of the U.S. understanding regarding intent.

The last version of the understanding, the one included in the Lugar-Helms-Hatch Sovereignty Package, differs substantially from the two that preceded it. Nonetheless, it deals with the same two issues that the earlier versions dealt with: the meaning of a part of a group and the element of intent. The understanding says that the United States understands a part of a group to mean a substantial part, and that the intent to destroy a group in whole or in substantial part must be a *specific* intent. It is primarily in this latter respect that the understanding in the Sovereignty Package differs from its predecessors, and we shall return to this point in our discussion of the intent element in the commission of genocide.

Looking back over the four decades of debate, we can see from the terms of the three different versions of the understanding regarding the phrase "intent to destroy, in whole or in part," that there has never been any doubt that the United States would claim that the intention of those who commit genocide must be to destroy at least a *substantial* part of a group. Yet those who made an issue out of this have themselves often seemed confused. The debate over what a part, or even a substantial part, of a group means has often degenerated into a numbers game: Is a part or a substantial part of a group 1 out of 5, 5 out of 20, 1,001 out of 2,000, 100,001 out of 200,000? The question is important, but it is unlikely that the answer lies in some rigid mathematical formula. Rather, in the final analysis the matter is one that calls for a judicial construction. Some more careful analysts pointed this out years ago. Gordon Tillott, for example, who represented the Section on Comparative and International Law of the ABA at the 1950 hearings (a section that favored ratification even if the association as a whole did not), made the point in response to questions from Senator Brien McMahon.

SENATOR MCMAHON: Let us assume there is a group of 200,000. Would that have to mean that you would have to murder 100,001 before a major part would come under the definition?

MR. TILLOTT: Well, I do not think that it would be possible, of course, to state the matter mathematically, but I think that is a matter for a judicial construction. I think that there you must have confidence in your court, realizing that the court will again look to the objective of the legislation or the treaty for an interpretation of the words.[27]

Even if one were to carry the point further and recognize that some guidelines might be established in the implementing legislation to assist the courts, those guidelines would still need to be interpreted by courts. The U.S. implementing legislation, the Proxmire Act, provides such guidance, and yet it still needs further interpretation. As regards the question of what constitutes a substantial part of a group, the act states: "the term 'substantial part' means a part of the group of such numerical significance that the destruction or loss of that part would cause the destruction of the group as a viable entity within the nation of which such group is a part."[28]

This portion of the Proxmire Act carries through on what the supporters of the understanding in the Committee on Foreign Relations had in mind when they insisted on its adoption. They wanted to eliminate the possibility that the convention could be interpreted as applying to "isolated acts of violence" against members of groups.[29] Another section of the act goes further. In the final stages of its deliberations on the bill, the Senate Committee on the Judiciary adopted an amendment sponsored by Senator Charles Grassley to require "more than one victimization as a predicate for a charge of genocide."[30] Hence, the committee altered an earlier House of Representatives version of the legislation and made it consistent with Article II of the convention; for example, it changed the phrases "kills a member of that group" to "kills members of that group," and "causes serious bodily injury to a member of that group" to "causes serious bodily injury to members of that group."[31] The committee noted, as analysts such as Ben Whitaker had done previously, that the plural is used throughout Article II of the convention. For itself, however, the committee stated that its use of the plural *did not* include the singular.[32] As a result, under the U.S. implementing legislation, it would appear that the murder or lynching of a single individual with the intent to destroy, in whole or in substantial part, a protected group within a nation would apparently not constitute genocide.

Proving the Intent to Destroy Groups

The second issue that the understanding addresses is the intent requirement in the commission of genocide. According to the understanding, the intent must be a *specific* intent. This requirement makes the understanding in the Lugar-Helms-Hatch Sovereignty Package unique when compared with its predecessors. Senator Jesse Helms was the main proponent of this change in the wording of the understanding. He argued that the understanding recommended by the Committee on Foreign Relations during the 1970s "was well intentioned, but would do little to clarify the definition of genocide or the standard of intent."[33] As he put it, "We cannot assume that the International Court of Justice, or any other court outside the United States, will view intent as it is viewed in the Anglo-American legal system. Nor even if it were, whether the standard set forth is a general intent or a specific intent. *A general intent might be inferred from circumstances, or the result of circumstances, which, when allowed by a government, might be interpreted as an intended consequence.*"[34]

Clearly, for Helms, the addition of the word "specific" in the U.S. understanding would eliminate what he considered undesirable interpretations of Article II. A person's guilt apparently could not be established without proving a specific intent to commit genocide; that is, it could not be inferred from the results of his or her actions—or at least this is what Helms claimed. As we shall see in chapter 5, similar considerations lay behind the adoption of a U.S. understanding regarding genocide committed during armed combat. There, the purpose of the understanding was to say that soldiers could not be convicted of genocide unless it were proven that they had the specific intent to commit the crime, which led some senators on the Committee on Foreign Relations to wonder if the understanding meant that the United States had something to hide. The same question could surely be raised here. The purpose of the U.S. understanding regarding the intent element in Article II was apparently to make it more difficult to prove charges of genocide.

In fact, the understanding exaggerates a problem that already exists in interpreting and applying the convention, a problem that is even more important than the question of what constitutes a part of a group; namely, the need to prove the *intent to destroy* a group in whole or in part regardless of the number of actual victims. The drafters devoted some attention specifically to the words "intent to destroy" when Article II was being discussed in the Sixth Committee of the General Assembly. The Soviet representative, supported by the French representative, proposed deleting those words and instead adopting language to guard against pleas of innocence on the ground of absence of intent. The notion of intent was retained, however, because it was perceived as an essential element in the definition of a crime, as the U.S. representative insisted; but the fears of the Soviet and French representatives proved prophetic, as two recent cases illustrate.

One case concerns the tragic plight of the Aché Indians in Paraguay. In *Genocide in Paraguay* Richard Arens and his colleagues provide evidence of genocidal acts, as enumerated in Article II, committed against that small group of primitive people.[35] When pressed on the issue, however, the Paraguayan government cloaked itself in the words "intent to destroy." In short, it claimed that there was no intent to destroy the Aché Indians, hence genocide was not being committed. The U.S. Department of State evidently concurred, though the reported atrocities provoked a storm of protest in the Senate. Relief could not be found in the United Nations or the Organization of American States. Arens himself, in his "lawyer's summation" of the tragedy, argued that the Paraguayan government's attempt to refute the charges of genocide on the ground of absence of intent defied "rational belief."[36]

The second case in which the notion of intent has figured prominently concerned U.S. involvement in the Vietnam War. During the 1960s and 1970s there were widespread charges, at home and abroad, that the United States was waging a genocidal war in Vietnam. The charges have been the subject of extensive investigation and analysis, and many points of view have been expressed on them. The International War Crimes Tribunal (the so-called Russell Tribunal), for example, which conducted a "trial" in Stockholm and Copenhagen in 1966–67, unanimously found the United States guilty of genocide in Vietnam.[37] Charges in which other states allied with the United States were implicated also received verdicts of guilty from the tribunal.

The most prominent argument on the notion of intent was advanced by Jean-Paul Sartre. Pointing out, quite correctly, that the Genocide Convention "was tacitly referring to memories which were still fresh," namely, to Hitler's "proclaimed . . . intent to exterminate the Jews," Sartre asserted that not all governments, including that of the United States, would be as stupid as Hitler's and proclaim such demonic intentions.[38] Hence, for Sartre the question was would it be possible, "*by studying the facts objectively, to discover implicit in them such a genocidal intention?*"[39] Sartre concluded that the "truth [was] apparent *on the battlefield* in the racism of the American soldiers."[40] The *authors* of such a genocidal plan would not necessarily be "thoroughly conscious of their intention." This would be "impossible to decide. We would have to plumb the depths of their consciences—and the Puritan bad faith of Americans works wonders."[41]

Many have taken issue with Sartre's claims, the judgment of the Russell Tribunal, and the various other charges of genocide in Vietnam. Some, such as Guenter Lewy, have looked to governmental statements (which, needless to say, never admitted a genocidal intent) and population statistics and health standards of the Vietnamese people and found the charge of genocide "grotesque."[42] Others, such as Cherif Bassiouni, have approached the charges through a more technical analysis of the provisions of Article II of the Genocide Convention and argued that there was no intent on the part of the United States to destroy, in whole or in part, any national, ethnical, racial, or religious group in Vietnam because the opposing "parties in Vietnam did not include a separate national, ethnical, racial, or religious group."[43] The United States, according to Bassiouni, took one side in a civil war and was engaged in activities directed against the Vietcong, a "term designating members of the insurgent military force," not a "separate national, ethnical, racial, or religious group."[44] Less certain conclusions have been reached by others. Hugo Adam Bedau, for example, after applying different models to discover intent, reached a "Scottish verdict. Not proven, not quite."[45]

Clearly, in any alleged case of genocide, the arguments are likely to concentrate on the need to prove intent, not on the number of victims. This is a serious hindrance to applying the convention, even if, as Bunyan Bryant suggests, "the number of victims may be of evidentiary value with respect to proving the necessary intent."[46] One might even conclude, from a reading of the Senate hearings on the Genocide Convention, that some proponents of U.S. ratification supported it with the expectation that no charge of genocide against anyone would stand because of the need to prove intent. As the Committee on Foreign Relations stated in a report to the Senate in

1976: "Harassment of minority groups and racial and religious intolerance generally, no matter how much to be deplored, are not outlawed per se by the Genocide Convention. Far from outlawing discrimination, article II is so written as to make it, in fact, difficult to prove the 'intent' element necessary to sustain a charge of genocide against anyone."[47] Still, an understanding regarding this issue was always perceived to be necessary, and the one included in the Lugar-Helms-Hatch Sovereignty Package states that the "specific intent" must exist to destroy a group "in whole or in substantial part." And, as we have seen, the U.S. implementing legislation, the Proxmire Act, follows up on the terms of the understanding.[48]

Is the Understanding Desirable?

Arguments can be made on both sides regarding the merits of the U.S. understanding of the phrase "intent to destroy, in whole or in part," in Article II of the Genocide Convention. On the one hand, it represents an improvement over earlier efforts in that it does not say that the United States understands Article II to mean that the intentions of the perpetrators of genocide must be to destroy an entire group, unlike the versions proposed in 1950 and throughout the 1970s, which stated that the intention must be to destroy an entire group. The latter were more like reservations to Article II inasmuch as they modified the plain meaning of the language of the article. For that reason, as suggested earlier, other parties to the convention would have had good grounds for objecting to the labeling of those statements *as* understandings and to insist that they were in fact reservations; they would also have had good reasons for objecting to the reservations on the ground that they were incompatible with the object and purpose of the convention. What about the understanding that was included in the Lugar-Helms-Hatch Sovereignty Package? Is it objectionable?

The understanding recognizes that an intention to destroy a (substantial) part of a protected group could constitute genocide. This part of the understanding was intended to rule out charges of genocide against single individuals or very small groups, as in racially motivated lynchings. Would other parties to the convention argue that the effect of this clause is to carve out an exception and therefore to modify the legal effects of Article II? No other party to the convention has ratified with a similar understanding or reservation, which gives us some idea as to what their practice in regard to this matter has been.[49] Perhaps they would be dissuaded from objecting to this part of the U.S. understanding out of a conviction that the convention was intended to apply to large numbers of people; perhaps not.

It would, of course, have been absurd for the United States (or the drafters of the convention) not to have recognized that genocide could be committed against parts of groups. Genocidal actions could be taken—and probably have been taken—against parts of groups for one or more of a variety of reasons: to intimidate or subjugate a large group by destroying only a part of it, which may explain the atrocities committed during the struggle over the creation of Bangladesh in the early 1970s;[50] to reduce any political threat a group as a whole might pose by virtue of its size, which appears to have been a factor in Burundi in the early 1970s;[51] or, perhaps, to eliminate a part of a group simply because the group as a whole is "in the way."[52] This last motive suggests that economic considerations can lie behind genocidal acts. In *Genocide in Paraguay*, anthropologist Mark Munzel describes the Aché Indians as a "stone-age tribe without social or political connections or aspirations that could make their existence dangerous to the Paraguayan elite," and he suggests that the "genocidal policy directed against them can only be explained by the fact that they are in the way."[53] In the way of what? In the way of economic development and progress. Another anthropologist, Shelton Davis, writes of a "silent war" being waged against aboriginal peoples and innocent peasants in Brazil—and more broadly against the rain forest ecosystem of the Amazon Basin—in the name of a specific "model of development." This model, he suggests, "is being implemented in several other frontier areas of the world."[54]

Questions could also be raised about the second main objective of the U.S. understanding, namely, the attempt to clarify the meaning of the word "intent." According to the understanding, there must be a *specific* intent to destroy a group entirely or in substantial part. Here, the proponents of the understanding were reacting to the findings of the Russell Tribunal, and especially to the arguments advanced by Jean-Paul Sartre quoted earlier, that the intent could be "apparent" in the actions. Again, no other party to the convention has made a comparable statement upon ratification. Perhaps the other parties consider this part of the U.S. understanding superfluous. After all, no one seems to think that genocide could ever occur "accidentally." But again, perhaps not.

Even though the U.S. understanding might be found unobjectionable by other parties on legal grounds, was it sound public policy to include it in the Lugar-Helms-Hatch Sovereignty Package? Other parties to the convention might find the understanding offensive even if legally unobjectionable. The fact that none of the other parties has ratified the convention with a similar understanding or reservation in itself is significant, and indicates that if the phrase "intent to destroy, in whole or in part," was the subject of any extensive discussion in those states when the convention was being considered, it was not thought to be so troublesome as to warrant ratification with either an understanding or a reservation. It suggests also that states that have already ratified the convention understand the phrase clearly enough for purposes of designing domestic implementing legislation. The Genocide Act of 1969 adopted by the British Parliament, for example, incorporates the whole of Article II as the definition of genocide.[55] Canadian law (1969–70) on the subject was drafted in a different way, but it does specify that genocide means certain acts "committed with intent to destroy in whole or in part any identifiable group."[56] These states, at least, are evidently prepared to let courts determine the precise meaning of words and phrases in Article II should the need arise. Clearly, they saw no need to ratify with an understanding or reservation. Why couldn't the United States do the same?

There is an additional reason why some parties to the convention might find the understanding offensive even if legally unobjectionable. The understanding is only one of a "package" of understandings and reservations, discussed in other chapters, that was imposed on the Reagan administration by the Senate, mainly by Republican senators. It is true that for political reasons of its own the administration capitulated to the critics of the convention and agreed to all the conditions of ratification, and even offered to assist in drafting appropriate conditions.[57] Nonetheless, the Sovereignty Package has no counterpart among any of the other instruments of ratification of the convention. It is unique in its breadth of coverage, and, given the atmosphere of acrimonious debate in which it was adopted, it could lead other parties to the convention to conclude that the United States is not ratifying in good faith. There is much to commend such suspicions, not only in the historical record of debate over ratification but also in Senate reports and debates that reveal the intentions of the most outspoken supporters of the Lugar-Helms-Hatch Sovereignty Package.

Proponents of the Sovereignty Package made much of their intention to fashion a "true sovereignty package." As Senator Orrin Hatch stated, the insertion of the words "which shall apply" before the list of understandings in the package accomplished that goal. He believed that the words transformed "the legal content" of the understandings "from merely recommendatory to legally mandatory," or *transformed the understandings into reservations if they should be challenged.*[58] Similarly, the majority on the Committee on Foreign Relations made their objectives clear in the committee's report to the Senate. They argued that the understandings were consistent with the drafting history of the convention, and that a "review of this history would yield no contrary interpretation of the obligation in question." They went on to say that "in the unlikely event there is some dispute about a term to which a Senate understanding applies, the Committee wishes to state unequivocally that the Senate understanding is controlling. The extent of the United States' obligation is defined by the Senate understandings. No contrary interpretation, whether the result of a decision of the International Court of Justice or some other tribunal, will supersede or nullify the U.S. understandings."[59]

Obviously, the majority of the Committee on Foreign Relations was determined to anticipate every potential problem—including any that might arise as a result of the provisions of the Vienna Convention on the Law of Treaties of 1969, specifically those provisions that pertain to the right of other parties to a multilateral convention to question even the labels that parties attach to their conditions of ratification. The Genocide Convention is a multilateral convention, but the most vociferous opponents of its ratification in the Senate took a staunch pro-sovereignty, unilateralist position. To them, the United States should set its own agenda and be accountable to no one. They were merely using the legal means of the Sovereignty Package to achieve their political agenda.

The majority on the committee also insisted that the Senate conditions would be binding on the administration; that, indeed, if the president did not want to accept the Senate conditions, he could not ratify the convention. This point seemed unnecessary, as the Reagan administration had agreed to the critics' terms. In fact, the committee claimed to have been assured by the administration that the conditions included in the Sovereignty Package would be included in the instrument of ratification that would be deposited at the United Nations.[60] The administration did carry through on this assurance.[61] However, the content of the committee's report suggests that it wanted to leave no room for doubt that its actions were binding on the executive branch.

All of this seems pointless, and may even come to naught. Despite the defiant attitudes of some senators, there is no way the Senate can prevent other parties to the Genocide Convention from objecting to any of the understandings or reservations in the Sovereignty Package. There is also no way the Senate can prevent any other party from declaring that it does not recognize the United States as a party. In fact, the objections of some parties (such as the Netherlands and Greece) to reservations made by other parties indicate that they will not consider the United States a party to the convention; furthermore, as we have already noted, nine European states raised objections to some U.S. conditions soon after the instrument of ratification had been deposited with the UN secretary general. Moreover, and perhaps most important, even though the majority of the committee emphasized that it considered the conditions of ratification binding on the executive branch, the minority, who strongly favored ratification with few conditions, as well as some senators who opposed ratification, expressed well-founded doubts about whether or not the Sovereignty Package could be *permanently* imposed on the executive branch. Indeed, it is far from certain that the conditions could actually bind future administrations.[62] We shall return to these points in chapter 9.

Chapter 4 Protected Groups and Political Groups

We must reject the claims of some that the treaty is worthless because it does not protect political groups. It protects national, ethnic, racial, and religious groups. I find it hard to imagine a nation defending itself against charges of genocide by saying, "We are not committing mass murder against an ethnic or racial group—we are only committing mass murder against a political group."
—Senator John Kerry, Senate floor debate, February 1986

The drafters of the Genocide Convention faced an issue of profound importance in seeking to identify the objects of protection. The General Assembly's Resolution 96 (I) refers to past instances of genocide when "racial, religious, political and other groups" had been destroyed. Article II of the convention, in contrast, identifies national, ethnic, racial, and religious groups as the objects of protection. The main difference between the resolution and the article, then, is that Article II does not extend protection to political groups as such. The drafters of the convention seriously considered the possibility of making it applicable to actions against political groups; in fact, a reference to them was included in Article II throughout most of the drafting stage. However, the word "political" was deleted from the article near the close of debate on the convention as a whole, and as a result its protection does not extend to political groups.

The drafters' decision has evidently been of little concern in most countries of the world, for the Genocide Convention has been widely accepted by states. However, it has always been of great concern, even an important obstacle to ratification, in the United States. Among other things, many critics of the convention have argued that the deletion of the word "political" from Article II created a loophole in the definition of genocide that could be abused by totalitarian states, especially the Soviet Union, which would fatally undermine its application. According to this interpretation of Article II, the Soviet Union could commit genocide against a national or ethnic group but claim that its actions were not genocidal at all because they were aimed at political enemies of the state, not at a national or ethnic group as such. Some critics have seen this possible evasion of charges of genocide as sufficient grounds for declining to ratify the convention. Others have argued that the United States should try to close the loophole by seeking an amendment of the convention that would make it applicable to genocide against political groups.

In this chapter we examine the arguments that have been made in the United States on the issue of the so-called political group exemption in Article II, and we explore the implications of the proposals that have been made to overcome the abusive interpretations of the article that the deletion of the word "political" allegedly makes possible. Why has this been such an important issue to critics of the convention in the United States? What arguments have been advanced on the issue, and how cogent are they? Should the convention extend protection to political groups? To provide the appropriate background for taking up these questions, let us look first at the groups that are protected under the terms of Article II and the reasons why the drafters decided not to extend protection to political groups as such.

The Groups Protected: National, Ethnic, Racial, and Religious

The drafters of the Genocide Convention engaged in very little debate over national, ethnic, racial, and religious groups as objects of protection. Issues related to these groups were, of course, discussed from the beginning of the drafting process, but the disagreements regarding them tended to be relatively minor and sometimes seemed to be related to specific ideological concerns. For example, Platon Morozov, the representative of the Soviet Union on the Ad Hoc Committee of the ECOSOC, argued that the convention should cover only racial and national groups, and that religious groups should be covered only in the sense that they are sometimes subgroups of national groups. In fact, Morozov maintained, "in all known cases of genocide committed for a religious motive, that motive had always been connected with other motives of a national or racial character."[1] He reiterated this argument in the Sixth Committee of the General Assembly.[2]

In general, throughout the negotiations the Soviets argued that the convention should affirm that genocide "is one of the gravest crimes against mankind," and that it should recognize that the crime is "organically bound up with fascism-nazism and other similar race 'theories' which preach racial and national hatred, the domination of the so-called higher races, and the extermination of the so-called lower races."[3] To most drafters, however, these concepts seemed propagandistic, and they felt that the convention should not be tied to any particular historical event or based on the idea that genocide is an exclusive product of any particular ideology. Accordingly, they decisively rejected the Soviet proposals regarding the link between genocide and fascism-nazism in the Sixth Committee and again in a plenary session of the General Assembly. Similarly, the drafters were strongly opposed to the Soviet proposal that religious groups should be considered as subgroups of national groups. They argued that there could be cases of genocide against religious groups within a single nation.[4] In fact, the vast majority of the drafters seemed to simply dismiss the Soviet position on religious groups. The Sixth Committee overwhelmingly rejected, by a vote of forty against, five in favor, and one abstention, an amendment of the Ad Hoc Committee's draft of Article II that would have put the word "religious" in parentheses following the word "national."[5]

Article II of the convention thus aims to protect two groups that are expressly mentioned in General Assembly Resolution 96 (I) as having been victims of genocide in the past—racial and religious groups. National groups are not expressly mentioned in the resolution, but there seems never to have been any doubt throughout the drafting stage that they should be identified as an object of protection in Article II. In fact, the matter was never really discussed; it was apparently assumed by everyone concerned that national groups should be covered.

The reference to ethnic groups, which are also not expressly mentioned in Resolution 96 (I), was inserted in Article II at the request of the Swedish delegation during debate in the Sixth Committee. It is not clear from the record precisely why ethnic groups were thought to be so important in their own right, but the Swedish delegation seems to have been concerned about possible future problems in interpreting the word "national" and wanted to draw a distinction between national and ethnic groups. Other representatives, however, argued that the word "ethnic" meant essentially the same thing as the word "racial," and that it was therefore unnecessary to specifically mention ethnic groups because the word "racial" was already in Article II. The drafters of the convention glossed over these difficulties, however, and adopted the Swedish amendment by a very narrow vote (eighteen in favor, seventeen against, and eleven abstentions).[6]

Defining the Protected Groups

It is noteworthy that the drafters, having agreed on the groups that were to be identified in Article II, decided merely to enumerate them, and not to define them in any detail. Had they decided to define the groups, they would have clarified the nature of the international obligation of any state that ratified the convention. In principle, it seems desirable to state such obligations as precisely as possible; if states are permitted too much discretion, confusion could arise in determining precisely what their obligations are.[7] At the same time, it seems clear from the discussions that took place during the drafting stage that it would have been extremely difficult, if not impossible, for the drafters to agree upon widely acceptable definitions of the groups. In fact, they made no serious attempt to do so. Precisely how the groups were to be defined, then, was presumably left to states' individual implementing legislation.

The discretion that parties to the convention can exercise in defining the protected groups may not be entirely satisfactory. A United Nations study of this matter showed that states that have ratified the convention have defined the groups in different ways, and it is reasonable to expect that other states would follow suit.[8] Thus, the methods of Canada,[9] the United Kingdom,[10] and many other countries are not exactly the same as the approach taken by the United States in the Proxmire Act.[11] While it is arguable that any difficulties arising from definitional differences could be resolved by the ICJ in accordance with Article IX of the convention, no such dispute has yet been brought to the court.

Despite potential definitional problems, it is probably just as well that no effort was made to define the groups more precisely in the convention itself, for it is unlikely that acceptable definitions could have been agreed on. The word "national," for example, seems to have acquired a meaning synonymous with citizenship in a state or country, regardless of its original meaning. The word "ethnic," in common usage, tends to refer to a group of people distinguished by certain cultural and linguistic characteristics. The word "racial" tends to be associated with physical characteristics of a people such as skin color. But these words could have different meanings (or perhaps no meaning) in different cultural contexts, and it could be difficult to translate these words from one language to another. By way of example, one hears frequently of the Soviet Union's treatment of *national* minorities and of Soviet *nationality* policies. The word "national" in such cases refers to Ukrainians, Georgians, and so forth, not to the citizens of the Soviet Union as a whole. In the English language, the word "ethnic" might seem more appropriate.

The Drafters' Intention to Protect Stable Groups

Although the drafters did not define the protected groups in detail, it is clear, as we shall see in a moment, that they intended to extend protection to *stable* groups only—groups having an enduring identity. This decision makes sense given the historical context in which the drafters were operating. Because the convention was obviously drafted in response to atrocities committed against the Jews, Poles, Gypsies, and other groups by the Nazis during World War II, Article II would apply to such a situation whether Jews were considered a religious, ethnic, or even racial or national group. Similarly, the convention would cover the Armenian genocide, and it would probably apply as well to numerous other instances of genocide that have occurred in Africa, Asia, and Latin America since World War II. Of the diverse legislation that parties to the convention have adopted on this subject, the Canadian legislation perhaps best reflects the intentions of the drafters. That legislation aims to protect "any identifiable group," a concept that "means any section of the public distinguished by colour, race, religion, or ethnic origin."[12]

Why Political Groups Are Not Protected

Although the drafters reached agreement relatively easily on most of the groups eventually identified in Article II, discord arose with respect to political groups. The issue consumed a vast amount of the time of both the Ad Hoc Committee of the ECOSOC and the Sixth Committee of the General Assembly.[13] As we have seen, Resolution 96 (I) specifically mentioned political groups among those that had been victims of genocide in the past. However, opposition to including them among those to be protected under the terms of the Genocide Convention soon developed. This became clear in the very narrow vote of four to three in favor of including political groups when the Ad Hoc Committee prepared its draft of Article II.[14] The committee's division into two groups carried over into the much larger Sixth Committee. The arguments put forth on the issue were essentially the same in both bodies, though the outcomes were different.

The Arguments Against Protecting Political Groups

Four different arguments were advanced against including political groups in Article II of the convention. Of these, two were of little importance as far as the ultimate decision was concerned. The argument of Platon Morozov, the Soviet representative, rested on allegedly scientific grounds. He argued that "genocide" referred to the destruction of races or nations, and that including political groups in Article II would have had the effect of expanding the meaning of the term beyond "the fundamental notion of genocide recognized by science."[15] But like the Soviet position on religious groups discussed earlier, this position was disregarded by the majority of the representatives of other states. This point deserves emphasis because, as we shall see, many scholars have concluded that the Soviet opposition to the protection of political groups was crucial to the outcome; and many critics of the convention in the United States have vilified the U.S. delegation to the United Nations for capitulating to the Soviets on the issue. The ABA, as well as extremist, right-wing groups such as Liberty Lobby, the Voters Interest League, and the American Coalition of Patriotic Societies, have argued that the U.S. delegation appeased or sold out to the Soviet delegation.[16]

A second argument, made by several representatives on the Sixth Committee, was that the protection of political groups ought to be considered in the broader context of human rights rather than the narrower one of genocide, and that the Human Rights Commission therefore seemed the more appropriate body in which to discuss the issue.[17] But this argument seems to have been introduced more as an afterthought—a convenient way of avoiding an issue full of conceptual and political difficulties.

The other two arguments were of much greater consequence and were dealt with at much greater length by the drafters of the convention. One had to do with a perceived lack of stability or permanence of political groups. This issue was vigorously and repeatedly raised by a number of Third World states. The representatives of Venezuela, Iran, Egypt, and Uruguay on the Sixth Committee were especially outspoken in this regard. They argued that political groups were different in kind from national, ethnic, racial, and religious groups, since persons tend to be born into the latter groups, or at least the membership of these groups does not change over relatively long periods of time. They did not perceive political groups to possess such stability or permanence. Precisely what did "political group" mean? Most delegates doubted that any precise and widely acceptable definition could be provided. The same arguments, of course, had to be made in connection with a proposal advanced by the U.S. delegation to include economic groups in Article II. Many states reacted strongly against this proposal, and the United States withdrew it.[18] As a representative of the Netherlands argued, economic groups would be even more difficult to define than political groups: "It would lead to the absurd result that certain professions, when threatened by economic measures which were required in the interest of the country might invoke the convention to protect their own interests."[19]

The Venezuelan representative's comments seemed to sum up the attitudes of most delegates on the purpose of the convention and the impact that purpose had on deciding which groups to protect: "The purpose of the convention was not to protect any and every group; if that were the case, other groups of workers, artists, scientists, etc., should also be taken into consideration."[20]

Finally, some representatives opposed including political groups in Article II out of concern that disputes over their inclusion might jeopardize support for the convention itself in many states. Some drafters felt that their governments might find it necessary to take action against subversive elements. Many representatives on the Sixth Committee, noting that the draft convention contemplated the creation of an international criminal court, feared that if political groups were protected under the terms of the convention, their governments might be reluctant to ratify it. As the Venezuelan representative stated:

> The inclusion of political groups might endanger the future of the convention because many States would be unwilling to ratify it, fearing the possibility of being called before an international tribunal to answer charges made against them, even if those charges were without foundation.
>
> Subversive elements might make use of the convention to weaken the attempts of their own governments to suppress them. . . . [While] certain countries where civic spirit was highly developed and the political struggle fought through electoral laws would favor the inclusion of political groups, . . . there were countries where the population was still developing and where political struggles were very violent. These countries would obviously not favor the inclusion of political groups in the convention.[21]

The Arguments in Favor of Protecting Political Groups

The views summarized above were widely shared, but the U.S. representatives, John Maktos on the Ad Hoc Committee of the ECOSOC, and Ernest A. Gross on the Sixth Committee of the General Assembly, took strong stands in favor of listing political groups along with national, ethnic, racial, and religious groups in Article II. Their insistence had the effect of prolonging the negotiations, especially in the Sixth Committee, until the United States was ready to compromise on the issue.

In the Sixth Committee, Ernest Gross advanced three main arguments in favor of extending protection to political groups. First, he argued that in practice many states defined political groups in their national legislation and decrees – for example, by banning political parties or by establishing a certain party as the only legal party of the state. Hence, he insisted, it could not be maintained that political groups were impossible to define. Second, he took issue with those who thought that extending protection to political groups would hinder the ability of governments to take action against groups involved in subversive activities. As he saw it, various types of groups, not only political groups, could engage in subversive activities, so it seemed unreasonable to think that states would be concerned only about the activities of political groups. And third, he invoked the terms of Resolution 96 (I), in which the General Assembly had declared that political groups had been victims of genocide, and he maintained that not to follow through on that earlier statement could weaken the credibility of the United Nations.[22]

Representatives of several states supported the U.S. position on political groups. An Ecuadorian delegate, for example, argued that the inclusion of political groups in Article II would not "assist subversive elements in revolt against the authority of a State, because there was a great difference between measures for maintaining order in such a case and measures employed in the perpetration of genocide."[23] In his view, it "would not be difficult to distinguish between" the two types of situations. In any event, it was the function of courts to "examine and reject" slanderous allegations of genocide. Therefore, the possibility that such allegations might be made against parties to the convention should not dissuade them from ratifying it. Like Ernest Gross, the Ecuadorian delegate also raised the issue of the credibility of the United Nations, saying that "public opinion will not understand it if the United Nations no longer condemned in 1948 what it had condemned in 1946."[24]

The Resolution of the Issue

The debate in the Sixth Committee over whether or not political groups should be made objects of protection under the terms of the convention was lively and prolonged; in fact, it was the most time-consuming issue that faced the drafters. Since the draft convention prepared by the Ad Hoc Committee of the ECOSOC contained a reference to political groups, the question for the Sixth Committee was whether or not that reference should be retained. Table 4.1 shows the results of a vote taken on a U.S. motion to retain the reference. The vote was twenty-nine in favor, thirteen against, with nine abstentions. In other words, half of the total membership of the United Nations at the time supported the U.S. proposal. But the three largest groupings of states (Asia, Americas, and Europe) were rather sharply

Table 4.1 Vote in the Sixth Committee on Political Groups (First Vote: *Include Political Groups*).

Area	Number (Percentage)	Yes	Abstain	No	No vote
Africa[1]		0	2	1	1
		(0)	(50.0)	(25.0)	(25.0)
Asia[2]		8	3	1	1
		(61.5)	(23.1)	(7.7)	(7.7)
Oceania[3]		2	0	0	0
		(100)	(0)	(0)	(0)
Americas[4]		10	2	5	5
		(45.5)	(9.1)	(22.7)	(22.7)
Europe[5]		9	2	6	0
		(52.9)	(11.8)	(35.3)	(0)
TOTALS		29	9	13	7
		(50.0)	(15.5)	(22.4)	(12.1)

Source: The data used in this table were made available by the Inter-University Consortium for Political Research. The data were originally collected by the International Relations Archive. Neither the original collector of the data nor the consortium bears any responsibility for analyses or interpretations presented here.

[1] *Africa:* Egypt, Ethiopia, Liberia, South Africa.

[2] *Asia:* Afghanistan, Burma, China, India, Iran, Iraq, Lebanon, Pakistan, Philippines, Saudi Arabia, Thailand, Syria, Yemen.

[3] *Oceania:* Australia, New Zealand.

[4] *Americas:* Argentina, Bolivia, Brazil, Canada, Chile, Colombia, Costa Rica, Cuba, Dominican Republic, Ecuador, El Salvador, Guatemala, Haiti, Honduras, Mexico, Nicaragua, Panama, Paraguay, Peru, USA, Uruguay, Venezuela.

[5] *Europe:* Belgium, Byelorussian SSR, Czechoslovakia, Denmark, France, Greece, Iceland, Luxembourg, Netherlands, Norway, Poland, Sweden, Turkey, Ukrainian SSR, USSR, United Kingdom, Yugoslavia.

divided. These divisions reflected the strong feelings of some delegates regarding the lack of stability of political groups and the relatively widespread belief that if they extended protection to political groups, many states would decline to ratify the convention out of fear that they would be unable to combat subversion effectively. Still, the measure carried.

In view of the long debate over the issue, the vote in favor of referring to political groups in Article II suggests that the arguments made by the U.S. representative were persuasive. The decision continued to be controversial, however, throughout the negotiations on other provisions of the convention. Indeed, it was the subject of the most serious disagreement during the drafting process. Near the close of debate on the convention as a whole, the issue was taken up again by representatives of Iran, Uruguay, and Egypt, who proposed that political groups be deleted from Article II.[25] The Egyptian delegate noted that as the discussion in the Sixth Committee proceeded, it had become clear that the inclusion of political groups in Article II would become a serious obstacle to ratification by many states. The word "political" should therefore be deleted from the article for this very practical reason.[26]

At this point, Ernest Gross took what he considered to be a "conciliatory" position, accepting the deletion of political groups from Article II *in exchange for* a provision in Article VI that contemplated the creation of an international criminal court.[27] The United States had supported the creation of an international criminal court throughout the negotiations on the convention, and the Ad Hoc Committee's draft convention included an article pertaining to the establishment of such a court. However, that article had been deleted by the Sixth Committee.[28] A number of states, including the Soviet Union, voiced strong opposition to the creation of an international criminal court out of concern that unfounded charges of genocide would be brought to the court against them if they took action against political groups.[29]

To the United States, therefore, it seemed wise to delete the political groups clause in Article II, particularly if the Sixth Committee delegates previously opposed would be willing to reconsider their rejection of the provision in Article VI regarding an international criminal court. This compromise proved acceptable to a large enough number of delegates and was significant, even though the court was never created (see chapter 7).

Once the United States withdrew its support for political groups, the Sixth Committee deleted the reference to them from Article II. However, it is noteworthy that on the second vote on the issue (see table 4.2), the number of states not voting more than doubled, increasing to approximately one-third the membership of the United Nations at the time. The number of states abstaining also increased. Only six member states (Burma, Chile, China, Ecuador, the Netherlands, and the Philippines) felt strongly enough about the issue to vote against excluding the reference to political groups from Article II. The U.S. proposal was adopted while a majority of member states either abstained or did not vote on the issue. A large increase in the number of abstentions among European states (from two, or 11.8 percent, to ten, or 58.8 percent) is especially noteworthy. The Soviet Union and its handful of consistent supporters (Byelorussian SSR, Ukrainian SSR, Czechoslovakia, Poland, and Yugoslavia) abstained, apparently to indicate

Table 4.2 Vote in the Sixth Committee on Political Groups (Second Vote: *Exclude Political Groups*).

Area	Number (Percentage)	Yes	Abstain	No	No vote
Africa		2	0	0	2
		(50.0)	(0)	(0)	(50.0)
Asia		5	0	3	5
		(38.5)	(0)	(23.1)	(38.5)
Oceania		1	1	0	0
		(50.0)	(50.0)	(0)	(0)
Americas		10	1	2	9
		(45.5)	(4.5)	(9.1)	(40.9)
Europe		4	10	1	2
		(23.5)	(58.8)	(5.9)	(11.8)
TOTALS		22	12	6	18
		(37.9)	(20.7)	(10.3)	(31.0)

Source: Same as table 4.1.

displeasure with the international criminal court compromise forged by the U.S. delegation.

It would be fair to say, then, that political groups fell victim to two major considerations when the convention was drafted. First, there were practical political considerations. The United States could have its way on political groups or on an international criminal court, but not both. In the end it took the court. Second, there were theoretical considerations. Political groups were widely perceived to be different in kind from national, ethnic, racial, and religious groups. Furthermore, they were perceived as essentially unstable, since membership in political groups is by choice rather than by birth, and such membership can change drastically over a relatively short period of time.

The Proposed U.S. Amendment on Political Groups

Ironically, while the United States agreed to the deletion of the reference to political groups in Article II, in part to remove an obstacle to the convention's ratification by other states, the decision to delete caused problems in the U.S. Senate. This becomes apparent from an examination of the record of debates on the question of ratification that dates back to the Truman administration. In fact, the issue continued to plague the Senate up to the adoption of the Lugar-Helms-Hatch Sovereignty Package in February 1986, and actions taken at that time suggest that the issue, at least as far as the United States is concerned, has not been laid to rest.

During debate over the Sovereignty Package on the Senate floor, two strategies were proposed to deal with the failure of the convention to extend protection to political groups. The most extreme proposal was advanced principally by Senator Steven Symms, and it entailed *amending* Article II of the convention by inserting the word "political" after the word "national." Symms defended his amendment as follows:

> Mr. President, I believe this amendment is an absolutely necessary prerequisite to the ratification of the Genocide Treaty.
>
> As my colleagues know, I have opposed the United States participation in this convention for some time. I believe it is essential that we make some structural changes in this treaty. This is the purpose of my amendment.
>
> My main objection would be removed by the adoption of this amendment which would simply add "political" groups to those protected from genocide under article II of the treaty.
>
> If this simple change is made, I think much of the opposition to this treaty would disappear instantaneously.[30]

The amendment enjoyed the support of a number of co-sponsors, including Senators Chic Hecht (R., Nevada), Jeremiah Denton, Strom Thurmond, John East, and Malcolm Wallop.[31] But it faced the combined opposition of the State Department and, more important, most senators. In fact, the amendment was one of the few important issues on which the State Department was able to stand firmly, its task undoubtedly made easier by the fact that Symms's proposal was so extreme. The State Department opposed the amendment on the ground that its adoption would have required renegotiation of the convention prior to ratification by the United States.[32] But Symms seemed unable to comprehend the real impact of his proposal, responding to the State Department's position as follows: "This is not true. We will simply send the treaty out with the message that the United States of America has ratified the Genocide Convention with one amendment. The other 96 nations who have signed the treaty would have the opportunity to either ratify our amendment or reject it."[33]

Senator Richard Lugar, who as chairman of the Committee on Foreign Relations, managed the floor debate on the resolution of ratification, also strongly opposed the adoption of Symms's amendment for the same reason given by the State Department. Graciously glossing over Symms's ineptitude, Lugar argued:

> Mr. President, the argument against the distinguished Senator's amendment is a simple one but it is an important one to understand. It is a method of procedure. It is a parliamentary argument. And I want to simply state it as concisely and clearly as I can; that when the Senate requires that an amendment to the treaty be adopted, the President of the United States must gain the consent of all other parties, as the Senator from Idaho has correctly stated, with 96 others at this point, before he—that is the President—may ratify the treaty on behalf of the United States.
>
> No amendment to the Genocide Treaty has been recommended by the Foreign Relations Committee for this obvious reason. As a matter of fact, *approval by the Senate of this amendment or of any other amendment would be tantamount to rejection of the treaty*, and of the convention, by the Senate. . . . The amendment that the Senator from Idaho has offered is *effectively a killer amendment. It is the same as a vote against the treaty.*[34]

On a roll-call vote, Symms's amendment was rejected by a vote of sixty-two against, thirty-one (of which twenty-seven were Republicans) in favor, and seven not voting.[35] But it was obvious that Symms was championing a cause that had considerable support in the Senate, and the second strategy that was proposed for dealing with the convention's failure to extend protection to political groups was a concession to him and others who had strong feelings about the issue. The second strategy was a compromise between the extremes of amending the convention and ignoring the so-called political group exemption altogether; namely, it advocated adopting a sense of the Senate resolution that calls for the United States to work toward persuading the United Nations to amend Article II to cover political groups. The resolution, which was passed immediately after the adoption of the Lugar-Helms-Hatch Sovereignty Package, was overwhelmingly approved by a vote of ninety-three in favor, one against (Senator Barry Goldwater), and six not voting. The resolution provides:

> Whereas the Senate has given its advice and consent to the ratification of the International Convention on the Prevention and Punishment of the Crime of Genocide (hereafter in this preamble referred to as the "Convention");
>
> Whereas such Convention excludes from its coverage genocide committed against political groups;
>
> Whereas the Senate finds that instances of political genocide have occurred in Tibet and Cambodia;

Whereas the Senate finds that politically motivated genocide is being carried out in Afghanistan;

Whereas the Senate believes that the protections afforded by the Convention should be extended to all forms of genocide;

Whereas Article XVI of the Convention provides that any party to the Convention may notify in writing the Secretary General of the United Nations of its desire to amend the Convention; and

Whereas Article XVI of the Convention also provides that the General Assembly of the United Nations may take action, after such notification, to amend the Convention: Now, therefore, be it

Resolved, That it is the sense of the Senate that—

(1) upon depositing the instrument of ratification to the International Convention on the Prevention and Punishment of the Crime of Genocide with the Secretary General of the United Nations, the President should notify in writing the Secretary General of the desire of the United States to amend the Convention to include acts constituting political genocide within the definition of the term "genocide"; and

(2) the President should instruct the Permanent Representative of the United States to the United Nations to take all steps necessary to see that such an amendment is adopted.

Sec. 2. The Secretary of the Senate shall transmit a copy of this resolution to the President.[36]

The resolution is nonbinding, and it was adopted amidst substantial skepticism about its potential effectiveness even among supporters such as Senator Malcolm Wallop, who stated in the discussion of the resolution's merits:

Mr. President, I strongly support this [resolution], too, but I have to tell my colleagues that they know as well as I do this will never take place. The reason it is not in the treaty at the present moment is that the Soviet Union refused to have it there. If we think we can persuade the United Nations, which is run by the Soviet Union and its client states, to buy off on a treaty amendment requiring a definition of political genocide, it is an act of self-deception which I think is unworthy of the Senate.

The appropriate place to have accomplished this was on the amendment of the Senator from Idaho. But we would not do that because, somehow or another, it would have been demeaning, I guess, to the treaty process. I do not know why we did not do it, but that amendment was the appropriate place, if the Senate really meant to have political genocide as a definition under the terms of the Genocide Treaty.

> That, Mr. President, is why I voted against the treaty. It does not do it, and neither will this. I strongly support the effort, but if anybody here believes that it will happen, I wish they would explain to me what process they think would achieve it.[37]

Other senators voted in favor of the resolution but, unlike Wallop, actually disagreed with its content and rationale. Senator Christopher Dodd (D., Connecticut), for example, admitted that he had voted in favor of the resolution for purely political reasons. Several days after the Senate adopted the resolution, Dodd stated on the floor that he had voted in favor of it as "a ransom to be paid for getting a final vote on the Genocide Convention." In fact, he had serious reservations about the content and implications of the resolution, suggesting that "anyone who talks about political genocide has missed the whole point of the Genocide Convention" and its entire history.[38]

Others expressed similar views or simply gave the issue very little attention. The near-unanimous vote in favor of the sense of the Senate resolution therefore does not reflect the true sentiment of all senators concerning genocide against political groups. Even so, the importance of the resolution should not be underestimated. Its adoption reflected—and all indications are that it continues to reflect—the strong feelings of many senators on the issue. After all, the more drastic proposal introduced by Symms to amend the convention was supported by thirty-one senators. Of those who opposed Symms's proposal, some felt that an amendment was not an appropriate way to approach the issue, even though they did not disapprove of the idea in principle. Moreover, President Reagan, in a "Dear Steve" letter, endorsed the strategy enunciated in the sense of the Senate resolution even before its adoption, which suggests that the issue was considered important by some members of the administration.[39] In short, even if the United Nations does not accede to U.S. wishes by amending the convention to cover political groups, there is support in the United States for keeping the issue alive. Let us thus explore the critics' main arguments relative to the issue of genocide against political groups.

Lack of Leadership by the U.S. Delegation

Historically, two main arguments have been made in the United States in connection with the failure of the convention to extend protection to political groups. Both arguments have shown the critics' preoccupation with the Soviet Union and its policies and practices, and thus together reveal that a profound anti-Sovietism, masked in legal and pseudolegal language, has been a major force operating in opposition to ratification of the convention.[40]

The first of these two arguments has been the charge that a lack of effective leadership on the part of the U.S. delegation to the United Nations was one of the main reasons why the word "political" was deleted from Article II. As we have seen, the U.S. delegation vigorously supported the inclusion of political groups in Article II throughout most of the drafting process, then changed its position to allow the deletion of the word "political" from the article. Opponents of ratification have criticized this change of stance ever since the first Senate hearings on the convention in 1950. Alfred J. Schweppe, for example, representing the ABA at the 1950 hearings, had this to say:

> Mr. Maktos proposed on behalf of the United States the inclusion of "political groups," which had been included in the General Assembly resolution of December 11, 1946. This position, . . . was at first approved in the Sixth Committee, over the opposition of Russia, and its satellites and a few others . . . and then the Sixth Committee reversed itself and excluded "political groups."
>
> As I shall . . . suggest a little later, the instrument with which our delegates came home, over their firm convictions on matters of principle, did not bear much resemblance to the convention they advocated. The losses which our representatives suffered are part of the reasons why our committee thinks the convention should not be ratified as submitted.[41]

Some twenty years later, in 1971, Schweppe reappeared before the Committee on Foreign Relations, once again representing the ABA in opposition to ratification of the convention. At that time he more vigorously denounced the deletion of the word "political" from Article II:

> I merely this morning would like to call attention to several items. There seems to be a misconception about the position of the United States in respect to the Genocide Convention. I find in the statement of the present Secretary of State, and I also find it in the committee report [of 1970], that the United States took great leadership in the creation of this Genocide Convention. As a matter of fact, if you gentlemen will read the testimony which I gave in the 1950 hearings, where I traced step by step, after having spent many hours browsing through the proceedings of the United Nations as to how the present text of the Genocide Convention came into being, you will find that the U.S. delegation instead of

exercising leadership, engaged in what I call a very pathetic case of followership. We retreated at every major point. I have described it as being like Napoleon's retreat from Moscow—a complete rout.

It was a complete rout of the American delegation. We took position after position in the negotiations in 1948 designed to make this a meaningful and effective convention, to protect people from destruction by governments or individuals acting in complicity with government. We lost the war when we acceded to the adamant Communist position, which is all a matter of record, that the word "political" must go out, and we fought and we fought, and we were outvoted on the question of political groups.

Once the word "political" was eliminated, the Genocide Convention, in my judgment, became ineffective and is today full of one of the worst holes that could possibly be put into print by not including that word.[42]

Eberhard Deutsch, who joined Schweppe in representing the ABA at the 1971 Senate hearings, provided equally colorful and alarming testimony:

The original United Nations declaration against genocide, adopted by the General Assembly in December, 1946, denounced genocide whether—and I am quoting—"committed on religious, racial, political, or any other grounds." When this declaration was being converted into the convention, the Communist nations insisted on omission of "political" from the listed categories, and the United States capitulated; so that none of the Communist nations could, for example, ever be charged under the convention, with committing genocide by inflicting intolerable "conditions of life" on a political group, or seeking to destroy its members.[43]

Deutsch claimed that in debate before the ABA's House of Delegates in 1970, some proponents of ratification of the convention had tried to explain away the U.S. delegation's "capitulation" on the word "political"; they had argued that the word was deleted in exchange for the insertion of the word "ethnic" in Article II. According to Deutsch, "ethnic" meant essentially the same thing as "race," and since the word "racial" was already in Article II, the exchange by the U.S. delegation "was acceptance of a stale, crumbling cracker for a carload of fine smoked hams."[44]

The ABA's representatives claimed to speak with considerable knowledge of the negotiations, but their arguments distorted and exaggerated what had actually occurred. For the most part, they portrayed the negotiations as a battle in which the U.S. delegation was unable to withstand the onslaught of a determined communist attack; and they gave the impression that had the word "political" not been deleted from Article II, they would have been inclined to support ratification of the convention. But several proponents of ratification took them to task for their distortions and misleading claims. Arthur Goldberg, for example, who had served as a cabinet secretary, Supreme Court justice, and ambassador to the United Nations, and who had had extensive negotiating experience, presented especially insightful testimony at the 1971 Senate hearings: "I listened with great interest to both witnesses who said that they would be for a genocide treaty if 'political' had been included. Well, that argument doesn't quite hold in light of their testimony. In the first place many of the legal objections would still presumably be advanced even if the word 'political' were in there. But I welcome converts even if they are somewhat belated."[45]

Goldberg presumed "that what had happened [during the negotiations] was that faced with an objection to the word 'political' a compromise was made, and a settlement was made on the basis, let us cover as much as we can even if we cannot cover everything, and I presume that is why the word 'political' was omitted from the treaty."[46] He concluded:

> I take it that we stand somewhat like this. Here we have a treaty. It is not perfect. It could have been made a lot better. It is a negotiated document. In my experience in negotiations, negotiated documents, domestic or foreign, are rarely perfect. You agree, and you agree on these compromises. We agree on the compromise. The test ought to be, does the compromise imperil anything sacred to us, and I say to this committee the answer is no, it does not imperil anything sacred to us.[47]

Goldberg's presumptions about what had happened during the negotiations were indeed correct, though there is no evidence that his arguments were persuasive, at least not with the ABA representatives. And these representatives had powerful allies in the Senate, among them Senator Sam Ervin, Jr. Nonetheless, it is a fact that in their testimony before the Committee on Foreign Relations, Schweppe and Deutsch greatly distorted the nature of the negotiations over the terms of the convention. The Soviet delegation did oppose listing political groups among those to be protected under Article II, but other delegations advanced much more persuasive and widely accepted arguments than the Soviets. Many delegates were concerned about the lack of stability of political groups and about whether or not extending protection to them would undermine support for the convention as a whole.

Moreover, there is good reason to think that the Soviet delegation felt outmaneuvered by the U.S. delegation on the eventual compromise. As noted in our discussion of table 4.2, the Soviet Union and its supporters abstained on the vote that resulted in the deletion of political groups from Article II. It is reasonable to assume that their abstentions were meant to show their displeasure with the compromise the U.S. delegation had been able to work out with others—that the reference to political groups would be deleted in exchange for a provision in Article VI regarding the creation of an international criminal court. While the Soviets vigorously opposed the reference to political groups in Article II, they even more vigorously championed sovereignty and nonintervention in the internal affairs of states throughout the negotiations on the convention, precisely the principles that were later so strongly defended by Schweppe, Deutsch, and various right-wing opponents of ratification in the Senate. The Soviets' vigorous defense of these principles led them to oppose both the creation of an international criminal court[48] and, though unsuccessfully, the reinsertion in Article VI of a provision concerning the court.[49]

Critics of the convention in the United States, such as Schweppe and Deutsch, either misunderstood the bargaining strategies of the U.S. delegation when the convention was drafted, or, as Goldberg suspected, they deliberately distorted what had occurred to suit their own purposes. Indeed, one of the many ironies of the debate over U.S. ratification of the convention is that the international criminal court provision of Article VI has been exceedingly controversial, stimulating disagreement reminiscent of the Brickerism of the 1950s. Even though no international criminal court has been created, great concern over the mere possibility that one might be created culminated in the inclusion of an understanding (discussed in chapter 7) in the Lugar-Helms-Hatch Sovereignty Package that states in part that the United States "declares that it reserves the right to effect its participation in any such tribunal only by a treaty entered into specifically for that purpose with the advice and consent of the Senate."[50]

Finally, it should be emphasized that in 1948 the Soviet bloc in the United Nations consisted of only five of fifty-eight states, six if Yugoslavia is included. This alone renders absurd the preoccupation of many of the convention's critics with the Soviet delegation's position on the issue of political groups. In fact, the United States was very ably represented during the negotiations, and the positions its representatives took enjoyed broad support. The data in table 4.3 show the coincidence of agreement of all the members of the United Nations with the U.S. and Soviet positions at the time the convention was drafted. Only roll-call votes taken in the Sixth Committee were used in making the calculations; few votes were taken in

Table 4.3 Support for U.S. and Soviet Positions on the Genocide Convention (Coincidence of Agreement, Yes or No, on All Roll-Call Votes).*

United States			Soviet Union		
Country	No. votes in agreement	% Agreement	Country	No. votes in agreement	% Agreement
Canada	15	100	Ukrainian SSR	15	100
New Zealand	14	93.3	Byelorussian SSR	15	100
Netherlands	13	86.7	Czechoslovakia	14	93.3
Brazil	12	80.0	Yugoslavia	14	93.3
Chile	12	80.0	Poland	13	86.7
United Kingdom	12	80.0	Venezuela	7	46.7
Uruguay	11	73.3	France	7	46.7
Belgium	11	73.3	Norway	6	40.0
Luxembourg	11	73.3	Argentina	5	33.3
Denmark	11	73.3	Denmark	5	33.3
India	11	73.3	Iran	5	33.3
Thailand	11	73.3	Egypt	5	33.3
Australia	11	73.3	Syria	5	33.3
Cuba	10	66.7	China	5	33.3
Dominican Republic	10	66.7	Philippines	5	33.3
Sweden	10	66.7	Australia	5	33.3
Norway	10	66.7	Haiti	4	26.7
Panama	9	60.0	Dominican Republic	4	26.7
Ecuador	9	60.0	Mexico	4	26.7
Bolivia	9	60.0	Colombia	4	26.7
Greece	9	60.0	Uruguay	4	26.7
Iran	9	60.0	Sweden	4	26.7
Turkey	9	60.0	India	4	26.7
Syria	9	60.0	Pakistan	4	26.7
China	9	60.0	Cuba	3	20.0
Peru	8	53.3	Panama	3	20.0
South Africa	8	53.3	Ecuador	3	20.0
Egypt	8	53.3	Peru	3	20.0
Afghanistan	8	53.3	Brazil	3	20.0
Venezuela	7	46.7	Bolivia	3	20.0
France	7	46.7	Greece	3	20.0
Mexico	6	40.0	Ethiopia	3	20.0
Colombia	6	40.0	Saudi Arabia	3	20.0
Argentina	6	40.0	Afghanistan	3	20.0
Pakistan	6	40.0	Netherlands	2	13.3

(continuation of Table 4.3)

United States			Soviet Union		
Country	No. votes in agreement	% Agreement	Country	No. votes in agreement	% Agreement
Philippines	6	40.0	Belgium	2	13.3
Haiti	5	33.3	Luxembourg	2	13.3
Saudi Arabia	5	33.3	Liberia	2	13.3
Nicaragua	4	26.7	South Africa	2	13.3
Paraguay	4	26.7	Yemen	2	13.3
Burma	4	26.7	Canada	1	6.7
Honduras	3	20.0	Guatemala	1	6.7
Yemen	3	20.0	Honduras	1	6.7
El Salvador	2	13.3	El Salvador	1	6.7
Liberia	2	13.3	Nicaragua	1	6.7
Lebanon	2	13.3	Chile	1	6.7
Guatemala	1	6.7	United Kingdom	1	6.7
Iceland	1	6.7	Turkey	1	6.7
Costa Rica	0	0	Lebanon	1	6.7
Poland	0	0	Burma	1	6.7
Czechoslovakia	0	0	Thailand	1	6.7
Yugoslavia	0	0	New Zealand	1	6.7
USSR	0	0	USA	0	0
Ukrainian SSR	0	0	Costa Rica	0	0
Byelorussian SSR	0	0	Paraguay	0	0
Ethiopia	0	0	Iceland	0	0
Iraq	0	0	Iraq	0	0

Source: Same as table 4.1.

*The United States and Soviet Union abstained or did not vote on two of the seventeen roll-call votes used in the preparation of this table. Hence, a 100 percent support score is achieved by any state that voted the same way, yes/no, as the United States or Soviet Union on the remaining fifteen roll calls. Note that Canada supported the United States on the fifteen roll calls the United States voted on. At the same time, Canada supported the Soviet position on one roll call, indicating that the United States and Soviet Union abstained or did not vote on different roll calls.

the plenary session of the General Assembly when the convention was adopted, and those taken upheld decisions reached earlier in committee. Moreover, only the coincidence of agreement on yes and no votes was taken into account. This method reduces the distortions that might otherwise occur if abstentions were included. A yes or no vote suggests stronger feelings on an issue than does an abstention. In addition, states might abstain for widely differing reasons; their coincidence in so voting would therefore tell us little.

In all, seventeen roll-call votes were taken in the Sixth Committee. In votes where no roll call was taken, an examination of the debate records suggests that the U.S. delegation managed as well as, if not better than, the data presented in table 4.3 suggest. Nonetheless, the data enable us to reach conclusions that are less impressionistic than conclusions based solely on the summary records. In addition, yes and no votes allow generalization about the extent of "support" for the U.S. and Soviet positions, respectively, and the sources of that support. As table 4.3 shows, the U.S. positions enjoyed substantial support across a broad spectrum of states. In fact, twenty-nine of fifty-seven member states supported the U.S. position more than 50 percent of the time (the dividing point being Afghanistan, which voted the same way as the United States 53.3 percent of the time). An additional group of nine states had relatively high support scores, ranging from 46.7 percent (Venezuela) to 33.3 percent (Saudi Arabia).

In marked contrast, the Soviet Union's position was meagerly supported. In fact, only five states, all members of the Soviet bloc, agreed with the Soviet Union on more than half of the issues. The table indicates a sharp and rapid decline in support for the Soviet positions after the very high scores of the Soviet bloc are taken into account. Although a high support score for either the United States or the Soviet Union often translated into a low support score for the other, there were states that exercised considerable independence in their voting behavior. For example, France's support scores for the U.S. and Soviet positions are identical at 46.7 percent.

The Perception of a Loophole

The second major argument of opponents of ratification concerned a perceived loophole in the convention's definition of genocide. This argument, like the alleged lack of U.S. leadership in the negotiations, reflected a preoccupation among the critics with the Soviet Union. The critics argued that the deletion of political groups from Article II made the convention inapplicable precisely where it should be applicable—to the treatment that totalitarian governments mete out to political opponents. In particular, the critics charged that the Soviet Union could commit genocide against any of the groups named in Article II while claiming that the acts were not genocidal because they were undertaken to suppress enemies of the state, not to destroy any specific protected group or groups. It was the omission of the word "political" from Article II that made this evasion of charges of genocide possible. This was one of the most important arguments made by the ABA representatives beginning with the 1950 Senate hearings on the convention. To George Finch, for example, the failure of the convention to protect political groups was reason enough to oppose ratification:

> The nonapplicability of the Convention to crimes of genocide now being committed by totalitarian governments behind the iron curtain is further emphasized by the requirement of article II of the convention that acts of genocide be committed only against a national, ethnic, racial, or religious group, as such. The inhuman treatment now being administered to members of these groups behind the iron curtain is said to be, not because they belong to any of the groups protected by the Genocide Convention, but because they are enemies of the state or dangerous to its security. The omission of political groups from the definition of genocide in the convention has made this evasion possible.[51]

Citing press reports of Soviet mass deportations of Jews, Greeks, and members of other ethnic groups, and the deaths of thousands of persons in Soviet-run concentration camps for political prisoners, Finch asked, "Of what avail to any of these poor unfortunate people will be this convention on genocide under which the only possible effective sanction will be the punishment of individuals by national courts? What can a national court in a country behind the iron curtain do to prevent genocide as defined in this convention? What real protection could the court of any country provide if an independent judiciary does not exist?"[52] Finch carried his opposition to the editorial pages of the prestigious *American Journal of International Law*, claiming that the Soviets could "liquidate those in favor of private enterprise on the ground that they are not covered by the Convention."[53]

The same arguments were made by ABA representatives Alfred Schweppe and Eberhard Deutsch in the 1970s.[54] Some groups, such as Liberty Lobby, continued to raise the issue after the ABA changed its position and declared itself in favor of ratification in 1976.[55]

The sense of the Senate resolution on political groups quoted earlier suggests that concern over a possible loophole in the convention's definition of genocide has had a tremendous impact on the Senate. The resolution's preambular clauses state that the Senate "finds that politically motivated genocide is being carried out in Afghanistan" and that "instances of political genocide have occurred in Tibet and Cambodia."[56] The Senate therefore concluded, by an overwhelming vote, that the convention should be amended to cover political groups. President Reagan, too, viewed an amendment as a way of dealing with "politically motivated" genocide by totalitarian states.[57]

Amending a multilateral convention, especially one such as the Genocide Convention, which has already been ratified by over one hundred states, would probably be impossible. One United Nations study during the 1970s showed that most states felt that their main objective should be to enforce the convention as it is rather than to amend it to expand its coverage.[58] A revised and updated version of this report prepared by Ben Whitaker and dated July 1985 provided no evidence that states had changed their attitudes. Whitaker himself did not strongly urge an amendment of the convention to cover political groups, though he indicated that such groups could be covered by the adoption of an optional protocol.[59]

Despite the apparent lack of enthusiasm for amending the convention to expand its coverage, at the time the Lugar-Helms-Hatch Sovereignty Package was adopted some senators were optimistic about the possibility of attracting sufficient support in the United Nations for an amendment, and they pressed for the adoption of the sense of the Senate resolution. Senator Richard Lugar, for example, did not think that pressing for an amendment after ratification "would be an empty gesture." He claimed that in August 1985 the matter had been discussed in the Subcommission on Prevention of Discrimination and Protection of Minorities of the UN Commission on Human Rights. According to Lugar, the Soviet delegate had succeeded in having the matter deferred. Nonetheless, he thought it might be possible to resurrect it with the help of Western states.[60]

The difficulty of amending a widely ratified multilateral convention is not the only consideration that should be weighed in assessing the U.S. strategy concerning political groups. It may even be argued that such considerations should be secondary. If an amendment of Article II is worth pursuing, it should be pursued regardless of the possible political difficulties. But is such an amendment necessary to achieve the objectives of the convention's critics? That is, is an amendment necessary to prevent states from evading charges of genocide? And even if an amendment is not necessary to meet the concerns of the critics, are there other reasons that would make it desirable?

Is an Amendment Necessary to Stop Politically Motivated Genocide?

The often expressed concern that the convention does not cover politically motivated genocide reflects a curious and probably erroneous interpretation of Article II and, more broadly, of the convention as a whole. The critics are preoccupied with motives. According to Article II, however, genocide is defined simply as the commission of certain acts "with the intent to destroy, in whole or in part, a national, ethnical, racial, or religious group, as such." Neither Article II nor any other article of the convention refers to the *motives* that must lie behind the commission of such acts. It is true that the drafters gave some consideration to the possibility of specifying motives. Article II of the draft convention prepared by the Ad Hoc Committee of the ECOSOC contained specific references to motives—the destruction of national, racial, religious, and political groups on grounds of their national or racial *origins*, religious *beliefs*, or political *opinions*.

These very precise references to motives were unacceptable to most representatives in the Sixth Committee of the General Assembly and they were deleted from the article. The representative of the United Kingdom offered the most trenchant criticisms, suggesting that references to motives should be deleted because they were at once "useless and dangerous": useless because Article II already included the notion of intent as a component of the crime of genocide; and dangerous because the terms of the draft had the effect of narrowing the grounds for charges of genocide.[61] Furthermore, requiring proof of motive might allow states to claim that vicious acts aimed at, say, religious groups had been committed on grounds other than the religious beliefs of the group. In such a situation, no charge of genocide could be made.[62]

Others on the Sixth Committee agreed with the United Kingdom's representative. Ernest Gross, for example, asserted that the "fundamental aim" of Article II was to "define the crime [of genocide] in terms of intention, as was normally done in national legislation," and that to "include motives in that definition would lead to ambiguity."[63] While a few representatives argued in favor of retaining the references to motives, the Sixth Committee ultimately decided to delete them and to insert the words "as such" in their place.[64]

In retrospect, there was more to be said for deleting the references to motives than for retaining them, precisely for the reasons advanced by the U.K. and U.S. representatives. The words "as such" in Article II have the effect of referring back to the groups as entities. Commentators on the convention have generally agreed that any of the acts stipulated in Article II committed with the intent to destroy, in whole or in part, one of the groups specified would constitute genocide.[65] Put another way, as Pieter Drost has maintained, no one could "plead that the deed was done for reasons other than those to be found in the constituent characteristics of the group," for the words "as such" "indicate that the *essential element* of the crime of genocide is the intentional attack against the existence of a group of human beings."[66] Under this interpretation of Article II, the reasons that national, ethnic, racial, or religious groups become victims of genocidal acts are irrelevant. It does not matter whether they become victims for political, economic, or other reasons; it matters only that they become victims. Thus, notwithstanding the critics' fears, a state would not be able to avoid charges of genocide by claiming that the motives that lay behind its acts against, say, a national group were solely political.

Proponents of ratification have sometimes made this point in their testimony, perhaps none more eloquently than Adrian Fisher, legal adviser to the Department of State at the time of the 1950 Senate hearings. The full-scale assault on the convention by representatives of the ABA led even some senators who supported ratification, such as Brien McMahon, to question if Soviet actions such as deportations, purges, and the establishment of labor camps would be considered genocide under the terms of Article II. McMahon noted that the Soviets stood accused of having "liquidated some 20,000,000 of their own people" since they had gained power, and he expressed doubt that the definition of the crime in Article II would apply to the Soviets' actions; perhaps they could evade charges of genocide by claiming that the victims were only political subversives.[67] Fisher replied:

> I do not agree with that, sir, because it depends on questions of fact. I would like to go a little bit into what I consider the crime today. If we were to ratify this convention, this country and other countries similarly affected . . . would be in a position to charge before the appropriate organs of the United Nations that these deportations, that these killings, were . . . for the purpose of exterminating a national group whose existence within the territorial boundaries of a particular state was considered by that state to be contrary to its objectives.
>
> Those facts would be determined not by one country alone pleading self-defense, but would be determined as is often done in the courts of our land. Those facts, in the real meaning of this convention, would be determined by the world.
>
> If we were not to ratify this convention on the ground that the plea of self-defense might be made, the Polish groups, the Estonian groups, all of whom appeared here to urge the ratification of this convention, would be denied even their day in court, their chance to be heard and to claim that this was not self-defense, to claim that this was rather a deliberate and purposeful act of genocide. Those groups have frankly urged the ratification of the convention, and they do so with a full understanding of what it means, and they do so with full recognition of the fact that in any international obligation terms of precision may involve questions of fact.
>
> . . . If we were not to ratify the convention they would not even get a day in court, a day before the bar of world opinion, before the bar of the conscience of the world, to contend that a deliberate act of genocide was being inflicted on them, and I believe it is for that reason they propose the

> ratification of the convention in its present form, not some theoretical "go back and start over" with the hope that 10 years from now, 5 years from now, we might come up with one which, in an unhappily imperfect world, was perfect.[68]

This interpretation of Article II, which is consistent with its terms and the intentions of the drafters, does not make proving charges of genocide easy, nor would Fisher have suggested that it would. Instead, it calls attention to a different, and equally vexing, problem in interpreting and applying the convention: proving the intent to destroy a group or groups. As we saw in chapter 3, disputes concerning intention, or the lack thereof, have already figured prominently in some recent allegations of genocide, such as those concerning the war waged by the United States in Vietnam and the treatment of the Aché Indians in Paraguay.

The difficulties that may exist in proving intent notwithstanding, the convention as written protects racial, national, ethnic, and religious groups from genocidal acts. As Adrian Fisher argued, the perpetrators of the crime could not evade charges of genocide by denying the objective characteristics of their victims and claiming that the motives that lay behind their actions were political. Should such a loophole exist, it could indeed be fatal. But, as Fisher noted, various ethnic groups (for example, Ukrainian, Armenian, and Greek) have never been persuaded that a fatal loophole exists in Article II that could be exploited by the Soviet Union or any other country. To the contrary, ethnic groups have supported ratification as a way of bringing pressure to bear on the Soviet Union for its alleged genocidal practices.[69]

Senator Robert Byrd (D., West Virginia) introduced a concurrent resolution in the Senate in June 1986 that calls upon the U.S. secretary of state to conduct an investigation of Soviet actions in Afghanistan as possibly being violative of the Genocide Convention, which the Soviet Union has ratified. Byrd cited United Nations studies and resolutions in support of his own.[70] By calling upon the U.S. secretary of state to conduct the investigation, Byrd's resolution bypassed the rule-supervisory mechanisms designated in the convention (Articles VIII and IX). Even though nothing has come of Byrd's resolution, it is characterized by a clarity of thought about the meaning of the Genocide Convention that is very rarely found in the Senate.

Is an Amendment Otherwise Desirable?

Even if the deletion of the word "political" from Article II did not create the sort of loophole regarding motives that critics of the convention allege, an amendment of the article to cover political groups might be considered desirable in order to outlaw large-scale political persecution. As a result of the drafters' exclusion of political groups, it appears that the convention does not apply to situations in which genocide-like acts, including mass slaughter, are committed, but the national, ethnic, racial, or religious identity of the victims is not clearly at issue. There is considerable evidence that many such instances have occurred since World War II.

Ted Gurr and Barbara Harff compiled data on forty-three episodes of mass killings that have occurred since World War II.[71] The data show that many more persons have died since the war as a result of mass killings than from natural disasters, international wars, and colonial and civil wars *combined*. As Gurr and Harff summarize the data, "On average, between 1.6 and 3.9 million unarmed civilians have died at the hand of the state in each decade since the end of WW II, compared with less than a million battle-related deaths in international wars (960,000 per decade) and civil wars (890,000 per decade)."[72] Five of the forty-three episodes appeared to constitute pure genocides, that is, cases in which the victims appeared to have become victims because of their communal identity. In contrast, Gurr and Harff classified nineteen of the episodes as "politicides," that is, episodes in which the victims "were defined in terms of their hierarchical position or political opposition to the state and dominant group."[73] The remainder of the episodes were classified as mixed, in which the victims were both political and communal groups, seven episodes being more like "genocides" and twelve being more like "politicides." Gurr and Harff argue that the "vast majority of the 6.8 to 16.3 million victims were ordinary people whose only 'offense' was to be on the wrong side of communal, separatist, or revolutionary conflicts."[74]

Episodes of alleged genocide since World War II have indeed been controversial, and the classification scheme employed by Gurr and Harff reflects the difficulties that attend efforts to analyze these episodes. It is not always clear whether or not the episodes would fall within the meaning of genocide as defined by the convention. For example, how does one classify the atrocities committed in Cambodia after the fall of the Lon Nol government in 1975? Did the acts constitute genocide under the terms of the convention? Hundreds of thousands of persons died, but was the senseless slaughter directed at specific groups on the grounds of their national, ethnic, racial, or religious identity?[75]

Cambodia ratified the Genocide Convention in 1950. The allegations of genocide in that country when it was ruled by the Khmer Rouge between 1975 and 1979 have been the subject of extensive investigation by private individuals and nongovernmental organizations. One nongovernmental organization—the Cambodia Documentation Commission—has attempted to persuade a party to the Genocide Convention to bring charges against the Khmer Rouge before the ICJ under Article IX of the convention.[76] Gregory Stanton, director of the Cambodian Genocide Project and chair of the ABA's Young Lawyers Division Committee on Human Rights, has also worked to persuade a party to the convention to bring charges against the Khmer Rouge to the ICJ.[77] No party has yet insisted on an ICJ ruling on this matter, reflecting a serious weakness in the rule-supervisory provisions of the convention (to which we shall return in chapter 9).

Other post–World War II cases have aroused controversy. Questions have been raised about whether or not the atrocities committed in Uganda during the reign of Idi Amin in the 1970s, and in the Soviet Union during the Stalinist purges of the 1930s, would constitute genocide under the convention.[78] Other cases could be cited in which the evidence seems to be inconclusive. In brief, widespread slaughter of populations can occur without, apparently, being covered by the convention. As one scholar has observed, the convention does not "outlaw all forms of barbarism."[79]

Many scholars and others concerned about genocide have been deeply disturbed about the possibility that the convention might not be applicable to situations such as those mentioned, and they have argued that its inapplicability reflects a serious weakness in the rule on genocide itself affirmed in the convention. The weakness would not exist had the reference to political groups been retained in Article II, because the one characteristic the victims appeared to share in all of those situations is that they were considered enemies of the state, or perhaps of a particular political leader or group of leaders. What is important in these cases is not so much the nature of the groups that became victims, but simply the fact that massive numbers of persons became victims. The horror and magnitude of the crimes have persuaded some that it would have been desirable to extend protection to political groups.

The liquidation of political groups is certainly deplorable, but it is nonetheless arguable that it would have been unwise and impractical to provide them protection under the convention. Most scholars and politicians who have seriously considered the question agree that violence against political groups may, in some circumstances, be legitimate. Kurt Glaser and Stephan Possony, for example, who feel that political groups should have been included in Article II, suggested that the convention "might have been broadminded and realistic enough to recognize that some groups may very well be hostile and threaten the security of the state, in which case the threatened state should be allowed to protect itself, albeit by *nongenocidal* means."[80] Similarly, Leo Kuper argued that the concept of genocide should not apply to some situations "which have some affinity with genocide, such as the large-scale slaughter of hostages taken from the opposing group, or the shooting down or bombing of passenger planes, or the striking at the soft underbelly of England by bombs in underground trains or subways."[81] And, as Senator Christopher Dodd explained on the Senate floor,

> not all political violence is illegal or immoral. There is simply no way to distinguish in legal terms between what may qualify for some as political genocide and what may be regarded as legitimate violence, for instance, a bitter and bloody fight by a subjugated people for its freedom. The use of this elusive concept would do nothing but provide ammunition for endless propaganda battles that we already have enough of. Opponents of the Genocide Convention never ceased to worry about American citizens who served in our military in Vietnam who may be accused of genocide as a result of their service. This was, of course, absurd. We were taking part in an armed political conflict, and were not trying to kill all Vietnamese, or all Buddhists, or any other objectively identifiable group.
>
> We, however, could arguably be accused of having tried to kill all Communists, or at least all Vietcong. This is the essence of war, ugly as it is. Do the champions of the concept of political genocide really want to expose our ex-servicemen to the charge of political genocide on this account? How about the Afghan freedom-fighters who certainly try to kill all who belong to the occupying Soviet powers and who are allied with them? Do the sponsors of this resolution really want to say they are committing political genocide?
>
> My point is, that the Genocide Convention omitted political groups from its definition with good reasons. The reason was not to excuse extreme political violence. The reason was to give a clear and objective definition, to try to raise a well-defined international standard that every nation can endorse, even if that endorsement is often hypocritical.[82]

As Dodd's remarks suggest, the inclusion of a reference to political groups could very well have resulted in the opposite of what the critics of the convention presumably wanted: It might have been much easier to prove charges of genocide against the United States during the Vietnam War had Article II of the convention extended protection to political groups.

These observations lead to a number of questions: Is it possible to make a widely accepted definitional distinction between political genocide and attacks against political groups that are made for legitimate reasons? Where does one draw the line between acceptable and forbidden political violence? If the convention is amended to include political groups among those it aims to protect, how should such groups be defined by member states and how would this provision be applied?

Ambassador Gross suggested that a political party provided a good example of a political group. While this might be true, it is only one example. Confining the meaning of political groups to political parties would result in an unduly narrow and vague definition. Groups and movements of various sizes commonly claim to be political in nature and to be persecuted for political reasons. Examples include groups of protesters and others who are attacked by their governments for their political views. It would be absurd to consider such cases as falling within the meaning of genocide as defined by the convention, but the examples illustrate the difficulties inherent in selecting criteria for determining what constitutes a political group. One possible criterion, of course, is the number of victims involved. But this criterion seems unreasonable. Why should the number of victims make any difference? Numerous cases already cited demonstrate that genocide can be perpetrated against small groups as well as large ones.

Political groups thus present problems of a sort that national, ethnic, racial, and religious groups do not. Consideration of these problems leads to a recognition of the wisdom of the drafters in deleting the reference to political groups from Article II. It does not appear possible to develop an acceptable definition of what constitutes a political group for purposes of the Genocide Convention; exceptions to any proposed definition come readily to mind. Yet who would argue that exceptions should be made in the more prominent cases of genocide, such as the wholesale slaughtering of Jews and Armenians. The Convention was obviously intended to apply to such situations, and does apply to them. It is arguable that it should apply only to such situations.

Is there any way out of this dilemma? Two possibilities present themselves; but, despite all that has been said and written about the subject, neither is likely to draw much support. One, mentioned earlier in connection with our discussion of Ben Whitaker's analysis of the issue, would be to draft a protocol to the Genocide Convention that would add political groups to those to which the convention extends protection. Those states that felt a need to protect political groups would then be able to ratify the protocol. A second possibility would be to draft a new, separate treaty or convention that would recognize the uniqueness of crimes against "political" groups. This is the position that has been taken by some scholars, notably Jordan Paust, who has suggested that to "the extent that violations of relevant human rights are criminally sanctioned, any gap in coverage by the Genocide Convention [of political groups] will prove to be of little import."[83] Paust nonetheless believes that "it may be important to emphasize these recognitions in a new international instrument," if only to further develop "criminal proscription and to provide additional guidance concerning the contours of present prohibitions."[84] In this connection he has proposed a draft convention on the prevention and punishment of the "crime of politicide." Paust's draft is analogous to the Genocide Convention, though it contains provisions that some might consider an improvement. For example, it expressly recognizes the principle of universal jurisdiction to try persons accused of politicide and related crimes.[85] While a full analysis of Paust's proposal is beyond the scope of this study, his ideas are worthy of further exploration.

Chapter 5 Genocidal Acts and Techniques

I have been at this longer than . . . the Department of Justice and most other agencies. The question about whether genocide is murder, I must say, stirs me. Genocide is murder and more. However, it may not qualify as murder under the criminal laws of many states. The reason is that genocide is mass murder by means other than those which might be declared murder in many civilized states.—Senator Jacob Javits, 1977 Senate hearings

The last issue that the drafters of the Genocide Convention had to deal with in developing the rule on genocide in Article II was the identification of the acts or techniques that would be considered genocidal. The General Assembly had provided little guidance on this matter. Implied in the terms of Resolution 96 (I), of course, was that members of groups could be killed. Indeed, for many people the word "genocide" is a synonym for "mass killing" or "mass murder." But the word was actually coined by Raphael Lemkin in part because he found the concept of "murder," or even "mass murder," inadequate to deal with the phenomenon he had in mind. In 1947, a few years after the publication of *Axis Rule in Occupied Europe*, Lemkin elaborated on how he perceived the concept of genocide in an article in the *American Journal of International Law*. He reiterated that genocide entailed the *destruction* of groups, which could be accomplished in a variety of ways, including, but not limited to, the killing of their members:

> The crime of genocide involves a wide range of actions, including not only the deprivation of life but also the prevention of life (abortions, sterilizations) and also devices considerably endangering life and health (artificial infections, working to death in special camps, deliberate separation of families for depopulation purposes, and so forth). All these actions are subordinated to the criminal intent to destroy or to cripple perma-

> nently a human group. The acts are directed against groups, as such, and individuals are selected for destruction only because they belong to these groups. In view of such a phenomenon the terms previously used to describe an attack upon nationhood were not adequate. Mass murder or extermination wouldn't apply in the case of sterilization because the victims of sterilizations were not murdered, rather a people was killed through delayed action by stopping propagation. Moreover, mass murder does not convey the specific losses to civilization in the form of cultural contributions which can be made only by groups of people united through national, racial or cultural characteristics.[1]

Since the General Assembly's resolution was not nearly as precise as Lemkin was on the subject of genocidal acts, the drafters of the convention were able to exercise substantial discretion in drafting the relevant provisions of Article II. In this endeavor they had to deal with two major issues. First, they had to decide whether or not to enumerate the acts, and, if so, whether or not to make the list closed or open-ended. Most drafters seemed to think that since the convention would deal with a new matter of criminal law, it would be essential to know what was envisaged, and they therefore agreed that the acts should be enumerated. Moreover, they were strongly in favor of a closed, not an open-ended, list. This was especially evident in the deliberations of the Sixth Committee, one of whose first decisions was to reject (by a vote of thirty-five against, nine in favor, and five abstentions) a Chinese proposal to amend the draft of Article II to state "including the following acts" rather than "any of the following acts," as the article now states.[2] If the Chinese proposal had been adopted, it would have had the effect of making the list of genocidal acts open-ended. Instead, Article II sets forth a strict enumeration of genocidal acts.

The second major issue the drafters had to deal with concerned the types of acts that should be considered genocidal. Should Article II list only physical acts of destruction, or should it also ban "cultural genocide"? Those who favored banning cultural genocide, or what is sometimes called ethnocide, argued that groups could be destroyed either through attacks against their physical existence or through actions taken to suppress their specific traits.[3] For the drafters, the issue was highly contentious. The UN Secretariat's draft convention, carrying forward Raphael Lemkin's ideas, proposed banning such acts as "forced and systematic exile of individuals representing the culture of a group"; "prohibition of the national language"; "systematic destruction or of historical or religious monuments or their diversion to alien uses," and so on.[4] Most delegates in the Sixth Committee believed that these were profoundly important issues, but they were turned away from serious discussion of cultural genocide by the emotion-charged argument of a Pakistani delegate who alleged that India was guilty of having committed cultural genocide in the breakup of India and the creation of Pakistan.[5] Charges to this effect were also aired in meetings of the Security Council and carried in media throughout the world.

The Pakistani delegation to the United Nations worked hard to achieve a compromise among the various states that supported the inclusion of an article on cultural genocide in the convention. But the subject was large and controversial, and it proved impossible to draft an article that would attract majority support. Many drafters were concerned about the implications an article on cultural genocide would have for the policies of governments regarding the treatment of minorities, particularly policies aimed at assimilation of minorities into a larger "national" entity. Some drafters thought that an article on cultural genocide would expose states to charges of having committed genocide when their intentions in pursuing policies of assimilation were in fact beneficial to minorities.[6] Proposals to include an article on cultural genocide were therefore rejected in the Sixth Committee and in a plenary session of the General Assembly.[7] As a result, Article II reflects a broad but nonetheless limited conception of the crime of genocide. It covers:

1. killing members of groups;
2. causing serious bodily or mental harm to members of groups;
3. inflicting conditions of life on members of groups that could bring about their physical destruction;
4. imposing measures intended to prevent births within groups; and
5. transferring children from one group to another.

All these acts are usually considered to be physical acts of destruction, though some commentators have suggested that imposing measures intended to prevent births within a group could be thought of as "biological" genocide. It could also be said that at least one of the acts, namely, transferring children from one group to another, is more nearly cultural genocide, even though the drafters expressly rejected draft articles on that subject. In any event, the acts are not mutually exclusive. In fact, varying combinations of the acts could be—and are likely to be—employed. Adolph Eichmann, for example, together with others, was convicted of having committed against Jews the first four acts listed in Article II.[8]

Virtually all the genocidal acts listed above were the subject of extensive debate and disagreement during the controversy over ratification of the

Genocide Convention by the United States, and some of them were dealt with in conditions of ratification specified in the Lugar-Helms-Hatch Sovereignty Package. In this chapter we shall take up each of these acts separately, looking, first, at the considerations that led the drafters to agree upon their inclusion in Article II, and, second, at the issues that each act raised in the debate over ratification of the convention by the United States.

Killing Members of Groups

Article II (a) stipulates that "killing members of [a national, ethnic, racial, or religious] group" is one form of genocide. Killing is the most efficient method of destroying groups, and its efficiency has been increased even more by modern technology. As one might expect, the drafters had no difficulty with this section of Article II. In fact, it was the only provision of the convention about which there was absolutely no discussion in the Sixth Committee of the General Assembly. The provision was adopted by consensus with no vote being taken.[9] When they adopted this provision, the drafters of the convention undoubtedly had in mind the mass extermination of Jews and others labeled undesirable by the Nazi regime during World War II. Perhaps they also had in mind the large-scale massacre of Armenians by the Ottomans during the earlier part of this century. Since World War II, massacres of differing magnitude exhibiting genocidal characteristics have occurred in numerous instances and have caused protest and great controversy.

None of the critics of the convention in the United States has ever objected to the content of Article II (a) by itself. However, beginning in the 1970s, some of the most outspoken critics claimed that the paragraph, combined with the terms of Article I of the convention, would expose American soldiers fighting in Vietnam to charges of having committed genocide in the conduct of the war, because Article I states that genocide is a crime whether committed "in time of peace or in time of war." The important implications of the phrase "killing members of groups," stipulated in Article II (a), had escaped notice until charges alleging the commission of genocide during the Vietnam War surfaced. At one point during the war the North Vietnamese authorities threatened to charge American prisoners with genocide. An article on this threat was carried by the *New York Times* on November 26, 1969, and it figured prominently in the Senate deliberations on the convention in the early 1970s.[10]

The charges of genocide in Vietnam provided critics of the convention such as Senator Sam Ervin, Jr., with a good reason for opposing its ratification in the early 1970s. As he stated in his wide-ranging testimony before the Committee on Foreign Relations in 1970:

> If the Senate should ratify the Genocide Convention, it would make American soldiers fighting under the flag of their country in foreign lands triable and punishable in foreign courts—even in courts in our warring enemy—for killing and seriously wounding members of the military forces of our warring enemy.
>
> This is made indisputable by article I which provides that genocide is punishable under the convention whether it is committed in time of peace or in time of war, *and by the fact that it contains no provision exempting soldiers engaged in combat from the coverage of the provisions of the convention.* When soldiers kill or seriously wound members of a detachment of the military forces of a hostile nation, they certainly do so with intent to destroy, in whole or in part, a national group as such. Hence, their acts in combat fall clearly within the purview of the convention.[11]

The Nixon administration was not quite as alarmed about the potentially adverse consequences of ratification. To the contrary, President Nixon resurrected the convention in 1970 after it had lain dormant in the Committee on Foreign Relations for about twenty years, and in his message to the Senate asking that it consider once again the question of ratification, the president stated that he was making the request in part because "some of our detractors have sought to exploit our failure to ratify this Convention to question our sincerity."[12] By 1970, charges that the United States was committing genocide in Vietnam were fairly widespread, and the Russell Tribunal had already rendered its "judgment" (discussed in chapter 3) that the United States and its allies had committed genocide in Vietnam. Those who believed the charges were evidently the "detractors" that President Nixon was referring to in his message. By ratifying the convention the United States would be demonstrating that it had nothing to hide. There was a certain plausibility to this reasoning. Quite a few proponents of ratification have argued that by becoming a party to the convention the United States would be better able to combat "false" charges of genocide.[13]

Senator Ervin was not the first, or the last, person who testified against ratification of the convention to raise the issue that it did not exempt soldiers from being charged with committing genocide during wartime. In fact, others have sometimes been more blunt about the issue. Eberhard Deutsch, for example, who represented the ABA at the 1971 hearings of the Committee on Foreign Relations, claimed that the United States would "regret Nuremberg" if it ever had to extradite members of the armed forces to stand trial on charges of genocide for having "acted under orders of their military commanders in doing this, that or the other."[14]

What did the drafters have to say about this issue? They discussed it extensively, but it is important to note that, unlike Senator Ervin and Eberhard Deutsch, the drafters debated whether or not the convention should expressly state that command of the law or superior orders *does not* justify the commission of genocidal acts. The Nuremberg Tribunal had expressly rejected such a plea as an *absolute* defense, though it recognized that such orders might be considered mitigating circumstances when imposing punishment if justice so required.[15] It was in this context that the drafters of the Genocide Convention discussed the issue. Platon Morozov, the Soviet representative on the Ad Hoc Committee of the ECOSOC, favored a proposal whereby the convention would state expressly that "command of the law or superior orders shall not justify genocide." He believed that this statement would be consistent with the view of the Nuremberg Tribunal and would have an "educative influence by warning those who might be led to commit the crime of genocide" that a plea of command of the law or superior orders would not exempt them from punishment.[16] Others argued that the Soviet proposal might not allow for flexibility in the application of the Nuremberg principle, and that it would therefore be best not to adopt it and to leave the issue up to the courts that would apply the convention. The same issues were debated again in the Sixth Committee of the General Assembly.[17] Table 5.1 shows how the members of the committee voted on a Soviet proposal to insert a provision in the convention that would ban the plea of command of the law or superior orders as a defense in cases of genocide.

As the table shows, the differences of opinion on the question of whether or not the defense of command of the law or superior orders in the commission of genocide should be expressly ruled out cut across the various geographical groupings of states at the time the convention was drafted. Among the largest geographical groups, the American states were the most unified in opposing the Soviet proposal, but only by a relatively narrow margin of 54.5 percent. The European states were virtually evenly divided, which is not surprising since the Soviet bloc constituted roughly one-third of that group at the time. The data suggest, however, that the issue was not one that pitted the Soviet bloc against everyone else. In fact, the Sixth Committee's rejection of the Soviet proposal did not mean that the delegates disagreed with the Nuremberg principle. To the contrary, the debate records indicate that everyone endorsed the principle. What the delegates disagreed on was

Table 5.1 Vote in the Sixth Committee on the Soviet Proposal on Command of the Law or Superior Orders.

Area	Number (Percentage)	Yes	Abstain	No	No vote
Africa		2	1	1	0
		(50.0)	(25.0)	(25.0)	(0)
Asia		2	3	5	3
		(15.4)	(23.1)	(38.5)	(23.1)
Oceania		0	0	2	0
		(0)	(0)	(100)	(0)
Americas		3	2	12	5
		(13.6)	(9.1)	(54.5)	(22.7)
Europe		8	0	8	1
		(47.1)	(0)	(47.1)	(5.9)
TOTALS		15	6	28	9
		(25.9)	(10.3)	(48.3)	(15.5)

Source: Same as table 4.1.

how best to affirm the principle and make allowances for the demands of justice at the same time. The drafters left the matter up to the courts that would have to apply the convention.

The subject of the Soviet proposal has only rarely been discussed by commentators on the convention. Ben Whitaker, however, in his 1985 report on the convention for the United Nations, argued that a case could be made for recognizing the Nuremberg principle in the convention. He pointed out that the tribunal's interpretation of the defense of superior orders was not "new at the trial," and that it "was perfectly familiar in national legal systems" and was also known in international law at the time. Consequently, "the doctrine was . . . not one that was invented *de novo* by the victors at Nuremberg," and there was "little doubt that courts today would hold that the concept of individual responsibility will override any defence of superior orders."[18] Nonetheless, Whitaker maintained

> since wider public education about this doctrine is highly crucial for the aversion of future genocide, . . . explicit wording should be added to the Convention, perhaps at the end of Article III, that "In judging culpability, a plea of superior orders is not an excusing defence." Similarly, wider publicity should be given to this principle in national codes governing armed forces, prison staffs, police officers, doctors, and others,

> to advise and warn them that it is not only their right to disobey orders violating human rights, such as to carry out genocide or torture, but their legal duty so to disobey. Such precepts should also be taught in all schools, and the United Nations Educational, Scientific and Cultural Organization might be asked to encourage this internationally.[19]

The principle at stake, and the arguments that have surrounded it, are important. However, it is noteworthy that those who favored U.S. ratification of the Genocide Convention avoided confronting the issue raised by Senator Ervin and others directly; that is, they did not generally argue *in favor* of the Nuremberg principle. The reason is not hard to find. It would have been politically unwise, if not suicidal, to make much of an issue out of the value of the Nuremberg principle at a time when there was so much concern, even if unfounded, that soldiers fighting in Vietnam could be charged with committing genocide if the United States ratified the convention. Therefore, rather than confronting the issue directly, the proponents of ratification concentrated on the obvious—that American military personnel or civilians could be charged with committing genocide in foreign lands, including Vietnam, even if the United States did not ratify the convention, even if the convention did not exist! Senator William Proxmire took the critics to task on this ground, arguing that it was "specious to say that the treaty allows American prisoners of war to be tried on charges of genocide"; and he suggested that to "even imply that ratification of the Genocide Convention would adversely affect our fighting men now prisoners of war in North Vietnam is patently absurd," that it was an argument that was "merely a blatant appeal to blind emotion with no basis in reality."[20] Proxmire's point was that American civilians or military personnel could be tried for genocide abroad under the law of any country even if there were no genocide convention. But even the Defense Department's 1976 endorsement of ratification of the convention was not sufficient to lay to rest the objections of the critics.[21]

The U.S. Understanding Regarding Genocide During Armed Conflict

During the 1980s, critics of the convention again raised the possibility of American soldiers being charged with committing genocide during conditions of armed conflict. On these occasions, however, the critics were in a much stronger position, especially after Senator Charles Percy (R., Illinois), the chairman of the Committee on Foreign Relations, was defeated in his bid for reelection in 1984. Percy had been tolerant of dissent (it came from within his own political party) regarding the convention, but he had resisted enlarging the number of conditions of ratification that would be recommended by the committee. He favored ratification subject to the same set of conditions that had been proposed by the committee throughout the 1970s. Thus, when the Committee on Foreign Relations favorably reported the convention to the Senate in 1984, the resolution of ratification it proposed was identical with the one it had proposed throughout the 1970s.[22]

Percy's defeat in his bid for reelection, and his replacement as chairman of the Committee on Foreign Relations by Senator Richard Lugar, had a tremendous impact on the eventual outcome regarding the convention. Lugar cooperated with Senator Jesse Helms, the arch-critic of the convention during the 1980s, at every turn, and helped to construct the Lugar-Helms-Hatch Sovereignty Package, which contains an understanding regarding genocide committed during armed conflicts that states:

> That acts in the course of armed conflicts committed without the specific intent required by Article II are not sufficient to constitute genocide as defined by this Convention.[23]

Different positions were taken on the understanding in the Senate debates. Senator Orrin Hatch, a main proponent of its adoption, seemed to have a broad view of the terms of the understanding. He argued that it would apply to "regular war or to guerrilla war" or a "combination of both, as in Vietnam," and that it meant that actions on the battlefield could not be "genocide without the combatants having the specific intent to commit genocide." According to Hatch, the Russell Tribunal's "judgment" on the Vietnam War demonstrated the need for the understanding. For Hatch, it was "not inconceivable that a similar situation could arise in the event of U.S. involvement in some form of hostilities with Nicaragua,"[24] which was a matter of great controversy at the time the Senate was deliberating ratification of the convention. By "insisting on the specific intent requirement in these situations," the understanding "effectively safeguarded a government fighting to defend itself against terrorism or fighting to assist other countries – or groups – in their struggle for independence and for the preservation of freedom."[25] In this connection Hatch also cited Israel, which has been accused by the PLO of committing against Palestinians all the genocidal acts listed in Article II.[26]

In contrast to Hatch, a group of senators on the Committee on Foreign Relations, including Claiborne Pell (D., Rhode Island), at that time the ranking Democrat, Joseph Biden, Jr. (D., Delaware), Paul Sarbanes (D., Maryland), Alan Cranston (D., California), Charles Mathias (R., Maryland), Christopher Dodd, Thomas Eagleton (D., Missouri), and John Kerry (D., Massachusetts), objected to the understanding on the ground that it was obvious that the intent element was required in every case to prove a charge of genocide. As they stated in the committee report:

> A new understanding had been added stating that "acts in the course of armed conflicts committed without the specific intent required by Article II are not sufficient to constitute genocide as defined by this Convention." Since it is obvious that any act committed without the specific intent required by Article II is not sufficient to constitute genocide, *a question arises as to what the United States is really seeking to accomplish by attaching this understanding. The language suggests that the United States fears it has something to hide.* Moreover, the relatively imprecise definition of "armed conflicts" in international law is an invitation to problems and will almost certainly draw adverse comments from other nations trying to figure out what the language is intended to do. *To call attention to our fears about being brought to account for acts committed in armed conflicts is really an embarrassment to the United States and should have no place in our ratification of the Genocide Convention.*[27]

There is much to commend this viewpoint, though it could be carried further. The entire Sovereignty Package could be thought of as embarrassing to the United States. It stands out among all the other instruments of ratification for its breadth of coverage, and the understanding concerning genocide in the course of armed conflicts is not its only provision that suggests the United States has something to hide. In fact, as I have pointed out, the acknowledged purpose of the Sovereignty Package was to reduce the convention to nothing more than a mere symbol of opposition to genocide. This fact alone raises the question of whether or not the United States ratified in good faith.

The U.S. understanding regarding genocide during armed conflicts is open to objection by other parties to the convention just like any other provision of the Sovereignty Package. They could object to the label that was used and argue that the understanding is in fact a reservation. Moreover, they could argue that the reservation is incompatible with the object and purpose of the convention. On the other hand, other parties might find that they have insufficient grounds for making such objections, since the understanding seems merely to restate the obvious, though someone could conceivably make a case that Hatch and others were attempting to modify the Nuremberg principle regarding command of the law or superior orders. No one, including Hatch, made an express statement to that effect in the

Senate debates, but the arguments they made could be construed to have implied such an intention. Whatever their intention, as in the case of the understanding regarding intent discussed in chapter 3, from a public policy perspective the understanding regarding the commission of genocide during armed conflicts might better have been left out of the Sovereignty Package precisely for the reasons stated by Senator Pell and other dissenting members of the Committee on Foreign Relations.

Causing Serious Bodily or Mental Harm

Article II (b) refers to "causing serious bodily or mental harm to members of [a national, ethnic, racial, or religious] group" as a genocidal act. This clause, too—in particular the words "mental harm"—has attracted the attention of many critics of the convention in the United States. The issues date back to the first hearings held on the convention by the Committee on Foreign Relations in 1950, and they persisted throughout the 1970s and into the 1980s. Throughout this period it was always assumed that if the convention were ratified, it would be with an understanding regarding the meaning of "mental harm," and an understanding regarding the words was included in the Lugar-Helms-Hatch Sovereignty Package. We shall examine the content and rationale of the U.S. understanding in a moment. Before turning our attention to this task, however, let us examine whether or not the drafters provided sufficiently clear guidelines for interpreting the meaning of the words "mental harm."

The Drafters' Intentions Regarding the Meaning of "Mental Harm"

The inclusion of "mental harm" in Article II (b) resulted from proposals initiated by Lin Mousheng, the Chinese representative on the Ad Hoc Committee of the ECOSOC.[28] He was concerned that everyone was preoccupied with Nazi genocidal actions during World War II and insufficiently concerned about atrocities committed in the Orient. He asserted that during the war the Japanese had built a huge opium-extraction plant in Mukden that was capable of processing four hundred tons of opium annually, producing fifty tons of heroin—at least fifty times the legitimate world requirements. Medical authorities estimated that the plant could have produced enough heroin to administer lethal doses to at least 200 million, and perhaps as many as 400 million, persons. According to Lin Mousheng, the sheer magnitude of the operation made it clear that the Japanese had intended to commit, and had committed, genocide. He felt the matter should be addressed in the convention, and he suggested that this could be done by including a reference to acts that would "impair the mental capacity" or "impair the health" of members of groups listed as objects of protection in Article II.[29]

The Ad Hoc Committee rejected the Chinese proposal. It was reintroduced in the Sixth Committee of the General Assembly, but again various delegates expressed reservations about it. Some argued that including the word "mental" in Article II (b) might lead to difficulties in interpreting the convention. As they saw it, acts that impaired the "mental capacity" of members of groups, if they resulted in "physical impairment," would be covered by the terms of the article. They were reluctant to allow acts that did not result in physical impairment to fall within the purview of Article II. The debate on this issue revealed how determined the drafters of the convention were to limit its application to physical acts of genocide.[30] At the conclusion of the discussion, a formal Chinese proposal to amend Article II (b) to state "impairing the physical or mental health of members of the group" was rejected by a vote of seventeen against, ten in favor, and thirteen abstentions.[31] Curiously, at the same meeting, the Sixth Committee reversed itself and adopted a joint proposal by India and the United Kingdom to include the words "mental harm." That proposal was supported by the Chinese representative.[32]

The official records of the Sixth Committee do not reveal clearly what the drafters of the convention intended by the words "mental harm." The Chinese representative initiating debate on the issue had in mind the administration of narcotics to groups. Yet his actual proposal did not seem to contemplate the physical destruction of groups, for "impairing the mental health" of groups certainly suggests something less extreme than the administration of lethal doses of narcotics. Nor do the official records clearly indicate why the representatives in the Sixth Committee were willing to accept the words "mental harm" but not the words "impairing mental health."

Commentators and others have attempted to clarify the matter. Nehemiah Robinson, for example, suggested that the measures must be extreme in light of the fact that the intention in inflicting mental harm must be to destroy a group.[33] Philip Perlman, solicitor general during the Truman administration, argued that the words "mental harm" were inserted in Article II in order to show that "disintegration of the mind, caused by stupefying drugs, or other permanent impairment of mental faculties was regarded as the evil to be condemned, equally with the outright slaughter of a group."[34] Thus, in their view, racial and religious epithets that could inflict mental harm, however deplorable, could not be considered genocidal. Others have suggested that the mental harm need not necessarily result in immediate physical destruction; nor would it even necessarily have to result in permanent injury. Brainwashing has sometimes been cited as an example of nonpermanent injury. Addiction to narcotics could also be considered nonpermanent.[35]

The U.S. Understanding Regarding Mental Harm

The vagueness of the concept "mental harm" has often been cited in debates over ratification of the convention by the United States. When the Senate Committee on Foreign Relations held its first hearings in 1950, opponents of ratification argued that the words "mental harm" might be used, especially by civil rights groups, to denounce segregation laws in the United States. In fact, they were concerned that the words might even make persons who utter racial and religious epithets susceptible to being charged with genocide. The ABA representatives were especially outspoken with regard to these possibilities. As George Finch stated:

> Can it be successfully denied that segregation laws are susceptible of being denounced as causing mental harm to all members of the group against which such laws discriminate? Minority groups in this country are now vigorously seeking to have such discrimination abolished by Federal legislation. Can there be any reasonable doubt that if Congress fails to enact the civil rights laws now being urged upon it and if this convention is ratified as submitted, members of the affected groups will be in a position to seek legal relief on the ground that this so-called Genocide Convention has superseded all obnoxious State legislation? By the United States Constitution, treaties are "the supreme law of the land, and the judges in every State shall be bound thereby, anything in the Constitution or laws of any State to the contrary notwithstanding." (Art. VI, sec. 2)[36]

Truman administration spokesmen attempted to calm the fears that these alarmist interpretations of Article II (b) generated. Adrian Fisher, for example, the State Department legal adviser, argued that the legislative history of the article made it clear that the words "mental harm" were not meant to apply to "embarrassment or hurt feelings, or even the sense of outrage that comes from such action as racial discrimination or segregation, however horrible those may be." Rather, the words would apply to "systematic attempts to cause permanent impairment of a man's mental faculties," "systematic terror," forced "lack of sleep," and the like. To Fisher,

> these things are vicious enough that they should be expressly prohibited and should not be left to any theoretical lawyers' argument as to whether or not this type of permanent impairment of the mental faculties is included in the definition of serious bodily harm or not. We should hit the snake where we see it, and not hope to catch him in a ricochet from something else.
>
> Again, I think the legislative history of this article makes it clear that Congress would be justified in living up to the international obligations of this country in writing a statute on the basis that all that was dealt with was permanent impairment of mental faculties, and I think that is a sufficiently horrible crime and a horrible method of carrying out crimes of this kind so that it should be mentioned by name.[37]

There was dissent on the issue even within the ABA's ranks. Thomas Dodd, who had served as a prosecutor at Nuremberg and would later become a U.S. senator, vigorously dissented from the official ABA position on the convention. Regarding the words "mental harm," he said,

> I would like to take just 1 minute to tell you that on this question of mental harm, I know what that means, having heard it from the mouths of people who knew what it meant subjectively. It was an established mechanism of the Nazi state, and it is practiced in other places as well, that the destruction, the disintegration of the human mind was a planned thing. It was one of the worst things that was done probably to individuals by the Nazis, and it is not too difficult for people who want to learn about it to read the records at Nuremberg, and they will have a very clear concept, when they have done so, as to what happens to people under a planned program of destroying their minds. There are all kinds of ways of doing it, and there are many, indeed.[38]

In general, the proponents of ratification at the 1950 Senate hearings argued that the ABA's official representatives trivialized the issue of mental harm in view of the necessity to prove the intent to destroy a group. Nonetheless, they were prepared to accept ratification with an understanding concerning "mental harm." The understanding was to say that the United States interpreted "mental harm" to mean "permanent injury to mental faculties." But even this interpretation was not considered restrictive enough, and some consideration was given to revising the understanding to state "permanent injury to mental faculties which results in physical disintegration." The reference to "physical disintegration" was proposed in order to appease the ABA representatives, and was, oddly enough, taken from the report of a committee of that association that favored ratification. In short, the 1950 understanding regarding mental harm was a political compromise—it was designed to assuage the fears and concerns of the ABA representatives and others who thought that racial epithets and segregation laws could be interpreted to mean genocide by mental harm. As Senator Elbert Thomas (D., Utah), one of the strongest supporters of ratification at the time, stated: "It seems to me that if there is an objection [to the words "mental harm," even among those in the ABA who support ratification], it would be awfully good to take a quote from them and accept their recommendation."[39]

This statement says much about the ABA's extraordinary influence in defeating the ratification effort in 1950. Portions of the 1950 hearings that were not published until 1976, in a compilation of executive sessions of the Senate Committee on Foreign Relations, are quite revealing on this point. Senator Tom Connally (D., Texas), the legendary chairman of the committee at that time, cited the opposition of the ABA as *the* reason why the committee would not even vote on the question of whether or not to report the convention to the Senate with a recommendation to ratify conditionally,[40] even though members of the subcommittee that had held the hearings were pressing the full committee to report the convention to the Senate with a recommendation regarding ratification.[41]

The same kinds of issues were raised again at Senate hearings during the 1970s. In apparent anticipation of difficulty, President Nixon urged ratification of the convention with an understanding regarding the meaning of the words "mental harm." The understanding was the *only* condition of ratification proposed by President Nixon.[42] Reflecting a modification of the 1950 version of the understanding, the one proposed by President Nixon did not include the words "physical injury." It stated "that the United States Government understands and construes the words 'mental harm' appearing in Article II (b) of this Convention to mean permanent impairment of mental faculties."[43]

This understanding was included in the proposed resolutions of ratification every time the Committee on Foreign Relations reported the convention to the Senate during the 1970s. It was also included in the draft resolution in 1984. The understanding was initially proposed by the Nixon administration to discourage what administration spokesmen called "frivolous" allegations of genocide through mental harm,[44] and those who supported it hoped that it would address the objections of the critics who were so concerned about possibly abusive interpretations of Article II. However, it did not appease them; to the contrary, some reacted to the understanding with profound skepticism and even hostility. Senator Sam Ervin, Jr., took the most extreme position, asserting: "If the Convention is ratified, article II (b) would impose upon the United States the duty to prevent and to prosecute and punish public officials and individuals who cause 'mental harm to members' of any one of the four groups named in the convention. What mental harm means in this context is totally incomprehensible, and what psychological acts or omissions are made punishable in this context are left in obscurity."[45]

Ervin went on to stress that in 1950 the subcommittee of the Committee on Foreign Relations that had held the hearings on the convention had recommended ratification with an understanding to the effect that the words "mental harm" meant "permanent physical injury to mental faculties." When pressed by Senator Frank Church (D., Idaho) to say whether or not he approved of the wording of that understanding, Ervin replied, "Yes, I think the United States would be very foolish to ratify it without putting in this understanding. In fact, I think the United States would be very foolish to ratify it even with this understanding."[46] Ervin was so determined to defeat ratification that he took his case to the Senate floor, going so far as to introduce an amendment to a resolution of ratification which provided that the U.S. government "understands and construes the words 'mental harm' appearing in Article II (b) of this convention as unintelligible and imposes no obligation upon the United States."[47]

Other opponents of ratification, like the ABA representatives in the early 1970s, argued that the understanding favored by the Nixon administration would not hamper victims of segregation laws from bringing charges of genocide against the United States. The U.S. Supreme Court's decision in *Brown* v. *Board of Education* (347 U.S. 483, 1954) figured prominently in these deliberations, indicating that the race issue was a major concern of the convention's critics. Thus, Eberhard Deutsch stated:

> In *Brown* v. *Board of Education*, the leading desegregation case . . . , the Supreme Court of the United States . . . held expressly that separation of Negro children—and now I quote from the opinion—separation—from others of similar age and qualifications solely because of their race, generates a feeling of inferiority as to their status in the community that may affect their hearts and minds in a way unlikely ever to be undone . . . and has a tendency to retard their education and mental development. . . .
>
> In light of this holding by the Supreme Court, such an understanding as this committee has proposed . . . that mental harm is to be construed

> "to mean permanent impairment of mental faculties," would hardly deter any tribunal from determining that any form of local segregation is within the definition of the international crime of genocide under the convention.[48]

Interestingly, according to Deutsch's argument the U.S. Supreme Court had itself provided the ammunition that civil rights groups could use to charge genocide.

Throughout the 1970s and early 1980s, most persons who testified before the Committee on Foreign Relations in support of ratification, such as Richard Gardner, Ambassador Rita Hauser, and George Aldrich, the Nixon administration State Department legal adviser, favored, or perhaps more precisely did not object to, the understanding that the Committee on Foreign Relations proposed regarding the words "mental harm." They maintained, of course, that local segregation laws, racial slurs, and the like could hardly be considered genocidal acts in light of the requirement established in the convention that the acts must be committed with the intent to destroy a group. Nonetheless, they believed that the proposed understanding was basically consistent with the drafting history of the convention in view of what the Chinese representative said when he opened debate on the subject; and they argued that it would have the effect of discouraging frivolous allegations of genocide by mental harm.

Whatever could be said in defense of the understanding, it probably would have been pointless to oppose it, because by the early 1970s it had already become obvious to all concerned that an understanding would be vitally important from the standpoint of securing enough votes in the Senate for ratification. In other words, whether or not an understanding was really necessary to clarify the meaning of "mental harm," it was necessary for political reasons. In fact, the Nixon administration was prepared to go beyond the understanding in clarifying the meaning of the words. The implementing legislation it submitted to Congress was drafted in a way that discouraged frivolous allegations of genocide by mental harm. The legislation stated that "permanent impairment of the mental faculties of members" of groups could be caused by "torture, deprivation of physical or physiological needs, surgical operation, introduction of drugs or other foreign substances into the bodies of such members, or subjection to psychological or psychiatric treatment calculated to permanently impair the mental processes, or nervous system, or motor functions of such members."[49] The same legislation was later recommended by the Carter administration. Obviously, in light of the way in which the draft legislation defined mental harm, one would have been hard-pressed to argue that local segregation laws were inflicting mental harm on their target populations sufficient to sustain a charge of genocide. But these concessions to the critics of the convention were still not enough to persuade them to support ratification.

With this background in mind, it could have been predicted that the Lugar-Helms-Hatch Sovereignty Package would contain an understanding regarding the words "mental harm." It states:

> That the term "mental harm" in Article II (b) means permanent impairment of mental faculties through drugs, torture or similar techniques.[50]

The language of this understanding is repeated in the U.S. implementing legislation, the Proxmire Act.[51]

According to the Committee on Foreign Relations, the understanding has two objectives. In the first place, it was designed to make it clear that the United States understands the words "mental harm" to mean "permanent harm."[52] Second, it was intended to stress that the United States understands that the "harm be the result of some physical intrusion into the body."[53] In other words, as the committee put it, "Psychological harm resulting from living conditions, differential treatment by government authorities and the like is excluded."[54]

The committee's reasoning demonstrates the lingering influence of the ABA critics who testified in 1950. Some senators were obviously very much concerned about the possibility that blacks might charge genocide on the basis of mental harm. While no one suggested in the 1980s that such charges might be forthcoming if the United States ratified the convention without the understanding (perhaps because it had been finally accepted that the charges could be made even if the United States never ratified the convention), their comments reflected an awareness of the possibility of such charges. Senator Jesse Helms, for example, favored including the words "permanent physical impairment" in the understanding, his view being that the words "permanent impairment of mental faculties" were not strong enough, that they did "not distinguish between objective impairment created by physical alteration or abuse of the organs of the body, and psychological impairment which might result from general economic and social conditions, or lack of opportunity for personality development."[55]

According to Helms, while "no one [could] approve a social context which results in psychological deprivation, the objective existence and extent of such deprivation is based on subjective assessment which could be highly politicized."[56] Of course, Helms had a political agenda of his own: he wanted to prevent ratification. But if it was to be ratified, Helms believed that it should limit "the definition of genocide to conditions specifically calculated to bring about the physical destruction of the group."[57]

Is the U.S. Understanding Necessary or Desirable?

The words "mental harm" in Article II are problematic, and the fears of Senator Helms, Hatch, and others are not totally unwarranted. The words are vague and give rise to various plausible interpretations. Moreover, the negotiating history of the convention does not provide much evidence as to the intentions of the drafters. Nonetheless, the understanding included in the Lugar-Helms-Hatch Sovereignty Package could be considered unnecessary and even undesirable for several reasons.

In the first place, no other party to the convention has ratified it with a similar understanding or reservation, perhaps because they have thought that vague provisions of the convention could be addressed in their own implementing legislation.[58] As we have seen, U.S. implementing legislation has been designed to discourage frivolous allegations of genocide. It is reasonable to expect that other states would do the same. Dealing with the issues in this way has the advantage of leaving it up to courts to reach judgments on the merits of allegations. But in the United States, the most outspoken critics of the convention have seemed extremely distrustful of courts, including the ICJ. This attitude is implicit in their views on a number of issues involved in interpreting the rule on genocide set forth in Article II, not just the issue of the vagueness of the words "mental harm." For these reasons the critics have sought to use understandings and reservations to close every conceivable loophole they have perceived emanating from vague provisions of the convention.

Second, an objection could be raised to the U.S. understanding by other parties to the convention. The grounds for objection could be similar to those discussed in connection with the understanding regarding the phrase "intent to destroy, in whole or in part," that were discussed in chapter 3, or the understanding regarding genocide in armed combat discussed earlier in this chapter. Other parties could object to the statement's label as an understanding, insisting that it is in fact a reservation; and they could object to the reservation on the ground that it is incompatible with the object and purpose of the convention. Criticisms of the earlier version of the understanding—the one proposed throughout the 1970s and in 1984—appear to be still valid and applicable against the understanding in the Sovereignty Package. Commenting on the earlier version of the understanding, Bunyan Bryant argued that nonpermanent or reversible mental harm—for example, that which could be caused by the administration of drugs and brainwashing—could eventually result in the destruction of groups. Consequently, he found that the understanding the Committee on Foreign Relations proposed during the 1970s might be no better a guide to interpreting the words "mental harm" than the ordinary meaning of the words construed in light of the object and purpose of the convention.[59]

Conditions of Life Leading to Genocide

Article II (c) states that "deliberately inflicting" on a national, ethnic, racial, or religious group "conditions of life calculated to bring about its physical destruction in whole or in part" constitutes genocide. The drafters of the convention did not clearly indicate what they meant by inserting this phrase in Article II, but it would seem from the context of the negotiations as well as the plain meaning of the language of the phrase that they had the Holocaust in mind when they adopted it. As commentators such as Nehemiah Robinson have suggested, the phrase presumably refers to such things as death camps established for the purpose of eventually destroying their inhabitants—that the conditions must be extreme.[60] This interpretation seems reasonable in view of the fact that Article II (c) expressly states that the conditions must be "deliberately" inflicted on a group to bring about its "physical" destruction in whole or in part.

Although the drafters apparently were thinking of the Holocaust when they approved Article II (c), many scholars have noted that there have been instances after World War II when conditions of life have been imposed on groups to bring about their destruction in whole or in part. Richard Falk, for example, noted the relationship between deprivation of basic human needs and genocide:

> The deprivation of basic human needs can be used to achieve explicit political ends, such as the denial of food in settling an ethnic conflict. Characteristically, the central government may deprive an ethnically distinct antagonistic component of its population of food so as to starve it into submission, as has been alleged in several African interethnic conflicts—Ibos in Nigeria and the Somalis and Eritreans in Ethiopia. If this deprivation results in the decimation of the target group, it amounts to genocide.[61]

While commentators and scholars agree that the measures covered by the terms of Article II (c) must be extreme, many critics of the convention in the

United States have asserted that the paragraph is exceedingly troublesome. In fact, the paragraph provided Senator Sam Ervin, Jr., with yet another opportunity to trivialize the convention and its purposes. In 1970 he had this to say:

> If the convention is ratified, article II (c) would impose upon the United States the duty to prevent and to prosecute and punish anyone who deliberately inflicts "on the group conditions of life calculated to bring about its physical destruction in whole or in part." *What this means, no mind can fathom.* Does it mean that a State or county official who refuses to give to a member of one of the four groups designated in the convention the amount of welfare benefits deemed desirable is to be punished or prosecuted for genocide? Does it mean that the Court of International Justice shall have power under article IX to adjudge that Congress or a State legislature which does not make available to members of one of the four groups what the court deems to be adequate welfare benefits has violated the convention?[62]

Outlandish comments such as these made it clear beyond any doubt that Ervin was determined to defeat the ratification movement, and that he would not be persuaded by any argument, however rational, that took issue with his stands. But he did not go unchallenged. To the contrary, Ervin's comments provoked impassioned, emotion-laden responses from some senators, especially Senator Jacob Javits, who suspected that critics such as Ervin were not interested in serious debate over the merits of the Genocide Convention, that in fact they were determined to prevent its ratification at any cost, even if they had to invent arguments to achieve their objective. Javits was incredulous that Ervin would actually oppose ratification,[63] and in 1970 he prepared a lengthy rebuttal of the various objections that Ervin had raised. Noting that Article II (c) was generally regarded as covering "slow death" measures, Javits pointed out the obvious: "Denial of adequate welfare benefits is of a completely different magnitude than measures calculated to bring about slow death. In addition, the requisite intent to destroy in whole or in part the members of a group . . . would be lacking."[64]

The exaggerations of the ABA representatives also irritated Javits. By 1971 there was already a movement within the ABA to reverse its long-standing opposition to ratification of the convention, and when Alfred Schweppe and Eberhard Deutsch appeared at the 1971 hearings, Javits challenged their credentials. There was substantial confusion about whether the witnesses were authorized to appear by the president of the association or by the association itself.[65] Conceding their right to appear before the committee, Javits took them to task for their arguments, exposing the political bias that lay behind their legal and pseudolegal arguments. When Deutsch claimed that he did not know of anyone within the ABA who had changed his mind about the Genocide Convention, but that the association itself had changed, becoming more "liberal" because of the influx of new members, Javits pressed him:

SENATOR JAVITS: Mr. Deutsch, do you consider genocide to be a liberal or conservative issue?

MR. DEUTSCH: No, sir. But I do consider the adoption of an international treaty to define domestic crimes and put them in the hands of international tribunals to be an expansion of liberalism tending toward world government for which I am satisfied the world is not yet ready, if it ever will be.

SENATOR JAVITS: And that is how you define this treaty?

MR. DEUTSCH: I do, yes.[66]

This deep-seated bias against ratification made it as clear as anything could that there was virtually nothing that the proponents of ratification could do to satisfy the opponents. A variety of legal, mainly technical, arguments were being made, but the real basis for opposition to ratification was a profound resistance to "liberalism tending toward world government," as Deutsch succinctly put it. Javits became increasingly frustrated. At the 1977 Senate hearings he said, "The numbers of rumors, innuendos, misconceptions, and scares that have been spread about this treaty are literally endless, and this has been done by people who are very, very competent and able in many other ways, but who somehow have an absolute blind spot on this one."[67]

Javits believed that the "imprimatur of the American Bar Association," which had officially endorsed ratification of the convention in 1976, was "really the most decisive answer" to the various objections because many of those objections were so "complicated."[68] But even the ABA's endorsement could not win over Senator Ervin, which suggests that Javits was being unduly optimistic. Ervin continued to oppose ratification even after he had left the Senate, urging Senator Charles Percy, in a "Dear Chuck" letter in 1984, to "forsake the Genocide Treaty" because it "contains the greatest foolishness ever presented to the Senate in the form of a treaty";[69] and he enclosed a copy of a speech he had made on the Senate floor in 1970 that explained "what a fool proposition the Genocide Treaty is."[70] On the issue of living conditions imposed on groups to bring about their destruction, however, Senator Ervin's arguments were disregarded by the Committee on Foreign Relations. At no time did the committee ever seriously discuss the possibility of drafting an understanding regarding that clause.

Preventing Births Within a Group

Article II (d) states that "imposing measures intended to prevent births within [a national, ethnic, racial, or religious] group" would constitute genocide. The drafters of the convention did not specify the measures that could be employed to prevent births, but here again commentators have generally been in agreement, saying that the drafters had in mind practices such as forced sterilizations and abortions, the purpose of which would be, as Raphael Lemkin noted, to prevent a group from replenishing itself so that it would eventually be destroyed. Whatever measures might be employed, they must be carried out with the intent to destroy a group in whole or in part. Moreover, some commentators have said that the measures must be forcible, or nonvoluntary, because Article II (d) specifically refers to "imposing measures" intended to prevent births. It would therefore seem reasonable to conclude that birth control programs, even if funded by governments, and even if the policies of those governments should be to promote birth control, cannot be considered "genocidal" within the meaning of Article II (d) so long as participation in such programs is voluntary. These points have been reiterated by many proponents of U.S. ratification of the convention, including William Rehnquist, who, as assistant attorney general during the Nixon administration, testified in favor of ratification of the convention in 1970.[71] The questions were put to him by Senator Frank Church as follows:

> Another extreme criticism leveled at the Convention is that it would make birth control efforts among the poor black an act of genocide. How would you answer this allegation?
>
> MR. REHNQUIST: I think that any birth control effort that might reasonably be contemplated in this country would certainly be a voluntary one, and would likewise be directed toward all individuals rather than any particular race. I think it is inconceivable that any sort of birth control effort that would ever receive public approval in this country would violate the provisions of this treaty.
>
> SENATOR CHURCH: Is it true that if any such effort were to be made, based upon some compulsory method and directed toward some particular group, that the protections of the Constitution would be

fully applicable whether or not the United States had ratified and become a party to the Genocide Convention?

MR. REHNQUIST: Certainly.[72]

Rehnquist's certainty to the contrary notwithstanding, some opponents of ratification made an issue out of the terms of Article II (d), claiming that if the United States ratified the convention, it would open itself to charges of genocide by groups, especially black Americans, because of birth control programs. At the 1971 Senate hearings Eberhard Deutsch called attention to a petition that a group of black leaders had published (titled "We Charge Genocide") and submitted to the United Nations, initially in 1951 and again in 1970, requesting, among other things, that the organization condemn the United States for its genocidal practices against black people. Nothing came of this petition, but Deutsch saw it as an ominous sign and made one hundred copies of it available to the Senate.[73]

The Genocide Thesis and Black Americans

The charges that were made in the petition "We Charge Genocide" have been made frequently, and could be made even in the absence of the ratification of the convention. Robert Weisbord has investigated these charges. In *Genocide? Birth Control and the Black American*, he noted that some blacks have long suspected that family planning "is just another means," along with "political oppression, economic exploitation, and outright brutality," used by whites to achieve the annihilation of blacks.[74] Although Weisbord states that from "the evidence available it is fair to conclude that contraception, abortion, and sterilization have never been systematically used to exterminate black Americans," and that there "has never been a genocidal master plan," he does point out that there is much in the "historical record and in contemporary societal developments to sustain black fears about the existence of such a plan."[75] In this connection he cites cases of involuntary sterilizations and a number of punitive sterilization bills aimed at welfare mothers which have been introduced in some state legislatures. None of the bills was adopted, but some of the involuntary sterilizations, when brought to light, became the subject of charges of genocide by black groups such as the Black Panthers and Black Muslims.[76] Other black organizations, such as the Urban League, while not calling such actions genocidal, have perceived them as opening the way for genocidal measures.[77]

Similarly, the legalization of abortion, and even family planning programs, have been attacked by some blacks on the ground that impoverished black women would be the ones most likely to take advantage of the laws and programs, and that this would run counter to the "strength-in-numbers" philosophy that opponents of abortion and family planning have advanced. According to this philosophy, "lots of babies is the best solution to [the] racial dilemma, a numerical antidote to discrimination, a kind of insurance against liquidation."[78] In contrast, some black leaders and groups, though not unconcerned about possible genocidal acts and plans, have seen family planning as a positive good that could help to improve the quality of life for black Americans. Weisbord cites W. E. B. DuBois and others as preferring "birth control" over "death control," that is, a high death rate.[79]

The black American genocide thesis has been embraced mainly, though not exclusively, by extremists; nevertheless, the charges have been made. This created some apprehension that ratification of the convention would open the way for litigation concerning the charges, implying again a basic distrust of courts' ability to dismiss frivolous allegations of genocide. Fortunately, the Committee on Foreign Relations disregarded the apprehensions of Deutsch and other critics of the convention on this issue and indicated in its report to the Senate in 1971 that the charges of genocide against black Americans have been made, and could be made in the future, even if the United States did not ratify the convention: "Charges have been made and will no doubt be made again, even though the United States has enacted historic civil rights legislation since 1951, but the committee cannot stress enough that such charges, domestic or foreign, do not constitute genocidal acts just because someone labels them so. Genocide is what the convention says and not what crusaders for human rights, no matter how well motivated, allege."[80]

The committee went on to say that it found it odd that the critics who were concerned that arbitrary charges would be made against the United States if it ratified the convention could simultaneously argue in favor of persuading the United Nations to negotiate a convention with "teeth in it." From the committee's viewpoint, even if the latter proposal had merit, "the practical difficulties of renegotiating" the convention were "formidable," and it urged the Senate not to be dissuaded from ratifying it out of fear that arbitrary charges would be made against the United States.[81]

Forcibly Transferring Children from One Group to Another

The last genocidal act listed in Article II is "forcibly transferring children of the group to another group." This provision was not included in the draft convention prepared by the Ad Hoc Committee of the ECOSOC; it was adopted by the Sixth Committee of the General Assembly on the urging of the Greek representative. It is one of the few provisions of the convention that gave rise to an open charge of political motivations, though such considerations were obviously present in the deliberations on many issues. The Greek representative defended his proposal on the ground that a similar provision had been included in the draft convention prepared by the UN Secretariat, and also in a draft submitted by the United States, but it was clear to everyone that he was attempting to call attention to a problem of great concern to his own government. Specifically, the Greek amendment to Article II addressed the abduction of thousands (by some estimates, 28,000) of Greek children by communists at the close of World War II and their transfer to several countries in Eastern Europe under communist control. There was little hope that the children would be returned, and characterizing the problem as genocide was a dramatic way of calling attention to it.[82]

The Greek amendment was adopted, but not enthusiastically (twenty in favor, thirteen against, and thirteen abstentions).[83] The primary opponents of the measure were, of course, the members of the Soviet bloc. The Polish representative, for example, who rarely diverged from the Soviet line during the negotiations on the convention, wondered whether or not the Greek representative had given genocide a "distinct political bent" by pressing his amendment.[84] Other representatives, genuinely concerned about the problem that the amendment addressed, nonetheless thought that it fell more appropriately within the subject of cultural genocide. But with the strong support of the United States, the Greek amendment to Article II was adopted.

It is noteworthy that at the same meeting at which the Sixth Committee adopted the Greek amendment it overwhelmingly rejected a Syrian amendment to Article II (twenty-nine against, five in favor, with eight abstentions) which stated that forcing members of groups to leave their homes constituted genocide.[85] It is arguable that the Syrian amendment should have enjoyed as much support as the Greek amendment if the decision were based on merit alone. In this instance, however, the decision was not based on merit—it was simply a matter that the Greek amendment enjoyed sufficient support to be adopted but the Syrian amendment did not. In particular, the Greek amendment enjoyed the great advantage of being supported by the United States, whereas the Syrian amendment was not. In retrospect, there was something to be said for the Polish representative's perspective—that the Greek amendment introduced a "distinct political bent" into the deliberations over the convention.

In view of the drafters' actions surrounding the adoption of Article II (e), it is doubtful that many of them took it seriously. It is the one provision that seems strangely out of place in the convention. This is not to say that the acts that Article II (e) aims to prevent and punish are not reprehensible. Surely they are. But it is debatable whether or not they should be considered to fall within the meaning of genocide. Experience suggests that perpetrators of genocide will not consider children of groups worthy of survival any more than adults, yet the terms of the clause imply that they would.

Article II (e) has rarely been raised in the debate over ratification of the convention by the United States. On those occasions when it has, the absurd proposition has been advanced that school busing of children to achieve integration might be considered genocidal within the meaning of Article II (e).[86] This objection is noteworthy only because it shows again that critics of the convention have never been without reasons for objecting to its ratification.

Part II Rule-Supervision: Measures of Implementation

Chapter 6 Domestic Implementing Legislation

There are those so pessimistic about the state of man that they believe it is futile to go through the formality of making Genocide an international crime. They would insist, as a prior condition to ratification, that we must be assured in advance that there will be enforcement of the treaty provisions. This, of course, is impossible. It is equally impossible to assure the observance of any treaty commitment by any contracting party. The same pessimistic outlook might apply as to any legislation on crimes: there is never any guarantee of compliance or assurance of enforcement. To insist that a treaty should never be adopted unless it prevents another Hitler from committing the crime of Genocide, is like demanding in advance of the enactment of a State Statute against homicide, that it must guarantee prevention of murder.—Bruno Bitker, 1970 Senate hearings

In the last few chapters we have been concerned with the basic elements of the rule on genocide affirmed in the Genocide Convention, and with the issues and problems that these elements have raised in the controversy over ratification of the convention by the United States. In this and the next three chapters we shall turn our attention to the rule-supervisory measures, or procedures, that are prescribed in the convention. The assumption that underlies these measures is that it is not enough simply to elaborate a rule on genocide and expect that everyone will abide by it; rather, it is necessary to indicate the specific measures that can be taken to ensure compliance with the rule among the states that are bound by it.

The convention prescribes a mix of international and domestic measures to ensure its implementation, though its thrust is to emphasize the domestic more than the international. This emphasis is understandable in light of the provisions of the convention as a whole. As discussed in chapter 2, genocide is a crime under international law. This has generally been understood to mean that the crime of genocide is a crime against the domestic law of the parties, which undertake an international obligation to make it a crime in their own legal systems. The point is carried further in Article V, which is generally regarded by most commentators as making the convention a non-self-executing treaty; that is, domestic implementing legislation is necessary to give it effect. Hence, as Joseph Kunz noted in commentary in 1949, genocide is not a crime *against* international law; it is a crime *under* international law. In this respect, Kunz found the convention to be "a thoroughly old-fashioned treaty."[1]

Although the convention is very straightforward on these matters, its critics in the United States have raised numerous troublesome questions regarding the rule-supervisory measures prescribed in it. It is obvious from the amount of time devoted to these issues over the years that ratification of the convention raised profound policy issues for the United States. Implicitly and explicitly, many critics denied that the subject matter of the convention was a matter of international concern, and they maintained that its ratification would be an improper and even unconstitutional exercise of the treaty-making power of the federal government. Some questioned whether or not the convention was truly a non-self-executing treaty, denounced what they perceived to be its potentially deleterious impact on federal-state relations within the United States, and quibbled about the terms of domestic implementing legislation. While many of the critics focused on the domestic impact of ratification, they were also concerned about the international rule-supervisory measures prescribed in the convention, particularly the international criminal court referred to in Article VI and the role of the ICJ spelled out in Article IX.

The issues and problems that arose in connection with these rule-supervisory measures were among the most important ones raised in the debate over ratification, and specific provisions of the Lugar-Helms-Hatch Sovereignty Package address them in some detail. We shall deal with these issues and problems, and with the provisions of the Sovereignty Package that address them, in this and the following three chapters. In this chapter we shall concentrate on the non-self-executing nature of the convention and the U.S. implementing legislation, the Proxmire Act. In chapter 7 we shall deal with the provisions of the convention that pertain to an international criminal court; in chapter 8 with the principles of jurisdiction of domestic courts and the related issue of extradition; and in chapter 9 with the role of the ICJ under Article IX of the convention.

The Convention as a Non-Self-Executing Treaty

All drafts of the Genocide Convention included articles that pertained to the enactment of domestic implementing legislation, indicating that the drafters always intended to make the convention a non-self-executing treaty for those states that wished to consider it such. The distinction between a non-self-executing treaty and its opposite, a self-executing treaty, in the case of the United States, is that the former requires an act of Congress to carry out the international obligation that is spelled out in the treaty itself, whereas the latter does not depend upon any legislative enactments to give it effect.[2] But while the drafters of the convention apparently agreed on the basic principle regarding domestic legislation, they differed on precisely what the convention should say about the content of that legislation.

The Content of Domestic Legislation

Different viewpoints were expressed in the Ad Hoc Committee of the ECOSOC, and later in the Sixth Committee of the General Assembly, on the question of how much direction the convention should give the parties regarding the content of their domestic legislation on genocide. In the Ad Hoc Committee, on one side, Soviet representative Platon Morozov argued that the parties to the convention should be obliged to "make provision in their criminal legislation for measures aimed at the prevention and suppression of genocide and also at the prevention and suppression of incitement of racial, national, and religious hatred . . . and to provide criminal penalties for the authors of such crimes."[3] In contrast, U.S. representative John Maktos argued that the convention should state simply that the parties would undertake to adopt necessary legislation in accordance with their constitutions to give effect to the provisions of the convention, and that it should not state specifically what that legislation should cover. He was concerned about the content of any article that referred to domestic legislation because, as he put it, in the United States the "passage of legislation in the field of criminal law fell principally within the province of the individual states."[4] Maktos believed that other states with federal systems or systems that were otherwise decentralized might be reluctant to ratify the convention were it to be too specific about the extent of their legislative obligations should they ratify.[5]

The argument advanced by Maktos seemed to carry the point to the extreme. Under the U.S. Constitution, the federal government alone has the power to conclude and enter into treaties and compacts with foreign powers. And the Congress clearly has the power to legislate in this field. The Supreme Court has dealt with a number of cases involving such matters. In *Missouri* v. *Holland* (252 U.S. 416, 1920), which involved the constitutionality of an act of Congress that implemented a treaty between Great Britain and the United States, the Court ruled that the Congress does have the power to adopt legislation implementing a valid treaty. Maktos's arguments seemed to question this authority. But in the context of the negotiations over the terms of the Genocide Convention, his arguments reflected the tendency among most negotiators to seek to harmonize the provisions of the convention with their own domestic laws, and not the other way around, even if his interpretation might have been exceedingly narrow.

The Ad Hoc Committee of the ECOSOC resolved the opposing positions on this issue by adopting an article that more nearly suited the interests of the United States. The article stated merely that the parties would undertake to adopt the necessary "legislation in accordance with their constitutional procedures to give effect to the provisions" of the convention.[6] The draft article was discussed further in the Sixth Committee. The Soviet representative once again argued that the convention should be specific about what the parties would be required to do with regard to domestic legislation on genocide; that is, it should state that the parties must ban such things as incitement to racial and national hatred.[7] Ernest A. Gross, who represented the United States in the Sixth Committee deliberations, opposed such precision for the same reasons given earlier by John Maktos during debate in the Ad Hoc Committee of the ECOSOC.[8] The Sixth Committee, like the Ad Hoc Committee, adopted an article that took into account U.S. concerns, and its decision was reaffirmed by the General Assembly in plenary session. Article V of the convention states:

> The Contracting Parties undertake to enact, in accordance with their respective Constitutions, the necessary legislation to give effect to the provisions of the present Convention and, in particular, to provide effective penalties for persons guilty of genocide or of any of the other acts enumerated in Article III.

Article III states:

> The following acts shall be punishable:
> (a) genocide;
> (b) conspiracy to commit genocide;
> (c) direct and public incitement to commit genocide;

(d) attempt to commit genocide;
(e) complicity in genocide.

The Soviet Union's delegation was not satisfied with how the Sixth Committee had resolved the matter of domestic legislation and insisted that the convention should provide more direction to the parties. Therefore, in a plenary session of the General Assembly just before the convention was adopted, the Soviet delegation proposed an amendment of the Sixth Committee's draft convention to add a new article to the effect that the parties would be obliged to disband hate groups. Table 6.1 shows how the member states of the United Nations at that time voted on this proposal.

The Soviet proposal was rejected by a substantial margin, with 53.4 percent of the total membership of the United Nations at that time voting against it. Since the six members of the Soviet bloc were the largest bloc voting in favor of the amendment, it obviously enjoyed little support among the member states. In this as in many other instances in drafting the convention, most states wanted to maximize the amount of discretion that the parties would be able to exercise in living up to their international obligations under the convention. Indeed, there is no reason why a party to the convention could not enact domestic implementing legislation that is more liberal in its content than the convention itself requires. Thus, a party

Table 6.1 Vote in the Plenary Session of the General Assembly on the Soviet Proposal Adding a New Article Disbanding Hate Groups

Area	Number (Percentage)	Yes	Abstain	No	No vote
Africa		1	2	1	0
		(25.0)	(50.0)	(25.0)	(0)
Asia		3	6	4	0
		(23.1)	(46.2)	(30.8)	(0)
Oceania		0	0	2	0
		(0)	(0)	(100)	(0)
Americas		0	5	14	3
		(0)	(22.7)	(63.6)	(13.6)
Europe		6	1	10	0
		(35.3)	(5.9)	(58.8)	(0)
TOTALS		10	14	31	3
		(17.2)	(24.1)	(53.4)	(5.2)

Source: Same as table 4.1.

can decide to disband hate groups on its own if it wishes. But the vote against the Soviet proposal suggests that the drafters did not want to impose such an obligation on the parties. Consequently, the obligation that the parties undertake under Article V is simply to "enact, in accordance with their respective Constitutions, the necessary legislation to give effect to the provisions" of the convention, including penalties for persons who commit genocide or any of the acts enumerated in Article III.

Taken together, Articles V and III are widely assumed by commentators to make the Genocide Convention non-self-executing, as least so far as countries that wish to treat it as such are concerned. In fact, it is usually assumed that Article V alone would have this effect, and whether or not it should even have been included in the convention was the subject of some discussion among the drafters. A minority of the drafters believed that Article V was superfluous and could be deleted. Basically, they argued that it was obvious without being said that the parties to the convention would have to enact legislation to implement it; among other things, the convention failed to specify the penalties that would be imposed on any persons who commit genocide or any of the acts enumerated in Article III. But most drafters maintained that Article V was necessary. Even if the article was arguably superfluous, the majority believed that it would do no harm to include it in the convention. Most commentators seem to have agreed with the majority viewpoint. The special rapporteur of a United Nations study of the convention during the 1970s, Nicodeme Ruhashyankiko, maintained that "it is never superfluous to recall in a particular convention the general obligation of States whose non-fulfillment would constitute an obstacle to the achievement of the desired goal."[9]

Article V and Domestic Implementing Legislation

Does Article V actually *require* the enactment of domestic legislation? This question has not been addressed often in commentary on the convention. When it has been addressed, it has usually been argued that the article does require the adoption of legislation. The special rapporteur of the UN study just cited expressed this opinion: "parties to the Genocide Convention are legally bound to adopt legislative measures dealing specifically with the crime of genocide and including provisions of criminal law and criminal procedure capable of ensuring effective prevention and punishment of that crime."[10] He was of the opinion that, "with a view to more effective prevention of the crime, the provisions in question should also make it a punishable offense to engage in propaganda in favor of genocide or to prepare for its commission."[11]

Other commentators have made statements to the effect that Article V requires the enactment of domestic legislation. Joseph Kunz, for example, in an editorial comment in the *American Journal of International Law* in 1949, stated that, at least so far as the United States was concerned, the convention "clearly does involve legislation" because neither Article II nor Article III could be directly applied by a court, not only because of vague definitions or a lack of definitions of key concepts in those articles, but also because of a "complete lack of penalties."[12] Along similar lines, William Jones has argued that implementing legislation is necessary to give effect to the convention, in part because "the words of Article V clearly contemplate legislation," and in part because no penalties are prescribed under the terms of Article III.[13] Hence, according to Jones, "even if the treaty were held to be self-executing, as no penalties are provided, no one, even if obviously guilty of one of the punishable acts, could be punished in the absence of congressional legislation."[14]

It is also generally agreed that Article V does not prescribe the enactment of *uniform* legislation among all parties to the convention. This is an important matter. The question has been raised whether or not the so-called constitutional clause in Article V refers to constitutional rules of form or of substance. The answer to the question would, of course, have important implications. If the clause refers to substantive rules, it would suggest that the domestic legislation need only conform to the substantive constitutional rules of the parties, and that the terms of their constitutions prevail over the terms of the convention; if the clause refers to matters of form, then it would mean simply that the parties must enact domestic legislation in accordance with their constitutional procedures.

Commentators on the convention have come to somewhat different answers to the question. The rapporteur of the UN study of the convention argued that the clause refers to constitutional procedures, and he pointed out that under Article 27 of the Vienna Convention on the Law of Treaties, no party to the convention could invoke a provision of its constitution or laws as a reason for not living up to its international obligations.[15] Nehemiah Robinson also reached the conclusion that the drafters were referring to constitutional procedures in the constitutional clause of Article V, since a party that did not want to live up to the substance of the terms of Articles II or III could enter a reservation to them.[16] But everyone, even those who avoid addressing the question directly, concludes that Articles V and III permit the parties to exercise broad discretion in determining the content of their domestic legislation, including the sorts of penalties they wish to impose for the commission of any of the acts specified in Article III. As Pieter Drost observed, the parties "are free to determine whatever legislative provisions and penalties they see fit to lay down and apply."[17] He suggests also that "wide discrepancies in theory and practice will unavoidably occur. The authors of the Convention will not have expected otherwise."[18] Similarly, Kunz argued that it is inevitable that the definitions and penalties in the "different domestic legislations" will vary.[19]

The Practice of the Parties regarding Domestic Legislation

The record shows that the practice of the parties to the convention regarding the matter of implementing legislation has varied. In some states, no specific implementing legislation has been adopted, and those states have given various reasons why none has been thought necessary. For example, some have claimed that the provisions of their constitutions and criminal statutes are adequate for prosecuting and punishing persons for committing genocide or any of the acts listed in Article III. It is noteworthy that the Soviet Union, whose representative at the United Nations when the convention was drafted took every opportunity to emphasize that stringent guidelines regarding the kind of domestic implementing legislation the parties must adopt should be specified in Article V, has not enacted any specific implementing legislation, claiming that its ratification of the convention "did not require any changes in or additions to Soviet legislation."[20] According to the Soviet government, "a system of guarantees designed to ensure the free development of national, ethnic, and religious groups existed in Soviet law long before the adoption" of the convention.[21]

Some states that have not adopted specific implementing legislation have made statements implying that they have treated the convention as a self-executing treaty; that is, that it has become directly applicable as law domestically. Finland and Poland are examples of such states.[22] Others have made highly unusual, seemingly bogus, claims. The Egyptian government, for example, stated that since "no national, ethnic, racial, or religious group exists in the structure of Egyptian society, making the crimes sanctioned by the Convention inconceivable," it had not been considered "useful to adopt special penal laws designed to prevent such crimes."[23] The Egyptian government deemed the provisions of its existing laws sufficient on the subject of genocide and related crimes enumerated in Article III of the convention.[24]

Some states have adopted implementing legislation. Generally, their legislation has consisted of basic definitions of the elements of the crime of genocide that are identical with or very similar to those used in the convention. In fact, in some cases the legislation incorporates verbatim the provisions of Article II into domestic law.[25] The states that have adopted legislation of this type are mainly East and West European states but include some Third World states.[26] But here again there are exceptions. States have adopted implementing legislation that may not be in conformity with the terms of the convention. The Israeli law, for example, is highly suspect. Though it is analogous to the Genocide Convention in that it defines the crime in terms of an intent to destroy, and so on, it apparently applies only to "crimes against the Jewish people," implying that the other types of groups mentioned in Article II of the convention are not covered.[27]

The implementing legislation adopted by states also varies with regard to the penalties for committing genocide or any of the related acts listed in Article III. The severity of penalties under Romanian legislation, for example, depends upon whether or not the genocidal acts are committed during peace or war: if during peace, the death penalty could possibly be applied; if during war, the death penalty is applied.[28] Irish legislation specifies less severe penalties, including life imprisonment if the acts result in the killing of any person, but only a prison term "not exceeding fourteen years" for any other acts.[29]

With regard to the domestic legislation of states on genocide, then, several possibilities exist: (1) states that have ratified the convention may adopt implementing legislation which may or may not be in conformity with the terms of the convention; (2) states that have ratified the convention may adopt no specific implementing legislation whatsoever; (3) states that have not ratified the convention may adopt domestic legislation consistent with, more liberal than, or more restrictive than, the terms of the convention.[30] All of these possibilities lead to one conclusion: substantial diversity, not uniformity, could exist and does exist in the rule on genocide that is to be applied by national courts. Some believe that greater consistency in the application of the convention might be achieved if the international criminal court contemplated in Article VI were created, provided that the parties to the convention would accept its jurisdiction. However, as will be discussed in chapter 7, there has been no sustained and serious effort to create that court since the convention was adopted; nor does it appear likely that one will be created in the near future.

It is also arguable that greater consistency in domestic legislation on genocide could be achieved, at least among the parties to the convention, if disputes regarding the interpretation of the convention were brought to the ICJ under Article IX. But no such disputes have been brought to the court, and approximately one-quarter of the parties to the convention have made a reservation to Article IX demonstrating their desire to prevent the court from resolving any such disputes to which they might be a party. Even if some parties should accept the jurisdiction of the court to resolve disputes among them, while the court could undoubtedly determine the "true" meaning of words and phrases in the convention, it presumably could not pass upon the adequacy of domestic legislation. Consequently, it can be expected that the diversity that prevails regarding the rule on genocide in the domestic law of states will persist into the future.

The Convention and the U.S. Constitution

In view of the great variety of domestic legislation on genocide among parties to the Genocide Convention, one might think that its terms and their implications would have appeared much less menacing to its critics in the United States. But the critics have never been satisfied by any rational exposition of facts and trends. To the contrary, ever since President Truman requested the Senate's advice and consent to ratification of the convention in 1949, serious questions have been raised about the implications of its ratification for the U.S. Constitution. In fact, the issues were sharply posed within the ABA even before the Senate Committee on Foreign Relations opened its first hearings on the convention in 1950; the ABA House of Delegates had already endorsed the report of its special committee, the Special Committee on Peace and Law through the United Nations, which resolutely opposed ratification of the convention.[31]

The ABA critics raised a host of issues, and they found powerful allies, notably Senator John Bricker, who introduced a controversial constitutional amendment during the early 1950s that would have had an impact on the exercise of the treaty-making power of the United States. The Eisenhower administration opposed and defeated the Bricker Amendment, but it paid a heavy price, retreating from the more activist stance on human rights issues of the Truman administration and resolving to use the treaty-making power only for more traditional concerns.[32] In fact, in a letter to the Committee on Foreign Relations in 1971, long after leaving the Senate, Bricker claimed that President Eisenhower had given him assurances that he would never transmit to the Senate any treaty that "violated either the wording or the spirit" of the amendment.[33] Accordingly, Bricker objected to President Nixon's resurrection of the Genocide Convention, which had lain dormant in the Committee on Foreign Relations for about twenty years.[34]

The Bricker Amendment was narrowly defeated in the Senate, but it had powerful effects that persisted throughout the 1960s and 1970s, and indeed persist to this day. Writing in *Foreign Affairs* in the mid-1960s, on the subject "Human Rights Treaties: Why Is the U.S. Stalling?" William Korey suggested that the Senate was suffering from "lingering Brickeritis."[35] Other scholars, too, such as Vernon Van Dyke[36] and Francis Boyle,[37] had noted the connection between the Genocide Convention and other human rights treaties, the ABA, and the Bricker movement.

More recent research by Natalie Hevener Kaufman and David Whiteman has demonstrated the lingering effects of Brickerism.[38] By comparing the results of a content analysis of the 1953 Bricker Amendment hearings with the 1979 hearings on four human rights treaties that President Carter sent to the Senate, Kaufman and Whiteman show that a very high degree of similarity existed between the arguments used in both hearings.[39] Although some concerns from the 1950s had diminished in importance by the late 1970s—for example, the opponents of the human rights treaties seemed less concerned that Americans would be subjected to trials abroad—the two main arguments that were used in the 1950s were used again in the late 1970s. These arguments were that the human rights treaties would undermine basic constitutional rights of Americans and adversely affect the powers of the states under the federal system of government in the United States.[40]

Kaufman and Whiteman suggest that the origins of the Bricker Amendment and the opposition to human rights treaties lie in the Genocide Convention hearings. For Bricker and his supporters the Genocide Convention was not an "isolated problem"; rather, it was part of a much larger and more menacing problem of international action on human rights that was under way in the United Nations in the late 1940s and early 1950s. The Genocide Convention was significant because the "arguments that germinated during [the 1950 Senate hearings on the convention] later blossomed into full-fledged opposition to all human rights treaties."[41]

Bricker and his supporters were concerned about a variety of legal and political issues that were reflected in the terms of his proposed constitutional amendment. These issues, raised during the Genocide Convention hearings, included the supremacy of the Constitution over international human rights law, the preservation of states' rights, and the prevention of abuse (and misuse) of the treaty-making power by the executive (through the conclusion of executive agreements rather than treaties) that might have an adverse impact on the constitutional rights and liberties of Americans. As Kaufman and Whiteman show, these concerns persist so far as the human rights treaties are concerned.[42] In the case of the Genocide Convention, as we shall see, opponents of ratification succeeded in inserting in the Lugar-Helms-Hatch Sovereignty Package conditions of ratification that reflect earlier Bricker Amendment provisions.

The U.S. Critics and Article V of the Genocide Convention

Is the Genocide Convention really a non-self-executing treaty? Some critics within the United States have expressed doubt about this matter since the Senate Committee on Foreign Relations held its first hearings on the convention in 1950. At that time, proponents of ratification, especially Truman administration spokesmen, asserted that the convention was obviously non-self-executing, and that its terms—particularly the constitutional clause of Article V—permitted substantial discretion to the parties in determining precisely what their domestic legislation would provide.[43] But the opponents of ratification and other skeptics who supported their position were confused about the meaning of Article V.

Senator Bourke B. Hickenlooper (R., Iowa) was one of the most outspoken senators on this issue at the 1950 hearings. He offered an interesting reason as to why he thought the convention was self-executing. According to Hickenlooper, the convention "is in effect self-executing because it binds us to pass laws implementing it," even if the "details of the execution may be left somewhat to us."[44] Other critics, such as the ABA representatives, were concerned that provisions of the convention might be used to attack discriminatory legislation then prevalent in the United States.

Truman administration representatives, including State Department personnel and Philip Perlman, solicitor general of the United States, took issue with Hickenlooper and other critics.[45] They pointed out that Hickenlooper's definition of what constitutes a self-executing treaty was basically in error. But facts such as this were rarely, if ever, accepted in the debate over ratification. In this instance Hickenlooper responded that he believed the United States would be committed "morally and literally" to adopt domestic legislation.[46] And who was to sit in judgment upon the adequacy of that legislation? Perlman suggested that under Article IX of the convention the ICJ could conceivably play a role in determining the adequacy of legislation, but that even if it did, it would have no "directive power," as Hickenlooper feared.[47] Still, Hickenlooper was persistent. He was concerned that ratification of the convention would "reduce somewhat" the sovereignty of the United States, and he suggested that ratification with a reservation regarding U.S. sovereignty might be necessary—a reservation to the effect that "we will adopt the convention, but we will have no one question the adequacy of our laws and no forum question the adequacy of our laws outside the United States itself."[48] He wondered if such a reservation "would destroy the effect of the genocide convention," or "violate some of the basic structure of this whole program." Perlman objected to Hickenlooper's proposal on the ground that it might set a bad precedent.[49] But Hickenlooper was persistent on the issue of national sovereignty, as indicated in the following exchange between him and Perlman:

SENATOR HICKENLOOPER: But we are in effect, in this Genocide Convention, as we undoubtedly have done in treaties in the past, dealing with the question of a certain area of sovereignty of the United States which amounts to a surrender of a certain area of sovereignty.

MR. PERLMAN: I do not understand that any sovereignty is being surrendered here at all. I do not know what you have in mind.

SENATOR HICKENLOOPER: If we submit the question of dispute as to the adequacy of our legislation to an international court, we surrender to that extent, do we not?

MR. PERLMAN: No, sir. We only agree that the international court, on the complaint of another contracting party, can pass on the question as to whether or not we have fulfilled our obligation. We do agree that that method of determining the good faith of all of the contracting parties to this agreement can be pursued. That is all we agree to. If the international court, on a proper submission, should find either that this Nation or some other nation had not properly fulfilled its obligation, they would state that for what effect it would have on our Nation and on the other nation.[50]

Hickenlooper's arguments were important inasmuch as they foreshadowed by almost forty years a dispute over a so-called constitutional reservation in the Lugar-Helms-Hatch Sovereignty Package, to which we shall return later in this chapter.[51] In addition, the arguments foreshadowed a provision of the Bricker Amendment that was aimed at making all treaties non-self-executing; that is, ensuring that treaties could become effective as internal law in the United States only through the adoption of domestic implementing legislation. Events during the early 1950s convinced many opponents of the Genocide Convention and other human rights treaties of the need to ensure that courts would not look upon treaties of that sort as self-executing instruments. For some, the 1950 California District Court of Appeal decision in the case of *Sei Fujii* v. *California* (217 P.2d 481) demonstrated the need for vigilance in this regard. In that case, the court declared the California Alien Land Law, which prohibited aliens who were ineligible for citizenship from acquiring real property in California, unenforceable on the ground that it violated certain provisions of the UN Charter, which the United States had by then ratified.

The California court's decision in *Sei Fujii* sent shock waves through some segments of the legal community. If provisions of the UN Charter could be considered self-executing and thus be used to strike down discriminatory legislation within the United States, what other treaties might be interpreted in that way? On appeal, the California Supreme Court rejected the lower court's ruling, holding that the terms of the UN Charter were not self-executing, but it nonetheless declared the California Alien Land Law unconstitutional as a violation of the Fourteenth Amendment of the U.S. Constitution.[52] However, as Francis Boyle has argued, "there was no guarantee that other state or federal courts would agree with the decision by the California Supreme Court." Other courts might indeed find provisions of the UN Charter and other treaties self-executing and use them "to strike down racially discriminatory state legislation and practices."[53] The *Sei Fujii* case therefore remained a matter of great concern to unilateralists and other opponents of U.S. involvement in the international human rights movement.

The debate over the Genocide Convention in particular was affected by these developments, and the arguments made initially by Hickenlooper persisted and were raised again during the 1970s and 1980s. While most of the convention's critics were eventually compelled to admit that Article V made the instrument non-self-executing, some of them pressed the argument that specific provisions might be interpreted as being self-executing even if the instrument as a whole were not. Senator Sam Ervin, Jr., anticipated perhaps the most far-reaching, if not devastating, consequences if the United States ratified the convention. Insisting that provisions of the U.S. Constitution, especially Article VI, made properly ratified treaties part of the "supreme law of the land," Ervin claimed:

> If the Senate should ratify the Genocide Convention, these constitutional provisions would automatically make the convention the law of the land, put all of its self-executing provisions into immediate effect as such, and impose upon the United States the obligation to take whatever steps are necessary to make its non-self-executing provisions effective. This means that the provisions of the Genocide Convention would immediately supersede all State laws and practices inconsistent with them, and would nullify all provisions of all acts of Congress and prior treaties of the United States inconsistent with them.

While Congress could repeal provisions of the Genocide Convention by future legislation, the States would be bound by them as long as the convention remained in effect. Moreover, the Genocide Convention would immediately require and authorize the Congress to enact legislation implementing its provisions, even though such legislation were beyond the power of Congress in the absence of the convention, and even though such legislation would deprive the States of the power to prosecute and punish in their courts acts condemned by articles II and III of the convention.[54]

In marked contrast to Senator Ervin, William Rehnquist, assistant attorney general during the Nixon administration, provided a much more restrained interpretation of Article V of the convention. Agreeing that properly ratified treaties are part of the "supreme law of the land," Rehnquist nonetheless denied that they "have superiority . . . over a statute."[55] Rather, he argued, the U.S. Constitution provides that treaties and laws are "of equal dignity."[56] Senator John Sherman Cooper (R., Kentucky) continued the questioning on this point:

SENATOR COOPER: Everybody is saying, though, this Convention is constitutional, and there has been the testimony to that effect. If we assume it is constitutional and a statute was passed which was not consonant with this treaty, then a question would be raised as to whether the statute controlled.

MR. REHNQUIST: I firmly believe that the treaty is entirely constitutional. Yet I also believe it is possible that Congress, in adopting implementing legislation, could very deliberately and carefully, as a matter of considered judgment, omit one section, say, of article II, and there would be no question that statute would be constitutional.

The United States might be called before the ICJ for failing to implement the treaty, but the treaty would not prevail over clear implementing legislation.[57]

Overall, it seems clear from Rehnquist's testimony that he perceived the views of critics such as Ervin as being nothing more than alarmist. To Rehnquist, the question of whether or not the United States could ratify the Genocide Convention was a matter of policy, not legal power.[58]

The U.S. Declaration on Implementing Legislation

Compared with the 1950s, the critics in the 1970s and 1980s seemed substantially less concerned about the impact that ratification of the convention would have on civil rights issues within the United States, but they still found reasons to think that some of the convention's provisions might be considered self-executing. As we shall see in chapter 8, the extradition provisions of Article VII have sometimes been viewed as self-executing. Whether or not the critics had a point on any of these isues, they demanded to know *in advance* of ratification what the U.S. domestic legislation would provide. The Nixon administration agreed to this demand, supplying a draft bill even before the Senate approved a resolution of ratification;[59] and agreeing also to the inclusion of a "declaration" in the resolution of ratification that the United States would not deposit its instrument of ratification at the United Nations *until* Congress had enacted the domestic implementing legislation. The declaration, included in the resolution the Committee on Foreign Relations proposed on several occasions during the 1970s and in 1984, provided:

> That the United States Government declares that it will not deposit its instrument of ratification until after the implementing legislation referred to in Article V has been enacted.[60]

This declaration did not, of course, win over enough senators to bring about ratification of the convention. To the contrary, the same issues continued to be raised at Senate hearings and in floor debate, especially after the Reagan administration endorsed ratification of the convention only weeks before the 1984 presidential election. President Reagan's endorsement virtually assured ratification of the convention, since it could no longer be maintained that ratification was a dream of liberal fantasizers. In fact, since the most outspoken opponents of ratification were all ideological allies of the president, they were really left with no alternative but to work toward converting the convention into what Senator Orrin Hatch would call a "mere symbol" of opposition to genocide.[61] Although not a member of the Committee on Foreign Relations, Senator Hatch had a major impact on the terms of ratification by virtue of his chairmanship of the Subcommittee on the Constitution of the Committee on the Judiciary. In 1985 this subcommittee held hearings on the constitutional issues relating to the proposed Genocide Convention.[62] These hearings, combined with those held by the Senate Committee on Foreign Relations,[63] then chaired by Senator Richard Lugar, revealed a great deal about the critics' intentions regarding the instrument of ratification that became known as the Lugar-Helms-Hatch Sovereignty Package. As a result of the Hatch hearings, the declaration quoted above was revised to state:

> That the President will not deposit the instrument of ratification until after the implementing legislation referred to in Article V has been enacted.[64]

Senator Hatch provided a straightforward explanation of what he thought the declaration would accomplish. In the first place, he believed that overall, the declaration *emphasized the non-self-executing nature of the Convention.*[65] Thus, according to Hatch, with the declaration in the Sovereignty Package the United States could not become a party to the convention without the implementing legislation. This strategy would presumably provide Congress with an additional opportunity to shape the nature of the international obligation the United States would assume by ratifying the convention. According to Hatch, the declaration was "mandatory in nature."[66] The president was specifically denied the authority to deposit the instrument of ratification until the legislation had been adopted. As Hatch put it: "One might say that this so-called declaration is in the nature of an executory contract between the Senate and the administration."[67] This was not a foolish claim on his part. Indeed, it was apparently to prevent arbitrary presidential action—or at least to attempt to prevent such action—in the use of the treaty-making power that the words "the President will not deposit" were put into the declaration.[68]

For its part, the Committee on Foreign Relations went along with Hatch's claims regarding the declaration. The committee did not feel, however, that the declaration had to be included in the *instrument of ratification*, for, unlike other conditions which had to be included in the instrument (in the committee's view, at least), the declaration established a *condition precedent* to ratification.[69] The declaration indeed had the effect of delaying U.S. ratification by approximately three years, until after the Proxmire Act was adopted in October 1988. The United States deposited its instrument of ratification at the United Nations in November 1988, including all provisions of the Sovereignty Package *except* the declaration regarding the implementing legislation.

The Use of the Treaty-Making Power and Federal-State Relations

Another question raised early in Senate deliberations was whether or not the subject matter of the Genocide Convention was truly a matter of international concern. The answer to this question was important from the standpoint of the use of the treaty-making power to deal with the matter of genocide. If genocide were properly a matter of international concern, then the treaty-making power could arguably be used to address it, although, of course, objections might still be raised to the content of specific provisions of the Genocide Convention on policy or perhaps even constitutional grounds. If genocide were not a matter of genuine international concern, then the use of the treaty-making power to deal with it would be at least improper, if not unconstitutional. In either case, since no one could ever be faulted for defending the U.S. Constitution, the question always demanded attention.

As noted above, Senator Bourke Hickenlooper and others expressed doubt at the 1950 Senate hearings that the subject matter of the Genocide Convention was truly a matter of international concern.[70] The State Department took issue with these critics, pointing out that the UN General Assembly had unanimously declared genocide "a matter of international concern" and a "crime under international law" in Resolution 96 (I). The United States had voted in favor of the resolution, and President Truman had endorsed it. Moveover, the Genocide Convention, which the U.S. representatives had played a vital role in drafting, and which the United States had signed, reaffirmed the thrust of Resolution 96 (I) in its preamble and Article I, which referred to genocide as a crime under international law. In light of these considerations, the Truman administration spokesmen wondered how the convention's critics could maintain that genocide was not a matter of international concern. And if it were a matter of international concern, then the treaty-making power of the federal government could undoubtedly be used to deal with it.[71]

Historically, critics of the convention could not rest their case on an argument to the effect that its ratification would constitute an improper or unconstitutional exercise of the treaty-making power. In view of the content of Resolution 96 (I), and the circumstances under which it was adopted, no one could seriously maintain that genocide was not a matter of international concern. Such a position would have been untenable at best. In fact, some scholars and practitioners have found it odd that the issue ever appeared as significant or was raised with as much vigor as it was. As the 1969 report of the Special Committee of Lawyers of the President's Commission for the Observance of Human Rights Year 1968 states, "it may seem almost anachronistic that this question continues to be raised."[72] The committee pointed out that the United States was an original member of the United Nations, whose charter states as one of its basic purposes the promotion of human rights for all. Moreover, the United States had already ratified a number of treaties and conventions that referred to human rights in one way or another.[73] Nonetheless, the issues raised by Hickenlooper and other critics of the convention at the 1950 Senate hearings continued to plague the deliberations over ratification during the 1970s and 1980s.

The critics of the convention have also fretted about the potentially negative impact of its ratification on federal-state relations. Specifically, they have been concerned about the possibility that ratification of the convention would alter the constitutionally mandated relationship between the federal and state governments. By ratifying the convention, would the federal government acquire powers at the expense of the states that it would not ordinarily be able to exercise? Would ratification of the convention further diminish states' rights? Although these concerns date back to the 1950s,[74] they were raised especially during the 1970s by the most outspoken critic of the convention at that time, Senator Sam Ervin, Jr. At the 1970 Senate hearings Ervin argued that ratification of the convention would result in its provisions immediately superseding all state laws that were inconsistent with them and thus deprive the states of the power to prosecute and punish persons for acts committed in violation of Articles II and III of the convention; that the convention would wreak havoc on the criminal justice system in the United States, making it difficult to ascertain whether it would be appropriate to prosecute in state or federal courts; and that the convention would expand the constitutional powers of Congress—that, in fact, the federal government would acquire powers with respect to genocide that it did not have in the absence of the treaty.[75]

Critics such as Ervin were especially concerned about these issues in light of the U.S. Supreme Court's judgment in *Missouri* v. *Holland* (252 U.S. 416, 1920). This 1920 case concerned the constitutionality of federal legislation and regulations that had been adopted and proclaimed to implement the Migratory Bird Treaty between the United States and Great Britain, acting for Canada, that pertained to the hunting of such birds. Missouri claimed that the states of the union had the power to regulate the hunting of migratory birds under the Tenth Amendment to the Constitution. However, the Supreme Court upheld both the treaty and the statute, indicating that a treaty might enlarge the powers of the federal government, permitting it to act in areas that it had not previously acted in. The Court did not say, of course, that a treaty need not conform to the Constitution. To the contrary, the Court's judgment in the case at least implied that a treaty could be found unconstitutional. But the Migratory Bird Treaty was not unconstitutional, nor were the act and regulations implementing it.[76] Kaufman and Whiteman argue that during the 1950s Senator John Bricker was interested in "reversing" *Missouri* v. *Holland* through his proposed constitutional amendment.[77]

At the 1970 Senate hearings various spokesmen of the Nixon administration took issue with Senator Ervin and those who supported his position, including representatives of the ABA. For example, William Rehnquist, then assistant attorney general, testified that while the issues raised by Senator Ervin had been "rather novel" when they were raised at the 1950 hearings, they were no longer so, and that as far as the Justice Department was concerned, the 1950 testimony of Truman administration representatives such as Solicitor General Philip Perlman was accurate. As I noted earlier, to Rehnquist the question of whether or not the United States could ratify the Genocide Convention was a matter of policy; there was nothing in constitutional law that prohibited ratification.[78]

In 1970 the Committee on Foreign Relations accepted the position taken by administration spokesmen. In its report to the Senate endorsing ratification of the convention, the committee dealt very briefly with the issue of congressional power to make genocide a federal crime. It noted that the arguments made to the contrary were "not persuasive," and that "Article 1, section 8, of the Constitution grants Congress the power to define and punish Piracies and Felonies committed on the high seas and Offenses against the Law of Nations."[79] The committee cited examples of laws enacted by Congress that made certain homicides federal crimes, including the killing of heads of foreign states and other designated foreign officials. Hence, the committee believed that it was "entirely within the power of the Congress to enact the legislation required by article V [of the convention, and make genocide a federal crime,] even in the absence of a treaty."[80] At other times during the 1970s representatives of the executive branch made similar arguments. At the 1977 Senate hearings, for example, representatives of the Carter administration suggested that concerns about the impact of ratification on federal-state relations had been exaggerated. Herbert Hansell, legal adviser to the Department of State, stated in his testimony that the implementing legislation the Congress would enact could indicate that the federal government did not intend to "occupy the field" at the exclusion of the states.[81] Deputy Secretary of State Warren Christopher made the same arguments in his testimony.[82]

Nonetheless, the opponents of ratification continued to argue that there were constitutional obstacles to ratification. They became even more strident after President Reagan endorsed ratification in 1984. In 1985, when Senator Orrin Hatch held hearings on constitutional issues relating to the proposed Genocide Convention in his Subcommittee on the Constitution of the Senate Committee on the Judiciary, he directed numerous questions to those invited to testify, and specific supplementary questions were later put to them by other senators on the subcommittee.[83] Many of the questions could be, and were, answered yes or no. "Can a treaty affect or nullify the provisions of the state constitutions?" Or a state statute? Or a judicial decision of a state supreme court? Or existing federal legislation on the same subject? All of these questions were answered "yes" by law professor John Norton Moore.[84] However, one of the more interesting questions raised by Hatch did not permit a yes or no answer: "*Why is it undesirable to federalize criminal law?*"[85]

The phrasing of the question implied that the conclusion was already known; there remained only the reasons for the conclusion to be ascertained. But the question produced a mix of responses. Distinguished law professors of different ideological orientations such as John Norton Moore and John Murphy looked to the past practice of the federal government and formulated responses that were mainly empirical in content. It was obvious that neither of them believed that it was *inherently undesirable* to federalize criminal law. Moore, for example, noted that Congress has already "enacted untold numbers of federal criminal laws, ranging from those protecting the President of the United States and other government officials, to those . . . implementing international treaties concerning aircraft hijacking and hostage-taking by terrorists."[86] He went on to say that "one of the primary areas of major congressional concern in recent decades has been the need to strengthen federal criminal laws." This was a movement that Moore saw as actually being supported by the American public.[87] Indeed, it is hard to imagine that many Americans would oppose such laws. The question, therefore, as Moore emphasized, was not whether or not there should be federal criminal law, but whether or not genocide should be added to the list of federal crimes.

John Murphy grounded his arguments in recent experience as well. He argued that ratification of the convention and the adoption of implementing legislation would not really "federalize" criminal law, that there was no intention on the part of Congress to preempt state criminal laws, and that it would be possible for the states and the federal government concurrently to exercise jurisdiction in cases of genocide as they can in a number of other areas of criminal law, including terrorism.[88]

If the responses provided by Moore and Murphy seemed skewed in favor of an expanded federal criminal law, it should be noted that others who testified provided responses consistent with the ideological position of the Reagan administration, or at least what they perceived the ideological position of the administration to be. Indeed, their willingness to provide such testimony perhaps best explains their being called to testify before the subcommittee. Rodolphe J. A. de Seife of the Northern Illinois University Law School, for example, responded to the heavily value-laden question "Why is it undesirable to federalize criminal law?" with an equally heavily value-laden response:

> Criminal law has been within the province of the states ever since this country was created. This is one area which is *best served* by the state systems with, as is the case now, a sort of supervisory capacity by the federal courts to see to it that the minimum requirements of justice guaranteed to American citizens, as opposed to state citizens, are respected. To create a federal criminal law system means the end of state sovereignties and the beginning of a centralized federal government at the national level, *which is certainly not something that this administration would want to propose.*[89]

Robert Friedlander of Ohio Northern Law School, later an aide to Senator Jesse Helms, provided testimony that was somewhat more restrained, but he, too, argued that to "federalize criminal law would disrupt the delicate balance of constitutional power which now exists between and among the state and federal governments."[90]

Undoubtedly, de Seife and Friedlander provided the sorts of responses that Hatch and others on the subcommittee who were opposed to ratification wanted to hear; that is, they were providing the "expert testimony" that contained the rationale for loading up the Sovereignty Package with provisions that would reduce the convention to a mere symbol of opposition to genocide. Presumably neither de Seife, Friedlander, nor Hatch would have opposed making terrorism or some other acts that Moore and Murphy referred to in their testimony federal crimes. At least one hopes that they would not. But they certainly opposed making *genocide* a federal crime. This was clearly a matter of preference regarding the policy the United States should follow, as William Rehnquist had pointed out in his more skillful testimony in 1970, and, before him, Philip Perlman in his testimony in 1950. However, legalistic arguments such as those used by de Seife and Friedlander always seemed to add an air of respectability.

The Hatch subcommittee put other questions to the witnesses:

> Should the treaty-making power be used as the basis for enactment of domestic legislation in the United States?
>
> Would the Genocide Convention alter the balance of authority between the States and the Federal Government by making genocide an international and Federal crime?

Does the Convention violate specific amendments to the Constitution?
Does ratification of the Convention limit our national sovereignty?
Does the Convention mandate changes in the independence of the American legal system?
What amendments, reservations, declarations, or understandings should be attached to the Genocide Convention?[91]

These questions all seem to have been legal in nature—even, in some cases, to have raised profound questions of constitutional law. But this is deceptive. In fact, sharp disagreements existed among the witnesses who responded to these questions, suggesting that there were no clear-cut legal answers, and that the answers indeed depended in large measure on political or ideological inclinations, if not affiliations.

The U.S. Constitutional Reservation

While Senator Hatch was holding hearings on the convention in a subcommittee of the Committee on the Judiciary, Senator Jesse Helms lobbied for several conditions of ratification in the Committee on Foreign Relations. One condition that grew mainly out of their efforts was the so-called constitutional reservation.[92] While Hatch and Helms conceived of this particular reservation, the idea was not original. As we have seen, Senator Bourke Hickenlooper had proposed something like a constitutional reservation at the 1950 Senate hearings.[93] Soon thereafter the Bricker Amendment raised the same sorts of issues. But Hickenlooper's proposal was not taken seriously by the Committee on Foreign Relations in 1950. Nor is there any evidence that the committee ever gave any serious thought to including such a reservation in its proposed resolutions of ratification during the 1970s. Even if the committee had proposed such a reservation, it probably would not have made any difference to the outcome. Proponents of ratification were always on the defensive. They could not even get the Senate to vote on a resolution of ratification. In such an atmosphere, it is extremely unlikely that even a constitutional reservation would have made any difference so far as the opponents of ratification were concerned.

The early years of the Reagan administration could only have encouraged the opponents of ratification. Senator Charles Percy held hearings on the convention when he took over the chairmanship of the Committee on Foreign Relations in 1981.[94] Percy strongly favored ratification; it was significant that not one representative of the Reagan administration came to testify.[95] This was in marked contrast to the hearings held during the 1970s, when high-ranking officials of the Nixon and Carter administrations provided abundant testimony, adding supplementary comments in writing upon the request of some senators. But in 1981, Reagan allies had every reason to be assertive; the Republicans had gained control of the Senate. Senator Strom Thurmond of the Judiciary Committee testified before the Committee on Foreign Relations and urged it to reject the convention. In fact, Thurmond seems to be the only senator ever to admit openly and on the record that he had urged a president to withdraw the convention from the Senate. He believed that any further consideration of the convention would be a "waste" of time. As he said at the 1981 Senate hearings:

> The point is this: The Genocide Treaty, where it should restrain atrocity, is not observed; and where it would be observed, it is unnecessary. In the barbaric nations of the world, the treaty is given lip service. In our civilized free republic, the treaty would be followed to the letter and thus could harm irreparably the fabric of our constitutional system.
>
> I welcome the opportunity to testify against the Genocide Treaty because, in my view, the time has come for the President to request the return of the treaty so that the Senate will not year after year face needlessly an issue which already has been effectively resolved and which is wasting the time of this institution to no good purpose whatsoever.
>
> I have today written to the President to express that opinion, and I am hopeful that he will request the return of the treaty without further delay. Thirty-two years of Senate consideration is long enough.[96]

Presidents can, of course, withdraw treaties that are pending Senate consideration, although this is rarely done. One of the most important recent examples was President Carter's withdrawal of the SALT II treaty in 1979 after the Soviet Union invaded Afghanistan. But even if the Reagan administration was indifferent about the Genocide Convention in 1981, it would have been imprudent for the president to withdraw it from the Senate. There were always many powerful and influential opponents of ratification of the convention, but it also always enjoyed substantial support among individuals and groups that would not give up the fight over its ratification. Moreover, withdrawing the convention would have been a grave insult to millions of Jewish voters who, for obvious reasons, strongly supported ratification. Withdrawing the convention therefore did not seem like a realistic option. In fact, when President Reagan endorsed ratification shortly before the 1984 presidential election, he did so in a speech to B'nai B'rith, a coincidence that provoked tremendous cynicism in the Senate. Democrats on the Committee on Foreign Relations were especially caustic, wondering why the review that the administration claimed it had begun in 1981 had taken so long and had been completed at such a convenient time.[97]

The timing of President Reagan's endorsement made the cynicism seem well justified. Be that as it may, since the president could hardly be considered some sort of liberal activist aligned with the United Nations, as promoters of the convention were sometimes portrayed, his endorsement significantly increased the chances of ratification. At the 1984 Senate hearings, Senator Helms spoke warmly of the president's endorsement and indicated that he too favored ratification "consistent with the U.S. Constitution."[98] This qualification was, of course, crucial, and Helms suggested that the problems he perceived to exist in the convention might be satisfactorily addressed through the inclusion of an "understanding" in the resolution of ratification stating that "the U.S. Government understands and construes the words 'in accordance with their respective Constitutions' in Article V [of the convention] to mean that the present convention or any provision thereof shall become effective as the domestic law of the United States only through legislation which would be valid in the absence of the convention."[99] Helms saw nothing unusual in his proposal, claiming that it merely reiterated the president's own wishes. But it actually repeated, though in slightly different language, the terms of the Bricker Amendment of the 1950s.

Although Helms claimed otherwise, the Reagan administration did not seem to share his views, since it had endorsed ratification with the same set of conditions that the Committee on Foreign Relations had proposed on several occasions during the 1970s and in 1984. Nonetheless, Helms was persistent in pushing his proposal, altering its language and finally labeling it a reservation in 1985. The Reagan administration endorsed the reservation, along with all other provisions of the Sovereignty Package. The constitutional reservation provides:

> That nothing in the Convention requires or authorizes legislation or other action by the United States of America prohibited by the Constitution of the United States as interpreted by the United States.[100]

While the language of this statement varies somewhat from the original one proposed by Helms, it seems to have the same effect. The fact that Helms upgraded his proposal to a reservation suggests the importance that he and others who supported his initiative attached to the primacy of the U.S. Constitution. The reservation was understood to have very broad coverage. Senator Hatch defended it on the Senate floor as covering "any legislation, executive conduct, or legal activity which would be contrary to the substantive and procedural protections of the U.S. Constitution."[101] For its part, the Committee on Foreign Relations decided to support the reservation because of difficulties it saw emanating from Article 27 of the Vienna Convention on the Law of Treaties, according to which no state can invoke the provisions of its internal law as a reason for not abiding by a treaty obligation. The committee thought that the reservation was necessary in the event that a conflict between the convention and the U.S. Constitution should arise. While the committee did not expect such a conflict, it felt that prudence dictated the adoption of the reservation.[102]

Some legal scholars doubted the need for the reservation. John Norton Moore, for example, pointed out that in accordance with the U.S. Supreme Court's judgment in *Reid* v. *Covert* (354 U.S. 1, 1957), "any treaty provision that is inconsistent with the United States Constitution would simply be invalid under national law."[103] Some senators on the Committee on Foreign Relations raised questions about the wisdom of adopting the reservation, suggesting that it might be understood as indicating that the United States was not ratifying the convention in "good faith," and that it might set a dangerous precedent for states that could easily change their constitutions, which would "undermine treaty commitments."[104] Nonetheless, there was little doubt that the Senate would either have to approve the Sovereignty Package as a whole or not give advice and consent to ratification. The critics of the convention had so dominated the debate that they could dictate the conditions of ratification, and the Reagan administration offered no resistance. It, too, had come to favor ratification at almost any price. At the time that the Sovereignty Package was adopted, the feeling was widespread that ratification was merely a symbolic act.

The passage of time has shown that those who opposed the constitutional reservation were justified in their concern about its reception by other parties to the convention. Of all the provisions of the Sovereignty Package, the constitutional reservation has attracted the most attention. The United States deposited the Sovereignty Package with the United Nations secretary general in November 1988. By December 1989 nine parties to the convention, all West European states (Denmark, Finland, Ireland, Italy, the Netherlands, Norway, Spain, Sweden, and the United Kingdom), had objected to the constitutional reservation using practically identical language.[105] In the main, they all expressed concern that the reservation raised a serious question about whether or not the United States was proposing to ratify the convention in good faith, pointing out that according to the rules of treaty law, a party to a treaty cannot invoke a provision of its domestic law as justification for not living up to its international obligations. Hence, in the view of these countries, the reservation created uncertainty as to the extent of the obligations being assumed by the United States. The similarities in the language used to object to the reservation, and the fact that the objections were reported to the secretary general all in the same month, makes it clear that the objecting states had discussed the issue in an effort to see if they could coordinate their objections. But none of these countries indicated in their statements that they did not consider the United States a party to the convention because of the reservation. They simply wanted to go on record that the reservation created uncertainty that was at best regrettable.

The Proxmire Act

The Proxmire Act, adopted in October 1988, makes the provisions of the Genocide Convention effective under U.S. law. The act was adopted by voice vote, not a roll call, so it cannot be said how many members of Congress in either the Senate or the House voted against it. Senator Jesse Helms, however, indicated in remarks on the Senate floor that he would vote against the act, claiming uncertainties about some of its provisions. He also claimed that his vote was an appropriate way to honor the late Senator Sam Ervin, Jr.[106] Helms's attitude about the legislation speaks volumes about what the proponents of ratification of the convention were up against.

The Proxmire Act follows through on the terms of Article V of the convention and, among other things, specifies penalties for those who commit genocide or any of the acts enumerated in Article III. While the act is named for Senator William Proxmire, it was not drafted by him. He did, of course, take an interest in it, and he testified in favor of its adoption at hearings of the Senate Committee on the Judiciary in February 1988. He also spoke in favor of its passage when it was discussed on the Senate floor in October 1988. But the appellation "the Proxmire Act" was proposed by the Committee on the Judiciary in recognition of the extraordinary work that Senator Proxmire did over a period of twenty years to secure the convention's ratification.[107]

By adopting the Proxmire Act, the United States joined other parties to the convention, mostly West and East European states, in the recognition that the implementation of the convention required the passage of special legislation. As we have seen, not all parties to the convention have enacted special implementing legislation.[108] But in view of the historic debate within the United States as to whether or not the convention as a whole or in any of its parts could be considered self-executing, and the provisions of the

Lugar-Helms-Hatch Sovereignty Package that were adopted as a result of that debate, it is not surprising that the United States took the same stance taken by most of the West and East European states, although this is not to say that its legislation is the same as that of the other states. In fact, the Proxmire Act adds to the variety of domestic legislation that has been adopted to implement the convention. Commentators on the convention have argued that the drafters would have expected nothing else.

The Basic Offense of Genocide and Related Acts

In the main, the Proxmire Act incorporates into U.S. federal criminal law the basic definition of genocide that appears in Article II of the Genocide Convention. Its enactment does not preclude the application of state or local laws on the same subject,[109] although presumably any state or local laws that may exist on the subject would have to be consistent with the federal law.

The act follows up on an understanding that was included in the Lugar-Helms-Hatch Sovereignty Package and stipulates that there must be a "specific intent" to destroy a national, ethnic, racial, or religious group "in whole or in substantial part."[110] Moreover, the act makes it clear that there must be more than one victim for a charge of genocide to be brought against anyone under the act. Thus, the lynching of a single individual, for example, even with the specific intent element required under the act, would not qualify as genocide. The legislation does, however, list each of the acts specified in Article II of the convention as offenses.[111]

In regard to the persons punishable for violating the act, it states that "whoever," being either a national of the Unites States or within the territory of the United States, commits the offense can be punished.[112] Put another way, under the Proxmire Act the United States claims the right to try persons for committing genocide or any of the acts enumerated in Article III only on the basis of the nationality and territorial principles of jurisdiction. This very narrow construction of the terms of the convention—particularly Article VI—is disappointing to those who think that the United States should have been more aggressive in claiming jurisdiction for its courts in suppressing genocide (see chapter 8 for a more detailed discussion). As it stands now, under the terms of the Proxmire Act a foreigner such as Pol Pot who commits genocide abroad could not be tried in U.S. courts.

Of the related offenses listed in Article III, only one, the "incitement" offense, was the subject of any extensive debate or controversy in the United States. In other words, no one ever expressed any reservations about whether or not U.S. criminal law could be made applicable to a conspiracy to commit genocide, an attempt to commit genocide, or complicity in the commission of genocide. There was extensive debate, however, over the issue of the "direct and public incitement to commit genocide" clause of Article III. The issue had been a serious one during the drafting stage as well, with a U.S. representative asserting that the incitement clause could create problems for the United States under the First Amendment constitutional guarantees to free speech and expression.[113] The issue had been treated even more seriously in light of Soviet proposals to ban hate groups and punish preparatory acts. But these seemingly more extreme proposals were rejected by the drafters, leaving only the incitement clause as it appears in Article III of the convention as a means of deterring the commission of genocide.[114]

Critics of the convention in the United States have questioned whether or not the clause would undermine First Amendment constitutional guarantees. The Committee on Foreign Relations was unable to agree on an interpretation of the clause before the adoption of the resolution. As its 1985 report to the Senate indicated, "how far the incitement provision reaches remains unclear."[115] The committee thought that "advocacy of abstract doctrine may be enough." In any event, since the drafters had not addressed the "probability of the result" of the incitement as a factor, the "types of incitement the parties to the Convention are obligated to punish is . . . not entirely certain."[116] The committee was concerned that the vagueness of the clause might make it impossible for the United States to live up to its international obligation because the only type of incitement punishable under current First Amendment jurisprudence was that stated by the Supreme Court in *Brandenburg* v. *Ohio* (395 U.S. 444, 1969).[117]

In this 1969 case, the Supreme Court had held that the constitutional guarantee of free speech "covers 'advocacy . . . of law violation,' but does not protect 'advocacy [that] is directed to inciting . . . lawless action."[118] Rehnquist and other legal scholars have contended that the Court's decision in *Brandenburg* meant that the incitement clause in Article III of the convention is not problematical,[119] but critics of the convention have not been willing to accept those assurances. Hence, the constitutional reservation discussed earlier was intended by the Committee on Foreign Relations to apply in uncertain situations such as this. And the Proxmire Act carries the point further, indicating in a section on definitions that "the term 'incites' means to urge another to engage imminently in conduct in circumstances under which there is a substantial likelihood of imminently causing such conduct."[120] The Judiciary Committee indicated in its report on the act that its definition of incitement "follows the Supreme Court's decision" in *Brandenburg* v. *Ohio*.[121]

Penalties for Commission of Genocide and Related Acts

The Proxmire Act also specifies penalties for the commission of genocide or any of the acts enumerated in Article III. The question of what these penalties should be was a matter of some dispute when the act was being drafted. The act was put in final form after the Democrats had regained control of the Senate as a result of the 1986 elections, but the prior philosophical disagreements regarding the sorts of penalties that should be applied for violations of the act remained. Senator Strom Thurmond, who had chaired the Committee on the Judiciary while the Republicans controlled the Senate from 1980 to 1986, and had now reverted to being the ranking Republican on the committee, argued in favor of the death penalty for the commission of genocide and related crimes. He introduced an amendment to this effect in committee, but it was rejected by a tie vote that cut across party lines.[122] Thurmond, and other senators who supported him, argued that the penalty should fit the crime, and they did not think that the penalties then proposed in the legislation met that objective. They pointed out that the death penalty is authorized for numerous federal crimes, including first-degree murder or kidnaping resulting in the death of a president, member of Congress, department head, or justice of the United States. According to these senators, genocide, "without a doubt, equals those crimes in terms of seriousness," and for that reason the death penalty should be applied. They found it "ironic" that the death penalty could be imposed for murder but not for genocide.[123]

Whatever might be said on either side of the issue, it was a bit more than merely ironic that Thurmond would take such an interest in the penalties that might be levied for committing genocide. For years he had been exceedingly hostile to the convention, and in 1981 had urged President Reagan to withdraw it from the Senate.[124] Moreover, he was one of only eleven senators to vote against ratification even with the Lugar-Helms-Hatch Sovereignty Package.[125] When the hearings on the Proxmire Act opened in February 1988, he attended the committee meeting and made a statement that indicated he still opposed the United States becoming a party:

> When the Senate gave its advice and consent to the treaty, several reservations and understandings were also passed in order to clarify the intent of the United States in becoming a party to this treaty. These

conditions were an attempt to address the concerns raised by myself and others. Further, after the Senate considered the treaty, a sense of the Senate resolution was passed which provided that when the President transmits the treaty, he must also seek an amendment to cover political genocide. While I believe that the conditions and the resolution were good faith attempts to address concerns that were raised, *they were insufficient to solve serious concerns regarding the treaty.*

In closing, I reiterate that genocide is a despicable act which should not be tolerated in any form on the face of the earth. With these views in mind, I look forward to hearing the testimony that will be presented today.[126]

By insisting that provision for the death penalty be made in the Proxmire Act, Thurmond was raising an issue that was guaranteed to provoke controversy and perhaps delay the adoption of the implementing legislation. Those who opposed the death penalty in principle would surely oppose its being established as a penalty even for genocide. Moreover, the way in which Thurmond raised the issue suggested that he was using the occasion to advance his own political agenda, which was to favor the imposition of the death penalty in cases of *other* federal crimes. The death penalty statutes for other federal crimes had been rendered "inoperative" by the U.S. Supreme Court, which had ruled that the penalty was "constitutional [only] when imposed in accordance with procedures designed to guide the factfinder in determining whether to impose such a penalty."[127] No such federal procedures were in place at the time the Committee on the Judiciary was debating the terms of the Proxmire Act. Hence, Thurmond actually wanted to amend the act "to provide for the death penalty for genocide *and other crimes as well as to provide the constitutional procedures.*"[128] Thurmond argued that the death penalty for genocide would provide "a sense of balance and proportion in the punishment prescribed for Federal crimes."[129] This philosophical reason notwithstanding, his proposal would have opened up the debate to the much broader question of the application of the death penalty for federal crimes in general, making the passage of the Proxmire Act even more complicated. Since the Democrats had regained control of the Senate at the time the Proxmire Act was being put in final form, Thurmond's delaying tactic could be rebuffed. Senator Howard Metzenbaum (D., Ohio), who chaired the hearing held by the Committee on the Judiciary, was a very strong proponent of ratification and made it clear at the hearing that the time had come to recommend the adoption of the act by the Senate.

According to the act, the penalty for offenses that result in the death of members of a protected group is mandatory life imprisonment and a fine of not more than $1 million. Moreover, in such cases the statute of limitations does not apply. In any other case the penalty is imprisonment of not more than twenty years and a fine of not more than $1,000,000, or both. Less severe penalties apply for the incitement offense—a fine of not more than $500,000 or imprisonment of not more than five years, or both. The Committee on the Judiciary accepted these different formulas on the recommendation of the Justice Department. An earlier draft of the legislation had called for mandatory twenty-year sentences for all offenses other than those that result in the death of members of protected groups. However, the Justice Department favored a more flexible formula in sentencing given the broad scope of genocidal acts covered by the convention and the legislation. The committee accepted this reasoning but indicated its intentions in its report to the Senate as follows: "At the same time, the committee believes that genocide crimes are, by definition, cruel and inhuman and that the U.S. Sentencing Commission should provide appropriately severe penalties for genocide offenses."[130]

Chapter 7 An International Criminal Court

The other criticism of the convention arose out of the possibility that, under article VI, a person accused of genocide could be tried by an international penal tribunal, possibly without trial by jury and other safeguards to which a U.S. citizen is entitled under our Constitution. . . . No such tribunal has been established. If one were established, parties to the Genocide Convention would have the option whether or not to accept its jurisdiction.

For the United States, that option would have to be independently exercised through the treaty power, that is, only with the advice and consent of the Senate by a two-thirds vote.—Ambassador Rita Hauser, 1970 Senate hearings

One of the most important issues that the drafters of the Genocide Convention had to resolve was the question of whether or not an international criminal court should be created as a rule-supervisory organ. Arguments on both sides of the issue were made at various times in the negotiations that led up to the adoption of the convention—in the Ad Hoc Committee of the ECOSOC,[1] the Sixth Committee of the General Assembly,[2] and even in a plenary session of the assembly.[3] Generally, those who favored the creation of a court argued that national authorities could not always be relied upon to bring persons to trial in their own countries on charges of genocide. In fact, most drafters seemed to assume that governmental authorities would inevitably be involved in any cases of genocide, and that since they would not be inclined to bring themselves to trial, an international mechanism that could conduct the trials was necessary. At every stage in the negotiations the U.S. representatives were at the forefront arguing in favor of the creation of an international criminal court.

Those who opposed the creation of a court invoked considerations of national sovereignty. The Soviet bloc representatives, especially the representatives of the Soviet Union itself, were outspoken in this regard. In the main, the Soviets took the position that the creation of an international criminal court with competence to try cases under the convention would constitute a "violation of the sovereign right of every State to judge crimes committed in its territory; and the sovereignty of States was the very basis of the United Nations."[4] Since there could be "no exception to that rule in the case of genocide," the Soviets wanted to recognize only the competence of domestic courts to try cases of genocide, and they were determined to prevent the adoption of an article that would even contemplate the creation of an international criminal court.[5] Ironically, the usually ultraconservative opponents of ratification of the convention by the United States made similar arguments throughout the 1970s and 1980s.

It is clear from the records of the negotiations that the drafters of the convention had serious *policy* disagreements regarding an international criminal court. They attempted to resolve those differences by adopting an article designed to accommodate both sides on the issue. Article VI of the convention provides:

> Persons charged with genocide or any of the other acts enumerated in Article III [conspiracy, incitement, attempt, and complicity to commit genocide] shall be tried by a competent tribunal of the State in the territory of which the act was committed, or by such international penal tribunal as may have jurisdiction with respect to those Contracting Parties which shall have accepted its jurisdiction.

At first glance, one might think that this article would not raise great concern among states, or the United States, for several reasons. In the first place, judging by the order in which the article takes up the issues it deals with, it actually seems to emphasize the competence of domestic courts to try cases of genocide. Second, it only *contemplates* the creation of an international criminal court, and no such court has been created. Third, in the event a court were created, it would not automatically exercise jurisdiction in cases of genocide. According to Article VI, the parties to the convention can decide for themselves whether or not they wish to accept the jurisdiction of any international criminal court that might be created.

The instruments of ratification of the states that have ratified the Genocide Convention suggest that the terms of Article VI have indeed been generally noncontroversial.[6] In fact, until the United States deposited its instrument of ratification, only a few of the parties (such as Morocco, Philippines, and Venezuela) had ratified with statements regarding the terms of Article VI.[7] Even then, their statements reflected more concern about the implications of the article for the jurisdiction of domestic courts than about the international criminal court clause. In the United States, however, the terms of Article VI had been a matter of highly contentious debate ever since President Truman recommended ratification of the convention, and two understandings regarding the article were included in the Lugar-Helms-Hatch Sovereignty Package. One understanding applies specifically to the international criminal court clause of Article VI.

> That with regard to the reference to an international penal tribunal in Article VI of the Convention, the United States declares that it reserves the right to effect its participation in any such tribunal only by a treaty entered into specifically for that purpose with the advice and consent of the Senate.[8]

The second understanding applies to the domestic court provisions of Article VI and to the related issue of extradition in Article VII, and states that "nothing in Article VI affects the right of any state to bring to trial before its own tribunals any of its nationals for acts committed outside a state."[9] Since the two understandings address different issues that arise out of the terms of Article VI, we shall deal with them in different chapters. In this chapter we shall focus on the understanding that pertains only to the proposed international criminal court. In chapter 8 we shall examine the understanding that applies to the jurisdiction of domestic courts and the related issue of extradition.

The understanding regarding the international criminal court clause of Article VI indicates that since the convention was drafted, attitudes in the United States toward the creation of such a court have undergone a significant change, and this change has had an impact on policy. Why did this change in attitude occur? Was an understanding regarding the international criminal court clause necessary, or was its adoption yet another example of the overreaction of critics of the convention to an essentially harmless article? To provide the necessary background information for answering these questions, let us look, first, at the considerations that led the drafters to include the international criminal court clause in Article VI, and, second, at the obstacles that lay in the way of the actual creation of a court.

The Proposed International Criminal Court

The possibility of creating an international criminal court to try cases of genocide was discussed from the earliest stages in the negotiations over the terms of the convention. The most far-reaching proposal on the matter was made by the experts who prepared the UN Secretariat's draft convention. One article of the draft stated that the parties to the convention would "pledge themselves to commit" offenders to trial by an international court in cases when (1) the parties themselves were "unwilling" to try the offenders or extradite them to another country that would try them, or (2) when the "acts of genocide [had] been committed by individuals acting as organs of the State or with the support or toleration of the State."[10] The experts envisioned such trials being conducted by a court that would have "jurisdiction [either] in all matters connected with international crimes," or only with regard to genocide.[11] Precisely which formula would be adopted was left to be determined through the process of negotiations on the convention as a whole. Although the Ad Hoc Committee of the ECOSOC later stripped these provisions from the draft convention, there was strong support in the committee for the *principle* of international criminal jurisdiction. The U.S. representative on the committee, John Maktos, joined with the representatives of China, France, and Lebanon voting in favor of the principle. The Soviet and Polish representatives were the only ones to vote against the principle, and the Venezuelan representative abstained.[12] Thus, by the time the issue was discussed in the Sixth Committee of the General Assembly, there seemed to be strong sentiment in favor of at least the principle of international criminal jurisdiction.

But the apparent widespread agreement in principle could not obscure the fact that there existed a number of issues related to the creation of a court, mostly of a practical nature, that had to be resolved. At the time the convention was being drafted, no international criminal court existed, which raised a series of questions. Should a statute for a court be included in the convention, or should the statute be a separate instrument? Should a court be created to deal exclusively with allegations of genocide, or should it be a court with broader competence to deal with criminal matters including, but not limited to, genocide? Under what conditions would a court exercise jurisdiction? Would parties to the convention be obliged to accept its jurisdiction or could they exercise an option in that regard?[13]

Additionally, the proposal to create an international criminal court had to be examined in the context of the convention as a whole. As we discussed in chapter 4, many of the delegates in the Sixth Committee, especially the representatives of Venezuela and Egypt, argued that states would be reluctant to ratify the convention if Article II extended protection to political groups and Article VI made it possible to bring cases before an international criminal court. They believed that political groups would seize the opportunity to make slanderous allegations of genocide against states, and that since states would not want to have to defend themselves against such allegations before an international criminal court, they would decline to ratify the convention.

Support for an International Criminal Court

The complexity of the issues required the delegates to the Sixth Committee to engage in extensive negotiations and strive to reach compromises that would accommodate the largest number of states. In fact, they took several votes during the negotiations as they attempted to work out these compromises. Since the draft convention prepared by the Ad Hoc Committee of the ECOSOC contained a clause relating to an international criminal court, the first question that arose in the Sixth Committee was whether or not the clause should be retained. The Soviet delegation, which consistently opposed even the principle of international criminal jurisdiction throughout the negotiations on the convention, led the way in the Sixth Committee in proposing the deletion of the clause. As table 7.1 shows, the Soviet proposal was narrowly adopted.

Slightly more than one-third of the total membership of the United Nations at the time (twenty-three states, or 39.7 percent) supported the

Table 7.1 Vote in the Sixth Committee on Article VI
(First Vote: *Delete Clause Pertaining to International Criminal Court*).

Area	Number (Percentage)	Yes	Abstain	No	No vote
Africa		0	1	1	2
		(0)	(25.0)	(25.0)	(50.0)
Asia		3	0	5	5
		(23.1)	(0)	(38.5)	(38.5)
Oceania		0	0	2	0
		(0)	(0)	(100)	(0)
Americas		10	1	7	4
		(45.5)	(4.5)	(31.8)	(18.2)
Europe		10	1	4	2
		(58.8)	(5.9)	(23.5)	(11.8)
TOTALS		23	3	19	13
		(39.7)	(5.2)	(32.8)	(22.4)

Source: Same as table 4.1.

deletion of the clause. At the same time, almost one-third (nineteen states, or 32.8 percent) opposed its deletion. A large number of states did not vote (thirteen, or 22.4 percent). Considering that the Soviet bloc was united in opposition to the clause, the inconclusive nature of the outcome reflected in table 7.1 suggested that a reconsideration of the issue might be in order, especially if the United States would change its position and allow the reference to political groups in Article II of the convention to be deleted.

Actually, the Sixth Committee's initial decision to delete the clause pertaining to an international criminal court left the drafters with only two plausible alternatives. As an Indian delegate argued, as amended, Article VI of the convention could be deleted in its entirety because it had become superfluous. Without the clause pertaining to an international criminal court, the effect of the terms of Article VI was to say that persons charged with genocide could be tried by competent tribunals of the state in whose territory the crime was committed.[14] In other words, as amended, Article VI affirmed the jurisdiction of domestic courts on the basis of the principle of territoriality. But since this principle is universally recognized even in the absence of the convention, the Indian delegate suggested that Article VI as amended be deleted on the ground that it was unnecessary.[15] His suggestion gave rise to a discussion of several principles of jurisdiction, to which we shall return in chapter 8.

The second alternative was to reconsider the terms of Article VI with a view to reinserting the clause pertaining to an international criminal court. Exercising this alternative required some negotiations, however, because the Soviet bloc was united in opposition to a clause. In addition, and perhaps more importantly from the standpoint of the number of votes required, some delegates were prepared to *support* a clause if it were written so that ratification of the convention would not *automatically* result in acceptance of the jurisdiction of the court. These delegates wanted acceptance of jurisdiction to be made *optional* and subject to a separate agreement.[16] Despite these difficulties, reinserting the international criminal court clause in Article VI carried the great advantage of at least recognizing the principle of international jurisdiction, which was important to the United States.

Once the particular interests of the states that favored the principle of international criminal jurisdiction were taken into account, the Sixth Committee took two additional votes on Article VI. One was to reconsider its earlier deletion of the clause regarding the international criminal court. Table 7.2 shows there was substantial support across a broad spectrum of states for a U.S. proposal to reconsider the earlier decision to delete the clause pertaining to an international criminal court in Article VI. Well over

Table 7.2 Vote in the Sixth Committee on Article VI (Second Vote: *Reconsider the Content of Article VI*).

Area	Number (Percentage)	Yes	Abstain	No	No vote
Africa		1	1	0	2
		(25.0)	(25.0)	(0)	(50.0)
Asia		8	0	2	3
		(61.5)	(0)	(15.4)	(23.1)
Oceania		2	0	0	0
		(100)	(0)	(0)	(0)
Americas		13	4	1	4
		(59.1)	(18.2)	(4.5)	(18.2)
Europe		9	1	6	1
		(52.9)	(5.9)	(35.3)	(5.9)
TOTALS		33	6	9	10
		(56.9)	(10.3)	(15.5)	(17.2)

Source: Same as table 4.1.

half the members of the United Nations at the time (thirty-three states, or 56.9 percent), including a majority of most of the geographical groups, supported the proposal; even the European group supported the proposal, despite the united opposition of the Soviet bloc.

Having decided to reconsider the content of Article VI, the Sixth Committee then voted on another U.S. proposal, which had itself been rephrased through a series of friendly amendments, to reinsert a clause pertaining to an international criminal court.[17] The clause, as adopted, makes acceptance of the jurisdiction of the court optional for any party to the convention. Table 7.3 shows how the Sixth Committee voted on the issue.

A comparison of the data in tables 7.2 and 7.3 shows very similar distributions of votes on reconsidering the deletion of the clause pertaining to an international criminal court and reinserting such a clause in Article VI. In fact, only four states—two American and two European—voted differently on the two issues. On the basis of the data presented in these two tables, it cannot be determined precisely how these states changed their votes. The largest change in the distribution of votes in the tables, however, occurred in the column showing states that did not vote. Ten states, or 17.2 percent of the UN's membership at the time, did not vote on the question of reconsidering the earlier decision to delete the clause, whereas fifteen

Table 7.3 Vote in the Sixth Committee on Article VI
(Third Vote: *Reinsert Clause Pertaining to International Criminal Court*).

Area	Number (Percentage)	Yes	Abstain	No	No vote
Africa		1	1	0	2
		(25.0)	(25.0)	(0)	(50.0)
Asia		8	1	1	3
		(61.5)	(7.7)	(7.7)	(23.1)
Oceania		2	0	0	0
		(100)	(0)	(0)	(0)
Americas		11	2	2	7
		(50.0)	(9.1)	(9.1)	(31.8)
Europe		7	1	6	3
		(41.2)	(5.9)	(35.3)	(17.6)
TOTALS		29	5	9	15
		(50.0)	(8.6)	(15.5)	(25.9)

Source: Same as table 4.1.

states, or 25.9 percent, did not vote on reinserting the clause. All things considered, the clause on the international criminal court in Article VI was supported by a good majority of the drafters. This conclusion is more compelling when one considers the figures shown in table 7.4.

Table 7.4 shows the results of a roll-call vote in a plenary session of the General Assembly on a Soviet proposal to delete the international criminal court clause from Article VI. This was one of the few votes taken in the plenary session, and it affirmed the decision that had been made earlier in the Sixth Committee by a substantial margin. Thirty-nine of the member states (67.2 percent) voted to affirm the earlier decision, a figure that is all the more impressive in light of the fact that the Soviet bloc (all six members) provided the only significant support for overriding the committee's decision.

Subsequent UN Actions Regarding an International Criminal Court

Consistent with its decision to include a provision relating to the creation of an international criminal court in Article VI, the Sixth Committee also adopted a draft resolution pertaining to further work that needed to be done to bring a court into existence. The resolution was approved by the Gen-

Table 7.4 Vote in Plenary Session of the General Assembly (Fourth Vote: *Delete Clause Pertaining to International Criminal Court*).

Area	Number (Percentage)	Yes	Abstain	No	No vote
Africa		0	1	3	0
		(0)	(25.0)	(75.0)	(0)
Asia		1	2	10	0
		(7.7)	(15.4)	(76.9)	(0)
Oceania		0	0	2	0
		(0)	(0)	(100)	(0)
Americas		1	4	14	3
		(4.5)	(18.2)	(63.6)	(13.6)
Europe		6	1	10	0
		(35.3)	(5.9)	(58.8)	(0)
TOTALS		8	8	39	3
		(13.8)	(13.8)	(67.2)	(5.2)

Source: Same as table 4.1.

eral Assembly in plenary session following its adoption of the convention. Resolution 260-B (III) states:

> THE GENERAL ASSEMBLY,
>
> CONSIDERING that the discussion of the Convention on the Prevention and Punishment of the Crime of Genocide has raised the question of the desirability and possibility of having persons charged with genocide tried by a competent international tribunal,
>
> CONSIDERING that in the course of development of the international community, there will be an increasing need of an international judicial organ for the trial of certain crimes under international law,
>
> INVITES the International Law Commission to study the desirability and possibility of establishing an international judicial organ for the trial of persons *charged with genocide or other crimes over which jurisdiction will be conferred upon that organ by international conventions;*
>
> REQUESTS the International Law Commission, in carrying out this task, to pay attention to the possibility of establishing a Criminal Chamber of the International Court of Justice. [emphasis mine]

Following up on this resolution, the fifteen-member International Law Commission (ILC) began discussion of the feasibility of proceeding with one of the options outlined by the General Assembly—either creating a free-standing international criminal court, or creating a criminal chamber of the ICJ—at its first session in April 1949. The UN Secretariat had prepared a background paper on previous work relating to the creation of an international criminal court to set the framework for the ILC's discussion of the matter.[18] Since the commission had other important matters to deal with, it decided to appoint two of its members as rapporteurs to prepare reports on the issues involved in pursuing either option, to be presented at its second session in 1950.[19] During that session the commission discussed the reports of the rapporteurs, which themselves indicated that serious disagreements were already beginning to develop on the questions of the desirability *and* feasibility of creating an international criminal court. In fact, the rapporteurs reached fundamentally different conclusions.

One rapporteur, Ricardo Alfaro, who had served as president of Panama and would later serve as a judge on the ICJ,[20] presented a lengthy, scholarly report that, among other things, summarized the efforts dating back to the early post–World War I period to create an international criminal court. According to Alfaro, there existed an "imposing array of official and unofficial thought and action which [had] manifested itself in favor of the establishment of an international criminal jurisdiction for the prevention and punishment of crimes against humanity."[21] As he put it: "The proposals of jurists, statesmen, thinkers, governmental bodies, and scientific institutions reflect the feelings of a generation which still shudders at the recollection of the atrocities of the last war and is gripped by the fear of a new conflagration. They also represent the considered opinion of the world with regard to war and its attendant horrors and respecting the imperative need of delivering humanity from those frightful evils."[22]

Alfaro stressed that the General Assembly had charged the ILC with studying the possibility and desirability of creating an international criminal court that could try persons charged with genocide *or other* international crimes. Thus, he argued that war crimes, crimes against peace, and crimes against humanity—Nuremberg principles—would probably also have to be included within the "scope" of a "prospective international penal code."[23] Furthermore, he suggested that jurisdiction might also be conferred upon an international criminal court for crimes such as piracy, the slave trade, traffic in narcotics, traffic in women and children, counterfeiting of currency, terrorism, injury to submarine cables, and "circulation of obscene publications."[24] All these crimes would have to be defined.

The thrust of Alfaro's report was overwhelmingly positive toward the creation of an international criminal court. He argued that a court was at once *desirable* and *possible:*

> That it is *desirable* to establish a judicial organ for the trial of international crimes, seems to be evidenced by all the facts, declarations, studies, proposals, recommendations, plans, and decisions which have marked for a period of over thirty years the birth and growth of the idea of an international criminal jurisdiction. In fact, more than something desirable, it is a thing desired, an aspiration of Governments, institutions, conferences, jurists, statesmen, and writers. . . .
>
> That it is *possible* to establish an international criminal organ of penal justice is demonstrated by actual experience. . . . [The international military tribunals at Nuremberg and Tokyo, for example,] did actually function and fulfill their mission. Seven different drafts for statutes of an international judicial organ have been formulated, plus the charters of [the international military tribunals], and their texts show that the constitution of an international court is possible and feasible, despite the many differences existing among them.[25]

For these reasons, Alfaro's answer to the questions of whether or not it was desirable and feasible to establish an international criminal court was "unhesitatingly in the affirmative."[26] He believed that if the "rule of law is to govern the community of States and protect it against violations of the international public order, it can only be satisfactorily established by the promulgation of an international penal code and by the permanent functioning of an international criminal jurisdiction."[27] While he clearly favored a free-standing court, he believed that it would also be possible to establish a criminal chamber of the International Court of Justice. Should that option be exercised, however, Alfaro pointed out that the statute of the court would have to be amended to make it possible for *individuals*, not just states, to be parties to a case before the court, because it would be necessary to establish that individuals could be tried for violating international criminal law.[28]

The second rapporteur for the ILC was Emil Sandstrom of Sweden.[29] He advanced a completely different interpretation of the General Assembly's resolution and reached completely different conclusions from those of Alfaro. Sandstrom argued that the General Assembly envisioned the international criminal court as a *principal organ* of the United Nations, analogous to the ICJ, and that such a court could be created only by amending the UN Charter.[30] This interpretation of the General Assembly's resolution meant, of course, that there were virtually insurmountable obstacles in the path of the creation of a court. According to Article 108 of the UN Charter, an amendment would have to be adopted by a two-thirds vote of the General Assembly, and then ratified by two-thirds of the member states, including all the permanent members of the Security Council. In effect, Article 108 gave a veto over all amendments of the UN Charter to the permanent members of the Security Council. Although Sandstrom did not say so in his report, it was obvious that the Soviet Union would be able to bloc the creation of an international criminal court simply by refusing to ratify an amendment of the UN Charter. He foresaw similar obstacles to the creation of a criminal chamber of the ICJ; the Soviet Union would be able to veto an amendment of the ICJ's statute. Despite these obstacles, Sandstrom acknowledged that it would be *possible* to create an international criminal court *or* a criminal chamber of the ICJ.[31]

With regard to the question of the *desirability* of pursuing either option, however, Sandstrom had serious reservations. He conceded that there might be an "urgent desire" among people "for such a jurisdiction," but he argued that even if it were established, "it is very uncertain whether it would have competence in an actual case, and as long as an important group of States are of the opinion that the repression of crimes—even such crimes which have an inter-State character—is a matter within the exclusive competence of the State and not a matter to be dealt with by the international community, there seems to be a very small chance that this uncertainty will be removed in the near future."[32] Consequently, the creation of an international criminal jurisdiction could do "more harm than good." As Sandstrom put it:

> The competence of the Court will be restricted to parties having submitted by convention to its jurisdiction. No organization does exist to enforce an appearance before the Court or the execution of its judgments, and it seems difficult to establish such an organization. The jurisdiction therefore is likely to be limited and brought into action in a haphazard way. There are great risks that culprits will not always be brought before the Court. On the whole, this will give the impression that the jurisdiction is being exercised in an arbitrary way. Its deterring effect will thus be very doubtful, if any.[33]

After discussing both reports, the ILC decided, by different margins, that Alfaro had the better argument and that the creation of an international criminal court was both desirable and possible. On the question of *desirability*, the vote was eight in favor, one against, with two abstentions. On the question of *possibility*, the vote was seven in favor, three against, and one abstention. This slightly more pessimistic—some would say realistic—assessment reflected the awareness of the members of the committee of heightening tensions in the cold war, in particular the outbreak of the Korean War, and their concern for the impact of these developments on the

United Nations and its role in furthering the development and strengthening of international law and institutions. While the commission thought that it would be possible to create a criminal chamber of the ICJ by amending its statute, it did not recommend that option.[34]

Different viewpoints were expressed when the Sixth Committee of the General Assembly discussed the ILC's report. Predictably, the Soviet bloc representatives raised objections to the establishment of a court on the ground that it would undermine the sovereignty of states. The Polish representative in particular reiterated the position taken by Sandstrom in his report to the ILC and argued that a court would constitute an organ of the United Nations that could not be created without amending the UN Charter.[35] But it was not only the Soviet bloc states that opposed the establishment of a court. The representatives of Australia, Brazil, Sweden, and the United Kingdom argued that the project would be impractical. From their point of view, no matter how "desirable anything might be in theory, if it was not a practical possibility the attempt to create it could only result in failure and therefore, in the realistic as opposed to the idealistic sense, the project was not in the circumstances desirable."[36] Those in favor of establishing a court (the representatives of China, France, Iran, and Mexico, for example) argued that it was a "logical consequence" of the existence of international crimes, and that it could make a contribution toward peace and security.[37] Most representatives, however, felt that the establishment of a court could not be discussed in abstract terms, that governments would have to know more specifically how the court would function before giving their approval to its creation. Moreover, they claimed to be concerned about the "dearth of positive law which the proposed court could apply."[38]

The Sixth Committee resolved the different points of view by recommending to the General Assembly that a seventeen-member committee meet during 1951 for the purpose of preparing draft conventions and proposals relating to the creation of a court.[39] The General Assembly approved this recommendation. Later, in 1953, the Committee on International Criminal Jurisdiction completed a draft statute for an international criminal court. But the idea was then linked with a draft code of offenses against mankind that the ILC was to draft, and it was eventually dropped from discussion.[40] The court has never been created.

Obstacles to Creating an International Criminal Court

Some scholars, practitioners, and activists maintain an interest in the creation of an international criminal court. The subject is occasionally addressed at conferences on international criminal law and on the further development and strengthening of international institutions and procedures.[41] Groups such as Campaign for UN Reform and the World Federalist Association are lobbying the U.S. Congress to press the executive branch to pursue the establishment of a court, and legislation to this effect has been introduced.[42] But progress—if it can be called that—in the direction of the creation of an international criminal court has proceeded at a glacial pace. In fact, most observers would likely say that if there has been any movement on the issue, it has been away from the creation of a court. As one participant in the First International Criminal Law Conference in 1971 remarked to a group of distinguished scholars and practitioners, "we should not be too disappointed if our effort sometimes seems to us to have some affinity to walking in space."[43]

There seems to be a consensus among those who have worked in this field on what the obstacles are to the creation of an international criminal court. For one, there is a broad divergence of interests between the developed and less-developed states on which important international crimes need priority attention. The developed states tend to emphasize the suppression of such crimes as terrorism, illegal drug trafficking, hijacking, kidnapping, and environmental pollution. In contrast, the less-developed states seem more concerned about such things as racial discrimination, intervention in their internal affairs, and some aspects of human rights. Beyond this divergence of interests, however, lies the older obstacle of national sovereignty and the reluctance of states to undertake obligations that would diminish their sovereignty. Despite occasional expressions of collective outrage in the wake of offenses committed against peoples, there seems to be no significant movement in world public opinion in the direction of demanding that governments accept greater accountability to international authorities, as the creation of an international criminal court would imply. Thus, while there is a substantial body of international criminal law in existence, there are formidable obstacles to effective enforcement. For this reason, some have suggested that perhaps a more modest beginning—a court with limited jurisdiction but with capacity gradually to expand, one that might perhaps emphasize more its protective and humanitarian rather than its penal nature—ultimately would prove a more prudent course.[44]

The United States and the International Criminal Court

One of the many ironies that have characterized the debate over the U.S. ratification of the Genocide Convention is that while the U.S. negotiators who participated in the drafting process prevailed over the strong opposition of the Soviet bloc and secured a clause in Article VI on the creation of an international criminal court, conservative critics of the convention have denounced the clause with at least as much vigor as the Soviet negotiators. The clause has been an issue in the debate over ratification from the beginning, although through the years the focus of the critics' concern has changed.

Bases of U.S. Opposition to an International Criminal Court

At the earliest Senate hearings on the convention in 1950, ABA representatives expressed alarm about the implications of Article VI, suggesting that under its terms American citizens could be carried off to an international criminal court for trial on charges of genocide, or any of the acts listed in Article III of the convention, without the constitutional protections such as the right to a fair trial that they would enjoy within the United States.[45] Given the text of Article VI, it is difficult to comprehend how the ABA representatives ever reached this conclusion. In fact, their argument was probably a scare tactic more than anything else, providing another illustration of how some ABA representatives disguised political arguments against ratification in legal language. Obviously, any court would have to have a statute, and if the United States should find that statute deficient, it could decline to accept it. The matter is fundamentally a policy issue that must be dealt with in the political arena. But ABA representatives often distorted issues to advance their own policy agenda, which was to defeat ratification.

Defeating ratification was at least the *official* position of the ABA until 1976. But there was always dissent in the ranks. In fact, in the case of the criminal court clause of Article VI, Gordon Tillott, who represented the ABA Section on Comparative and International Law, which favored ratification even if the association as a whole did not, argued at the 1950 Senate hearings that the criticisms of the official representatives were "obviously fallacious." According to Tillott, "it was clearly stated in the convention" that the provision relating to the international criminal court would not be binding upon parties unless they had accepted it by a separate affirmative act.[46] Solicitor General Philip Perlman, representing the Truman administration at the 1950 Senate hearings and himself a member of the ABA, pointed out that the president had stated in his report to the Senate that no international criminal court as yet existed, and that the "consent of the United States to an agreement establishing such a tribunal would be necessary before it could be binding upon the United States."[47]

During the 1970s issues were once again raised concerning the terms of Article VI. As though reading from an old script, some critics argued that American citizens would be carried off to face trial in a hostile international criminal court. Again the supporters of the convention were on the defensive, stressing that a treaty would be necessary to create a court. At the 1970 hearings, for example, Senator William Proxmire argued:

> Mr. Chairman, some concern has been voiced that if we ratify the convention, Americans would be hailed before an international penal tribunal and tried there. There has been a great deal of confusion on this point.
>
> First, I would like to clearly point out that the international penal tribunal referred to in article VI of the convention is not yet in existence. If such a court should ever be established no American citizen could ever come within its jurisdiction unless the Senate specifically ratified a new treaty providing for this.
>
> Second, the International Court of Justice which now sits at The Hague (and is commonly known as the World Court) is given a purely interpretative function by the Genocide Convention. It will have no power to try persons accused of genocide.
>
> Third, as there is no existing international penal tribunal to try genocide cases, local courts in the territory where the crime is alleged to have occurred, whether in foreign countries or in America, will have jurisdiction to try the cases. It is as simple as that. American ratification of the Genocide Convention, furthermore, will do nothing to create a new cause of action in foreign courts.[48]

Others who testified in favor of ratification in 1970, including Ambassador Rita Hauser and Bruno Bitker, an attorney and tireless advocate of ratification within the ABA, argued along similar lines. In fact, both emphasized, like Proxmire, that the United States could only accept the jurisdiction of an international criminal court through the ratification of a treaty.[49] The critics of the convention tried to overcome this response by introducing a somewhat different argument. Senator Sam Ervin, Jr., for example, suggested that the terms of Article VI imposed on the Congress an "implied commitment" to participate in the creation of an international criminal court.[50]

So far as the Committee on Foreign Relations was concerned, the majority of its members evidently agreed with Proxmire, Hauser, and others, and believed that Ervin's argument exaggerated the impact of Article VI, as indeed it did. In its report to the Senate recommending ratification of the convention in 1970, the committee stated that "only brief reference" need be made to the part of Article VI that referred to the creation of an international criminal court because it was "a dead letter" at that time. No court existed, and should one come into existence, the United States would be able to decide then what policy it wished to pursue with regard to it. In any event, the committee was of the view that "separate action either through ratification of a treaty or enactment of a law" would be required for the United States to accept the jurisdiction of such a court.[51]

Again the argument shifted, becoming more sophisticated, at the 1971 Senate hearings. Eberhard Deutsch raised the possibility that the international criminal court contemplated in Article VI could be created by an *executive agreement*, not necessarily by a treaty.[52] In brief, Deutsch was concerned that a president might commit the United States to acceptance of the jurisdiction of an international criminal court on his own authority, avoiding congressional involvement. He even attacked the position of the U.S. drafters of the convention regarding the provisions of Article VI. His attitude was clearly expressed in response to questions raised by Senator John Sherman Cooper:

SENATOR COOPER: Another provision states that they shall be tried by such international penal tribunal which may have such jurisdiction with respect to such contracting parties which have accepted its jurisdiction.

The response of the State Department was that there is no international penal tribunal and if one should be established we wouldn't have to accept their jurisdiction. Does that follow logically?

MR. DEUTSCH: I think it is absolutely correct that we would not have to. We don't have one now, and there would be no compulsion on us to accept that jurisdiction. *But in my opinion, good faith probably would require us to do so, and further it would be done.*

You must bear in mind, as I stated, reading rather rapidly from my formal statement, that the United States representative at one of these conferences assured the other nations that it was the intention of the United States to proceed, as to itself, on its own part, to create such a tribunal, to submit plans for such a tribunal. The United States expects to have it and to participate in it. That is what was said.

Now of course they can, the United States can, change their mind, but I don't think there is the slightest question, sir, and I have been involved in this phase of international law for many years—I am approaching the 50th year of my practice of the law—and I don't think there is the slightest question that that could be done by an executive agreement without the advice and consent of the Senate.[53]

The U.S. representatives who had participated in drafting the convention had, of course, strongly supported the international criminal court clause in Article VI. In fact, as discussed in chapter 4, they were willing to delete the reference to political groups in Article II in exchange for the inclusion of a provision on the international criminal court in Article VI. Deutsch thought that the delegation had firmly expressed the determination of the United States to accept the jurisdiction of the court, and he saw this as proof that the executive authorities could not be trusted to call upon the Congress to consent to their wish to accept the jurisdiction of an international criminal court. While Deutsch conceded that the plain language of Article VI made it possible for the United States to exercise an option with regard to accepting the jurisdiction of an international criminal court, he suspected that the option might be exercised by a president acting without congressional approval. In this respect he was distorting the position of John Maktos and Ernest A. Gross, but he was not without precedent to cite in support of his suspicions. He referred to the case of the International Antidumping Code, concluded in Geneva in 1967, that had been treated as a treaty by seventeen parties other than the United States. According to Deutsch, the United States alone among the parties had treated the code as an executive agreement because some of its provisions conflicted with acts of Congress and the administration wanted to get around any difficulties with the Senate in having the code ratified.[54]

The objections Deutsch raised were important, and they became the most potent arguments surrounding Article VI during the 1980s. Deutsch effectively shifted the reason for concern over the meaning of Article VI away from the procedural technicalities of whether or not Americans would be dragged before an international court that did not afford them procedural and substantive guarantees—an argument that seemed to be dismissed by all intelligent participants in the debate—to a concern with the possibility of executive *abuse* of the treaty-making power by accepting the jurisdiction of an international criminal court through an executive agreement rather than through a treaty. It was this preoccupation with the possible abuse of power that resulted in the inclusion of the understanding regarding the international criminal court clause in the Lugar-Helms-Hatch Sovereignty Package. In 1971, however, the Committee on Foreign Relations paid relatively little attention to the issue. Rather, as discussed more fully in chapter 8, the committee was more concerned about the principles upon which domestic courts would be able to exercise jurisdiction in cases arising under the convention, and with extradition, than it was about the possibility of arbitrary executive action in accepting the jurisdiction of an international criminal court. If anything, during the 1970s the committee seemed to assume that the acceptance of the jurisdiction of an international criminal court would require congressional involvement. For that reason, at no time did it propose including either an understanding or a reservation that would require such involvement in resolutions of ratification. The committee's attitude changed fundamentally in 1985.

The U.S. Understanding Regarding the International Criminal Court

By the time serious negotiations were under way on the content of the Lugar-Helms-Hatch Sovereignty Package in 1985, it was clear that a condition relating to the international criminal court clause in Article VI of the convention would be necessary, and the understanding quoted at the beginning of this chapter, and cited again here, was adopted:

> That with regard to the reference to an international penal tribunal in Article VI of the Convention, the United States declares that it reserves the right to effect its participation in any such tribunal only by a treaty entered into specifically for that purpose with the advice and consent of the Senate.

The adoption of this understanding became absolutely essential as a result of testimony by Reagan administration officials at the 1985 hearings of the Committee on Foreign Relations.[55] At the hearings, Ralph Tarr, acting assistant attorney general, and Davis Robinson, State Department legal adviser, provided conflicting testimony on the question of whether or not the United States could adhere to a statute of an international criminal court by means of an executive agreement. It is not surprising that the question was raised, and vigorously pressed, by Senator Jesse Helms. Reciting the terms of Article VI, Helms asked: "Does the U.S. Government have any plans to accept the jurisdiction of such an international penal tribunal?"[56] To Robinson's reply that no tribunal existed and that he imagined the United States would want to "give any such proposal the most serious analysis,"[57] Helms insisted on considering a hypothetical situation: "Now, let me get hypothetical. Would the acceptance of such jurisdiction require a treaty ratified with the advice and consent of the Senate, or could we accede by executive agreement?"[58]

Robinson thought Article VI clearly contemplated a treaty, and that the United States would so interpret it.[59] Tarr was of the opinion that sound legal precedent existed to support acceptance of such a statute by executive agreement, especially if done in pursuance of congressional legislation.[60]

These conflicting views bothered Helms and other critics such as Senator Orrin Hatch. Even upon further reflection, administration spokesmen such as Robinson and Tarr could not categorically state that a treaty would be required for the United States to accept the jurisdiction of an international criminal court. They could affirm that the Reagan administration had no intentions of accepting the jurisdiction of an international criminal court by executive agreement, but they could not speak for *future* administrations.[61]

Senator Helms summarized the problem. As he saw it, once the convention was ratified a "new political dynamic may take over," and "in a changed political climate, five, ten, or even fifteen years from now, a future President might claim that the mere approval of the resolution of ratification by the Senate has given him authority, under Article V, to accede to an international penal tribunal by executive agreement, by-passing the Senate."[62] Helms claimed that there already existed precedents for such action and that the understanding would therefore put "both future Presidents and other Contracting Parties on notice that the United States will not accede to a statute or treaty for an international penal tribunal without the advice and consent of the U.S. Senate."[63]

Senator Hatch vigorously defended the understanding on the Senate floor during debate over the resolution of ratification. He had written a letter to the *New York Times* about the problem but claimed to have received no "effective reply."[64] In particular, he found the reply of Ernest A. Gross, who had represented the United States on the Sixth Committee when the convention was drafted, to the effect that "gentlemen do not do such things," ineffective. According to Hatch, the State Department had long ago "confused the nature of treaties with the nature of executive agreements."[65] The understanding was essential for that reason alone. But Hatch had an additional reason. As he stated in floor debate: "Considering that President Daniel Ortega of Nicaragua has already accused the United States of supporting genocide in Nicaragua, the consequences of such jurisdictional authority vested in an international penal court would be disastrous from the standpoint of constitutional protections and guarantees. That is why the requirement of a treaty approved by the Senate prior to any U.S. adherence to, and participation in, a penal tribunal is so important."[66]

The Use of Executive Agreements in the Conduct of Foreign Policy

Do the critics have a point? Are there reasons to be concerned that a president might use an executive agreement to accept the jurisdiction of an international criminal court? A number of studies in recent years have examined presidential use of executive agreements in the conduct of foreign policy. Much of the interest in this field dates back to the 1960s and 1970s when serious political disagreements erupted over the possibility that presidents could conclude even secret executive agreements that would bind the United States to take certain courses of action. The issue was especially controversial during the course of the Vietnam War and culminated in the adoption of the Case-Zablocki Act in 1972, which requires the U.S. secretary of state to report to the Congress on agreements other than treaties to which the United States is a party; in the case of secret agreements, they must be reported to the Senate Foreign Relations and House Foreign Affairs committees only.[67]

The use of executive agreements in the conduct of foreign policy has a history dating back to the early years of the republic, though it is only in the post-World War II period that there has been an enormous increase in the number of such agreements. According to data compiled by Lawrence Margolis, until the twentieth century, presidents concluded on the average only one executive agreement per year. In more recent years, however, presidents have concluded as many as three hundred, and sometimes more, executive agreements in a single year.[68] The agreements have covered a variety of issues, including what Margolis calls "procedural matters," that is, agreements relative to postal services, aircraft landing rights, reciprocal trade, and the like, things that make it possible for states to interact peacefully on a day-to-day basis; agreements relative to the delivery of material goods, for example, providing agricultural and technical assistance; and defense-related agreements, such as the sending of military missions and loans of military equipment.[69]

Although there is reason to doubt that the founding fathers would have favored the use of executive agreements in the conduct of foreign policy, Margolis suggests that they would almost certainly have come to accept them in view of the changed circumstances of the international system since the founding of the republic. Indeed, it would seem impractical to expect that the Senate could deal in treaty form with every issue that is presently dealt with in the form of executive agreements. The sheer number of such agreements would overwhelm it. Moreover, it is doubtful that most senators even think that they *should* have a voice in the conclusion of the vast bulk of the executive agreements, particularly those that deal with routine matters.[70] As Louis Henkin and others have pointed out, many executive agreements are adopted with prior congressional approval. In fact, Henkin divides executive agreements into two broad categories: "congressional-executive" agreements, that is, agreements that are concluded by executive action with congressional approval; and "sole" executive agreements, "international agreements contemplated by a treaty, or which [presidents] considered appropriate for implementing treaty obligations."[71] In regard to the former category, there could hardly be any doubt that the president could conclude an agreement authorized by Congress; as regards the latter category, according to Henkin, "no one seems to have questioned" the authority of presidents to make such agreements.[72] Loch Johnson, in his study titled *The Making of International Agreements: Congress Confronts the Executive*, uses a somewhat different classification scheme from that used by Henkin. He found that the use of executive agreements is widespread in important areas of foreign policy, and that "the members of Congress have been asked to give and have given an official green light to the vast majority of overseas commitments—most initiated by the executive branch."[73]

Although the Constitution does not speak of presidents concluding executive agreements, it does recognize that there can be international agreements that are not treaties. Article I, section 10, permits U.S. states to enter into "agreements" or "compacts" with other states or foreign powers with the consent of Congress. Such agreements or compacts as are entered into with foreign powers would, of course, by definition be international in nature. But the Constitution does not specifically say that presidents can conclude such agreements, or that such agreements could be made by either the U.S. states or the president without congressional approval.[74] However, as Margolis and others have pointed out, since the founding, through a succession of Supreme Court cases, executive agreements have moved from being considered provisional international arrangements to having the same legal status as treaties, including supremacy over state law. *United States* v. *Belmont* (301 U.S. 324, 1937) and *United States* v. *Pink* (315 U.S. 203, 1942) are usually considered landmark cases in this field. In these cases the Supreme Court held that international compacts and agreements that are concluded by the president on his own authority can override the public policies or law of the individual states. As with treaties, however, executive agreements can be overridden by subsequent acts of Congress. Moreover, since treaties could be declared unconstitutional (though none has yet been), the same presumably applies to executive agreements. In *Reid* v. *Covert* (354 U.S. 1, 1957), the Court ruled that a civilian abroad could not be deprived of her right to a jury trial as recognized by the U.S. Constitution through an executive agreement with a foreign power. Nonetheless, the Supreme Court has not provided all the answers with regard to the limitations on presidential power regarding the conclusion of executive agreements, and scholars such as Henkin and

Margolis argue that, for this reason, in practice the principal restraint on the use and abuse of executive agreements is likely to have to come from Congress.[75]

Be that as it may, it does not really seem to be the quantity of executive agreements that has given rise to problems. It is even arguable that it is not the constitutional issue of presidents concluding executive agreements without going through the constitutionally prescribed process for the ratification of treaties that has given rise to problems. Rather, it is the quality of the agreements themselves, and the potential for abuse in the exercise of executive power in this field, that have led some to question whether or not presidents can be trusted to consult with the Senate in all cases in which it would seem appropriate to do so. Martin Goldstein quotes former senator and chairman of the Committee on Foreign Relations William Fulbright (D., Arkansas) as once lamenting: "The Senate is asked to convene solemnly to approve by a two-thirds vote a treaty to preserve cultural artifacts in a friendly neighboring country. At the same time, the chief executive is moving military men and material around the globe like so many pawns in a chess game."[76]

The quotation is instructive, even if it exaggerates the situation at hand, for it suggests that the issue at stake here really cuts across the political spectrum. Fulbright would probably have had little in common politically with senators such as Helms and Hatch. Yet he expressed the same sort of concern about how presidents might use executive agreements for the most important matters and treaties for relatively trivial ones. On this issue, both sides have a point. As Margolis has suggested, "those relatively rare occasions when presidents do use executive agreements just to avoid the Senate and its treaty process are often, as one might suspect, very significant agreements." He cites as an example the U.S.-British exchange of naval destroyers for bases in the Caribbean during World War II that facilitated American involvement in the war.[77]

The Effects of the U.S. Understanding

Returning specifically to the international criminal court contemplated under Article VI of the Genocide Convention, we can see that what senators such as Helms and Hatch were concerned about was the possibility that a president—a *future president*, as Helms put it—would abuse executive power and accept the jurisdiction of a court without Senate approval. Of course, neither Helms nor Hatch would ever likely vote to approve even a treaty that would achieve the same objective. Nonetheless, they were determined to ensure that no president could try to accept the jurisdiction of an international criminal court on his own authority. Accordingly, they pressed to include an understanding pertaining to Article VI in the resolution of ratification for the convention. The Committee on Foreign Relations followed through on this, and in its 1985 report to the Senate indicated that "accession [to a statute of an international criminal court] by an executive agreement would be barred" by its proposed understanding.[78]

Despite the committee's conviction, it is doubtful that the understanding could be imposed on a future administration. This doubt was expressed even by some members of the committee, who opposed the understanding and stated that in their "view it had no more binding authority than a 'sense of the Senate' resolution."[79] The extensive debate record on this issue, however, and the extraordinary lengths to which the critics of the convention went to set down all of the Senate's intentions in giving approval of the treaty, would provide significant evidence upon which to build substantial *political* opposition to any president who might attempt to accept the jurisdiction of a court by executive agreement. There are indications that Helms had this in mind in pressing for answers to his questions at the hearings. At the 1985 hearings, for example, in the midst of Robinson's and Tarr's conflicting testimony on whether or not a president could accept the jurisdiction of an international criminal court by executive agreement, Helms said, "I have just one final question. Do you or do you not suggest that whatever position you take here, making legislative history as you have, is that binding on any future administration?"[80]

The responses to the question were confused, though it is clear that faced with defeat on the question of ratification, Helms wanted to build up the most impressive "legislative history" on the convention that he could get. The Reagan administration put up token opposition to a reservation to Article VI on the ground that one was not necessary, that in the event an international criminal court were created the United States could study the policy options available to it at that time and decide what to do.[81] But Helms got both the understanding he wanted and the abundant record of legislative history, including the confusion and inconclusive debates. Thus, even if the understanding should prove to have no legal significance, its terms, combined with its legislative history, could have substantial political significance.

Chapter 8 Jurisdiction of Domestic Courts and Extradition

I studied the legislative history at the U.N., and other countries were very much concerned about this, and the legislative history is very clear that concurrent jurisdiction is reserved, we still have the right to try our own nationals, and the legal committee acquiesced in that, and appropriately so, so that we really don't have to worry about that in light of the legislative history and our implementing legislation. And I don't think there will be a peep about this since nearly all countries share the view that they would have the right to try their own nationals in their own courts within constitutional limits for acts committed abroad.—Arthur Goldberg, 1971 Senate hearings

Besides contemplating the creation of an international criminal court, Article VI of the Genocide Convention addresses the issue of the conditions under which domestic courts and tribunals can exercise jurisdiction in cases of genocide or any of the acts enumerated in Article III. Specifically, Article VI states that persons may be tried "by a competent tribunal of the State in the territory of which the act was committed." In other words, the clause incorporates into the convention what is known in international law as the territorial principle of jurisdiction. The notion that the courts of a state can exercise jurisdiction when crimes are committed within the territory of that state is accepted by all states, including the United States. Consequently, one might think that the endorsement of the principle in Article VI would be readily acceptable to the United States. Yet, as we shall see in this chapter, the fact that Article VI singles out only the territorial principle of jurisdiction, and is silent on alternative principles, became an important factor in the debate over ratification of the convention. The issue became especially important beginning in the early 1970s in the light of Article VII, which states that the parties to the convention agree that genocide shall not be considered a "political" crime for purposes of extradition, and they "pledge themselves" to grant extradition "in accordance with their laws and treaties in force."

During the 1970s many critics of the convention questioned whether or not the combined effects of Articles VI and VII would be to compel the United States to extradite Americans—including, perhaps, U.S. soldiers who had fought in Vietnam—to stand trial on charges of genocide abroad. By the time the Lugar-Helms-Hatch Sovereignty Package was being fashioned in 1985, the controversy over both articles had become so intense that it was obvious that a condition regarding both the territorial principle and extradition would be necessary. That condition is in the form of an understanding, and it states:

> That the pledge to grant extradition in accordance with a state's laws and treaties in force found in Article VII extends only to acts which are criminal under the laws of both the requesting and requested state and nothing in Article VI affects the right of any state to bring to trial before its own tribunals any of its nationals for acts committed outside a state.[1]

In this chapter we shall explore the rationale and implications of this understanding. The fact that it was included in the Sovereignty Package suggests that Articles VI and VII address significant policy issues that the United States believed were in need of clarification. But specifically why was the understanding considered necessary? What arguments were advanced for and against its adoption, and how cogent were they? What are the implications of the understanding? Would other parties to the convention have any bases on which to object to the understanding, or is it basically unobjectionable? As a matter of policy, is the understanding desirable?

Principles of Jurisdiction of Domestic Courts

Part of the U.S. understanding quoted above states that Article VI does not preclude any state from trying its own nationals for committing genocide or any of the acts enumerated in Article III, even when they commit those acts abroad. The understanding therefore implies that since the drafters expressly mentioned only the territorial principle of jurisdiction in Article VI, they intended to recognize only that principle, and that an understanding was necessary to indicate that the United States could claim the right to try its own nationals if they should commit the acts abroad. But even though the drafters settled upon the territorial principle of jurisdiction, they were surely aware of other principles, and indeed they discussed them during various stages of the drafting process. The records of the Sixth Committee of the General Assembly in particular make this clear. The territorial principle was especially attractive to the delegates precisely because it was so widely accepted by states. However, some delegates believed that the courts of states in which genocide occurred would not be likely to try the offenders, especially if they were government officials. As we discussed in chapter 7, this was the main reason why some delegates believed that it would be necessary to create an international criminal court. It was also the reason why some believed that another principle or principles of jurisdiction of domestic courts should be recognized under the terms of Article VI.[2] The question was, what should those principles be? When the drafters turned to a discussion of these other principles, they found it very difficult to arrive at a consensus.

Alternative Principles of Jurisdiction

One of the main questions discussed by the drafters in connection with the principles of jurisdiction of domestic courts was whether or not a party to the convention should be able to try its *own nationals* for committing genocide or any of the acts enumerated in Article III of the convention *even when those acts were committed abroad.* This is precisely the issue that the U.S. understanding addresses. It was also a matter of great concern to a large number of delegates in the Sixth Committee when the convention was drafted. The issue was raised most pointedly by an Indian delegate, who wondered if the effect of mentioning only the territorial principle in Article VI might be interpreted as eliminating the possibility that trials could be conducted on the basis of the nationality of the offender, that is, on the basis of the *nationality principle.*[3] This was an especially important issue because Article VII of the convention states that the parties will not consider genocide a "political" crime for purposes of extradition, and indeed seems to encourage the extradition of offenders. Be that as it may, the Indian delegate thought that the nationality principle should be recognized, and to achieve that end he proposed the addition of a paragraph to Article VI.[4] It stated that "nothing in this article shall affect the right of any State to bring to trial before its own tribunals any of its nationals for acts committed outside the State."[5]

Most delegates seemed to agree with the idea expressed in this proposed paragraph, so it seems odd that the Sixth Committee did not adopt an amendment to Article VI in order to formally recognize the validity of the nationality principle. But the discussion of the article as a whole ranged over several controversial topics, including the clause on the creation of an international criminal court and other principles of jurisdiction, to which we shall return in a moment. Therefore, if the drafters had given serious consideration to adopting the Indian amendment, they might have been faced with numerous other amendments that also had merit but were not supported by the overwhelming majority. For this reason a proposal to amend Article VI was not well received, and even the Indian representative came to think that it would suffice to recognize the nationality principle by the inclusion of a statement in the Sixth Committee's report to the General Assembly on the negotiations over the terms of the convention as a whole. The statement would be to the effect that "none of the provisions of article VI affected the right of any State to bring any of its nationals to trial before its own courts for acts committed outside its territory."[6] There were no objections to this proposal, and the chair ordered it included in the report.[7]

But the Indian proposal, though not rejected by anyone, was not accepted by everyone as the definitive statement on the matter of jurisdiction because it meant that under Article VI the courts of states could exercise jurisdiction under two principles—the territorial and the nationality principles—only one of which was expressly recognized. The Swedish representative on the Sixth Committee argued that it should be possible under Article VI for a state to try *aliens who commit genocide against its own nationals abroad*, provided that the offenders were apprehended within the home state of the victims. The Swedish representative felt that this principle, the so-called *passive personality principle*, could be recognized by amending the terms of the Indian statement to include the following: "Furthermore, article VI should not be interpreted as depriving a State of jurisdiction in the case of crimes committed against its nationals outside national territory."[8]

It was precisely this kind of proposal that revealed the difficulties the drafters would have encountered had they been willing to seriously entertain amendments to the provisions of Article VI that pertained to the jurisdiction of domestic courts. The representatives of several states, especially the United States, took a strong stand against the Swedish proposal on the ground that the Sixth Committee did not have any obligation to "reconcile conflicts of law to codify international law in the matter."[9] While this formal objection gave the impression that the disagreement was legal in nature, in fact it reflected serious policy differences—the U.S. representative simply did not want to recognize the passive personality principle, at least not at that time. In general, Western states have had reservations about the principle. As international legal scholars have noted, many states are reluctant to recognize the principle out of fear that their own nationals might be subjected to arbitrary charges of having committed crimes against nationals of another state abroad.[10] There are some recent indications that views on this issue are changing, especially in the light of international terrorism, and we shall return to this point later. For the moment, it should be noted that even in 1948 not everyone was hostile to the Swedish proposal. In fact, some representatives, such as those of Egypt and Syria, supported it and offered perfecting amendments that the Swedish representative accepted.[11] As in many other instances when the drafters faced strong sentiments on both sides of an issue, they worked out a compromise that embraced the essential elements of the different viewpoints. That compromise was to revise the Indian statement for inclusion in the Sixth Committee report as follows: "The first part of Article VI contemplates the obligation of the State in whose territory acts of genocide have been committed. Thus, *in particular*, it does not affect the right of any State to bring to trial before its own tribunals any of its nationals for acts committed outside the State."[12]

Ordinarily, this statement might be understood to mean that the drafters of the Genocide Convention thought that Article VI, while expressly recognizing the territorial principle of jurisdiction, did not prohibit states from bringing to trial their own nationals for genocidal acts they commit abroad. But in the light of the background discussion that preceded the adoption of this statement, it means more than that. The insertion of the words "in particular" in the statement made it acceptable to the Swedish representative.[13] Hence, the statement means that Article VI does not rule out the application of *other* principles of jurisdiction—in addition to the nationality principle—in suppressing genocide. But does the statement have any special legal significance? On this matter there is some doubt. As the representatives on the Sixth Committee were well aware, if a body such as the ICJ were ever asked to provide an authoritative interpretation of what Article VI says, it would look first to the text of the article, and only if it were to find the text lacking would it look elsewhere, including to the legislative history of the convention, for guidance in interpreting it. Moreover, as Nicodeme Ruhashyankiko, a rapporteur for a UN study of the convention during the 1970s, pointed out, the clarifying statement that was inserted in the report of the Sixth Committee does not have "an inherent interpretative value different from that of the other preparatory work of the Convention."[14]

The fourth, and last, principle of jurisdiction that the drafters discussed was the *universality principle.* Given the subject matter of the convention, one might think that the drafters would have expressly recognized this principle. As described by Buergenthal and Maier, the universality principle "recognizes that certain activities, universally dangerous to states and their subjects, require authority in all community members to punish such acts wherever they may occur, *even absent a link between the state and the parties or the acts in question.*"[15] Few crimes have generally been thought to be so offensive as to lead to the application of the universality principle in suppressing them; piracy on the high seas is an example. But there are others, and since World War II some have argued that crimes such as genocide, crimes against humanity, aircraft hijacking, some aspects of terrorism, and acts against internationally protected persons should also be subject to universal suppression. In fact, specialized multilateral conventions have been concluded on some of these subjects in recent years.[16]

In the case of the Genocide Convention, however, the principle of universal jurisdiction actually enjoyed very little support. The outcome on the issue would have been different if the experts who participated in preparing the UN Secretariat's draft convention had prevailed. An article in the draft titled "Universal Enforcement of Municipal Law" stated: "The High Contracting Parties pledge themselves to punish any offender under this Convention within any territory under their jurisdiction, irrespective of the nationality of the offender or of the place where the offense has been committed."[17] But this article, along with others proposed by the Secretariat, was rejected for political reasons. As noted in chapter 2, the Ad Hoc Committee of the ECOSOC had stripped the Secretariat's draft of many of its most important provisions and had retained only some of its more "technical" ones. Later, representatives on the ECOSOC and on the Sixth Committee of the General Assembly expressed the opinion that the Secretariat's draft was flawed from the beginning because it was prepared by "experts," not by the representatives of states who would be more attuned to "political realities."

Even if the principle of universal jurisdiction had been supported by a large number of representatives on the Sixth Committee, its chances of being included in the convention were extremely remote in view of the fact that both the United States and the Soviet Union were opposed to it. In fact, this was one of the few issues of any consequence on which the two powers agreed, even in the Ad Hoc Committee of the ECOSOC.[18] Those who favored recognizing the principle argued that the national courts of states could not be relied upon to bring to justice the perpetrators of genocide because the state authorities would most likely be implicated in the acts. Hence, they believed that it was necessary to recognize that the perpetrators could be tried by the courts of *any* state. The U.S. and Soviet representatives, however, defended national sovereignty, asserting that the principle of universal suppression could lead "national courts to judge the acts of foreign Governments," possibly resulting in "dangerous international tension."[19] These seemed like strange positions for states that had only recently participated in the international military tribunals in Nuremberg and Tokyo. Nonetheless, their joint opposition to the principle of universal suppression would have been extremely difficult, if not impossible, to overcome during the negotiations on Article VI even if a large number of states had supported the principle. But it had relatively little support anyway. The Sixth Committee gave some consideration to a system proposed by the U.S. representative in which the courts of other states could try offenders if the courts of the state in which the crime was committed did not do so.[20] In general, however, most members of the committee were strongly in favor of recognizing the territorial principle of jurisdiction. Their inability to come to a broad-based agreement on any other principle resulted in the adoption of Article VI and the clarifying statement, which did not rule out the application of other principles, though the statement was apparently not intended as an endorsement of the universality principle.

The passage of time since the convention was adopted has not resulted in any appreciable change of attitude toward the principle of universal suppression of acts of genocide or any of the acts enumerated in Article III. To be sure, the issue could be resolved by any state in its own domestic implementing legislation, and we shall return to this point below. But from the standpoint of officially recognizing the principle for violations of the convention, there has been no significant change in attitude. The question of whether or not a protocol to the convention recognizing the principle should be adopted was put to states in a UN survey conducted in the 1970s. A few governments replied in favor of a protocol, including Bulgaria, the Netherlands, Romania, and Ecuador.[21] Canada favored recognition of the principle of universal jurisdiction as a transitional measure on the way to establishing an international criminal court.[22] But other states either declined to respond to the part of the survey that addressed the issue or opposed the adoption of a protocol. Even some well-known international nongovernmental organizations opposed the idea. The International Association of Penal Law, for example, took the position that the time for the adoption of a protocol was not "opportune." The International Commission of Jurists, a human rights nongovernmental international organization, expressed reservations to a protocol on the ground that "such proceedings would be likely to be, or be regarded as being, politically motivated."[23] A July 1985 revision and updating of the 1970 report, conducted by Ben

Whitaker, provided no evidence of any increase in support for officially recognizing the principle of universal jurisdiction under the terms of the convention. However, Whitaker himself urged either the creation of an international criminal court or the recognition of the principle of universal jurisdiction, arguing that failure to adopt either option would be "indefensible."[24]

The practice of parties to the convention in making reservations to it also suggests that, if anything, they want to preserve the authority of their own courts to try persons for violations of the convention, especially when the acts are committed within their own territory. Very few parties have seen a need to make a reservation concerning Article VI, but some have done so and stressed the importance of the territorial principle. Algeria, for example, upon ratification in 1963, declared that "no provision of article VI . . . shall be interpreted as depriving its tribunals of jurisdiction in cases of genocide . . . which have been committed in its territory or as conferring such jurisdiction on foreign tribunals."[25] Burma, in 1956, made a reservation that nothing in Article VI "shall be construed as depriving the Courts and Tribunals of the Union of jurisdiction or of giving foreign courts and tribunals jurisdiction over any cases of genocide or any of the other acts enumerated in article III committed within the Union territory."[26] Morocco, in 1958, added a reservation to Article VI stating that "the Government of His Majesty the King considers that Moroccan courts and tribunals alone have jurisdiction with respect to acts of genocide committed within the territory of the Kingdom of Morocco."[27] The Philippines, too, in 1950, made a similar reservation.[28] A few parties, Brazil and Greece, for example, have objected to the reservations, but they have not made an issue of them.[29]

U.S. Critics and the Nationality Principle

At the 1950 Senate hearings on the Genocide Convention, most of the criticism of Article VI focused on the clause relating to the creation of an international criminal court. In fact, no one seemed concerned about the matter of jurisdictional principles regarding domestic courts. However, beginning at the 1970 hearings, many critics focused on the issue, for several reasons. As discussed in chapter 5, the United States was involved in the Vietnam War, and some critics were concerned about the fact that Article I of the convention established that genocide was a crime under international law whether committed in times of peace or war. Since Article VI expressly recognized the territorial principle of jurisdiction, critics became alarmed that ratification of the convention would bestow legitimacy on trials of American soldiers that might be conducted by North Vietnamese authorities. The issue became of even greater concern when the terms of Article VII regarding extradition were taken into account.

In fact, judging from the amount of time devoted to it, the clause relating to jurisdictional principles in Article VI was one of the most important issues at the 1970 hearings. Senator John Sherman Cooper was one of the most persistent in raising questions about the implications of the article. Cooper was concerned that according to the plain meaning of Article VI, trials of persons accused of violating the convention would be conducted in the state in whose territory the acts were committed, and this raised the possibility that American soldiers could be tried in North Vietnam.[30] The same would be true, of course, in any other circumstances in which Americans committed genocide abroad. In fact, the same would be true for any crime. As Senator William Proxmire argued at the 1970 hearings:

> Some have expressed the fear that if America became a party to this treaty American citizens could be tried in foreign courts on charges of genocide. This is clearly specious. Right now with no treaty in force, an American citizen in the physical territory and/or control of a foreign nation can be charged and tried for any offense from shoplifting, to robbery, to espionage, to murder, even to genocide. The Genocide Treaty does not alter this, and does not expand the jurisdiction of foreign courts in any way whatsoever.[31]

Numerous other witnesses who testified in favor of ratification at the 1970 hearings made the same point. Consider, for example, the following exchange between Senator Frank Church and William Rehnquist, testifying as assistant attorney general during the Nixon administration:

> SENATOR CHURCH: In regard to the argument that if we become a party to the convention, U.S. citizens can be tried abroad without the constitutional guarantees of trial by jury and other safeguards, is this not the case now if our citizens commit crimes abroad?
>
> MR. REHNQUIST: Yes. My understanding of the state of international law in that regard is that if a U.S. citizen commits a crime under Bulgarian law in Bulgaria there is nothing in the world the United States can do to prevent him from being tried by the Bulgarian courts.[32]

Rehnquist, Proxmire, and others who testified in favor of ratification in 1970 recalled the legislative history of Article VI, particularly the Indian/Swedish statement that had been included in the report of the Sixth Committee to the General Assembly, and argued that both the territorial and nationality principles of jurisdiction were consistent with the terms of Article VI.[33] From their viewpoint, then, *should American soldiers who had returned to the United States* be charged with having committed genocide while they were in Vietnam, the United States would be able to claim jurisdiction for its own courts to conduct trials if necessary. But Senator Cooper was not satisfied, and he expressed displeasure with what he perceived as a tendency on the part of proponents of ratification to defend the convention but then to say that the United States could interpret its provisions in ways that were at variance with their plain meaning.[34] To Cooper, Article VI expressly recognized *only* the territorial principle of jurisdiction; the witnesses were saying that it also recognized the nationality principle, even if not expressly. The witnesses also maintained that in some instances it was to be expected that *concurrent jurisdiction* could be claimed, especially when American nationals committed acts abroad and then returned to the United States before being arrested and brought to trial.[35] This did not seem unusual to Rehnquist, for example, who argued that concurrent jurisdiction could be claimed within the United States as well; that is, both federal and state courts might be able to try persons accused of genocide because there was nothing in the convention that would preclude a state of the United States adopting legislation against genocide.[36] The Proxmire Act in fact expressly provides that the federal law shall not be "construed as precluding the application of State or local laws" on genocide.[37] The possibility of concurrent jurisdiction came up again in connection with the discussion of extradition under the terms of Article VII.

The U.S. Understanding and the Nationality Principle

Although the exchange of views on jurisdictional principles was prolonged and intense at the 1970 hearings, in its report to the Senate the Committee on Foreign Relations professed not to be unduly alarmed about the substance and implications of Article VI. Nonetheless, in another of its concessions to the critics of the convention, the committee recommended ratification subject to an understanding regarding jurisdictional principles that stated:

> That the United States Government understands and construes Article VI of the Convention in accordance with the agreed language of the Report of the Legal Committee of the United Nations General Assembly that nothing in Article VI shall affect the right of any State to bring to trial

before its own tribunals any of its nationals for acts committed outside the State.[38]

The wording of this understanding was suggested by the Justice Department in a memorandum supplied by Rehnquist in response to questions raised by Senator Jacob Javits during the hearings.[39] Javits was a strong proponent of ratification, and he was interested in an understanding as a way of overcoming the objections of the critics. Rehnquist was not convinced that such an understanding was necessary, but he recommended the text that was adopted to be used "if a statement" on the subject was "thought necessary."[40] The committee thought a statement was necessary for political reasons. There were numerous and powerful opponents of ratification of the convention, including the ABA and outspoken critics like Senator Sam Ervin, Jr. Prudence dictated that some compromise on the matter was necessary—that an understanding regarding principles of jurisdiction was a price that had to be paid to secure ratification, especially in view of the deep-seated suspicions of critics such as Ervin that ratification would open the way for trials of American soldiers in Vietnam. For all practical purposes, then, the issue for the committee was not whether or not it would recommend ratification subject to an understanding regarding jurisdictional principles, but what the substance of that understanding would be.

As the text of the understanding that the committee chose to propose during the 1970s makes clear, Rehnquist was sensitive to the difference between a reservation and an understanding, and he was determined to draft a "pure" understanding. He pointed out, however, that another party might object to the understanding, that "as a practical matter, the description that either the Senate or the Executive gives to a declaration is not conclusive."[41] Although objections could have been forthcoming, other parties to the convention would have been hard-pressed to find good reasons for objecting to Rehnquist's understanding. As indicated earlier, other parties already seemed to understand that Article VI does not prevent them from claiming jurisdiction for their own courts to try cases of genocide involving their own nationals, though a few states have seen a need to make a reservation to this effect. Nonetheless, the U.S. understanding during the 1970s simply emphasized that it understood Article VI in the same way that the drafters had indicated they understood it in their report to the General Assembly. If anything, the understanding advanced an even *narrower* interpretation of Article VI than the drafters themselves had assumed, which, as we have seen, was that the article did not exclude the application of principles *other* than the territorial principle, presumably including the nationality *and* passive personality principles.

The understanding drafted by Rehnquist became a permanent fixture of the proposed U.S. resolutions of ratification during the 1970s. It was also included in the resolution that was proposed in 1984. By the time the Lugar-Helms-Hatch Sovereignty Package was adopted in 1986, it was obvious that the understanding would not be discarded. In fact, it was merely revised to address as well the related question of extradition (discussed below). The understanding states in part that "nothing in Article VI affects the right of any state to bring to trial before its own tribunals any of its nationals for acts committed outside a state."[42]

This understanding reflects, as its predecessor did, the concern of critics of the convention that the phrasing of Article VI might lead to situations in which Americans would be tried abroad under circumstances that the U.S. government would find objectionable. The problem was perceived to be more serious in view of the extradition provisions of Article VII, which give rise to the possibility that Americans might be extradited to stand trial in hostile foreign courts. The critics wanted to prevent that from occurring. But their obsession with this objective led them to reject a broader, and arguably better, understanding of Article VI. For the same reasons given in connection with our discussion of the Rehnquist version of the understanding, other parties to the convention would seem to have no grounds on which to object to the U.S. understanding regarding the nationality principle of jurisdiction. By this understanding the United States is actually adhering to a *narrow* construction of Article VI. And the implementing legislation, the Proxmire Act, was drafted in such a way as to reiterate this narrow construction. It states that *whoever* commits certain acts within the United States (the territorial principle) or is a national of the United States (the nationality principle) can be tried and punished under U.S. law; the federal law does not, of course, preclude the application of state or local law on the same subject.[43]

The U.S. approach to this subject is disappointing to those who have argued that a more aggressive approach to matters of international criminal law is desirable. In fact, during the debate over ratification, some witnesses expressed the opinion that the United States should consider incorporating the principle of universal suppression of genocide in its implementing legislation. The subject came up especially in connection with the discussion of the relationship between Articles VI and VII. John Murphy, for example, when testifying before the Subcommittee on the Constitution of the Senate Committee on the Judiciary in February 1985, suggested that the

United States consider making it clear that it did not understand the convention as precluding "the United States from trying any individual regardless of nationality, for genocide under its law."[44] He argued that this "would be in keeping with the idea that genocide is a crime against the world community, the same as piracy." It would surely not have been unprecedented for the United States to adopt this principle, for, as Murphy pointed out, the "antiterrorist conventions, such as the conventions against aircraft hijackings or sabotage, provide for the extradite or prosecute approach to [those] crimes." Hence, under those conventions "the state where the individual has been apprehended has its choice. It can either extradite that person back to where the crime was committed, or it can assert jurisdiction over that person on the ground the crime is subject to the jurisdiction of any state that apprehends the alleged offender." To Murphy, it would have "made sense to apply this approach to genocide."[45]

Murphy took up the case again when testifying before the Senate Committee on the Judiciary when it was considering the Proxmire Act in February 1988. Appearing jointly with Joseph Griffin to represent the ABA, Murphy provided cogent arguments in favor of broadening the scope of the act. As a recognized expert on the law of terrorism and chair of the ABA's Subcommittee on United Nations Activity, he was most concerned about the "exceedingly narrow" scope of coverage of the act then in draft form; that is, that it covered "only genocide that occur[red] in the United States or genocide that occur[red] abroad committed by a U.S. national." According to Murphy:

> The problem with this is that it is highly unlikely that genocide is going to be committed in the United States. It is also highly unlikely that Americans are going to be committing genocide abroad. The more likely prospect is that persons other than U.S. nationals are going to be committing genocide abroad. And one can envisage a situation where such an individual might come to the United States and be apprehended.
>
> Under the legislation, as currently drafted, the United States would have no jurisdiction to prosecute such an individual for the crime of genocide. And it would, of course, be very uncertain as to whether anybody would seek extradition of such an individual in order to prosecute him.[46]

Murphy and Griffin urged the Judiciary Committee to revise the draft of the Proxmire Act to take these issues into account. As Murphy put it, it "would seem unfortunate for U.S. jurisdiction to be so narrow in scope as to be dysfunctional with respect to prosecuting and punishing this crime."[47]

He and Griffin argued for language that had been used in a 1970s version of draft implementing legislation to the effect that "whoever, being a national of the United States or otherwise under or within the jurisdiction of the United States," commits genocide could be tried in U.S. courts. They believed that this language "more clearly state[ed] the interest of the United States in asserting jurisdiction over those, for instance, from another country who may be found in the U.S." than did the language of the act the Judiciary Committee was considering.[48]

But the Judiciary Committee went ahead and reported out the Proxmire Act with the "exceedingly narrow" and "dysfunctional" provisions that Murphy had argued against. Murphy had hoped that once the United States ratified the convention it would "actively pursue those individuals and, indeed, those countries that engage in genocide." In this connection, he suggested that a "variety of means," including recourse to the ICJ, the Security Council, and the General Assembly, would be available to the United States.[49] However, in the presence of members of the Judiciary Committee such as Senators Strom Thurmond and Charles Grassley, who had voted against even the Lugar-Helms-Hatch Sovereignty Package and were now preoccupied with ensuring that the Proxmire Act "closely track"—as Grassley put it—the treaty language and the Sovereignty Package,[50] his ideas were not likely to be widely accepted. The opponents of ratification had long ago come to dominate the debate, and in the end they determined the conditions of ratification. They were now going to determine the conditions of the convention's enforcement, at least under U.S. law. Far from doing anything that might strengthen the convention or contribute to its more effective enforcement, their objective was to weaken it and undermine its effective enforcement. While some revisions of the draft legislation were made, mostly to follow through on the language of the Sovereignty Package, the Proxmire Act remained anchored in the territorial and nationality principles so far as the exercise of jurisdiction of courts in the United States is concerned.

Extradition under the Convention

The understanding in the Lugar-Helms-Hatch Sovereignty Package that relates to the principles of jurisdiction of domestic courts also concerns the matter of extradition that is addressed in Article VII of the Genocide Convention. The United States had already concluded a large network of bilateral extradition treaties with countries throughout the world, so it is obvious that well-established law and practice on the matter of extradition already existed. Why, then, was it believed necessary to include an understanding in the Sovereignty Package regarding the matter? Let us approach this question by looking first to the terms of Article VII and the considerations that led the drafters of the convention to adopt it. Article VII states:

> Genocide and the other acts enumerated in Article III shall not be considered as political crimes for the purpose of extradition.
>
> The Contracting Parties pledge themselves in such cases to grant extradition in accordance with their laws and treaties in force.

The drafters of the convention had relatively little difficulty with the principle affirmed in the first paragraph of Article VII. It was discussed extensively in the Ad Hoc Committee of the ECOSOC[51] and in the Sixth Committee of the General Assembly,[52] but it was not controversial. Indeed, everyone seemed to agree with the British representative on the Sixth Committee that the crime of genocide is "inherently political," and that this made the adoption of Article VII essential so that it would be clear to all concerned that persons who committed genocide, or any of the acts enumerated in Article III, could not avoid extradition by pleading that their actions were political in nature.[53] Many states do not extradite persons accused of political crimes. In fact, political crimes are commonly excluded from the ambit of extradition treaties. Determining precisely what criteria should be applied in distinguishing political crimes from other crimes has, of course, given rise to serious disagreements completely outside the framework of the Genocide Convention. These disagreements need not concern us here. What is important is that, for the purposes of the Genocide Convention, the commission of genocide does not fall within the category of political crimes, however defined, and it is therefore an extraditable offense. The drafters of the convention believed it was important to make this point clear and unequivocal.

But while they agreed on the principle affirmed in the first paragraph of Article VII, they had some difficulty reaching agreement on precisely how to frame the second paragraph. What obligations regarding extradition should the parties assume by ratifying the convention? Should they be obliged to grant extradition in all cases? Or should they be able to exercise some discretion in making such decisions? These questions were important, and several formulas were put forth to resolve them. The draft of Article VII prepared by the UN Secretariat, for example, stated that the parties to the convention "pledged themselves to grant extradition in cases of genocide,"[54] implying that there would be no exceptions and that extradition would have to be granted. This formula, however, was unacceptable to most members of the Sixth Committee. It is clear from their discussions of Article VII that they wanted to maximize the amount of discretion that the parties would be able to exercise in reaching decisions on extradition. In the main, they wanted to harmonize the provisions of the convention with their own laws, not the other way around. Illustrative of this attitude was the argument of Ernest A. Gross, the U.S. representative on the committee, to the effect that "it would not be possible" to "surrender a person accused of a crime not already extraditable" under existing U.S. law, and that any new law could not have retroactive effect.[55] The United States wanted to avoid any great inconsistencies between its own law and the terms of the convention and thus would not have been able to accept the kind of statement on extradition that had been recommended by the Secretariat.

Other important issues surfaced during the debates in the Sixth Committee. Should parties be obliged to extradite their own nationals? Should those parties that extradite only if they have already concluded an extradition treaty with the requesting state be obliged to conclude a new treaty if the existing one does not already cover genocide?[56] The drafters recognized that most states had already developed practices regarding these issues, and that they would probably be reluctant to change those practices in order to ratify the convention. This is why the second paragraph of Article VII permits substantial discretion to the parties by stating that they "pledge themselves . . . to grant extradition in accordance with their laws and treaties in force." Some drafters assumed that this provision meant that states that do not extradite their own nationals would be under no obligation to do so under Article VII; some also assumed that it did not impose upon the parties a formal obligation to conclude new extradition treaties or amend existing treaties to cover genocide.[57]

Whatever Article VII was intended to accomplish, and whatever the plain meaning of its words, there are some indications that it has not worked as well as the drafters hoped. The government of the Federal Republic of Germany, in response to a United Nations survey on the subject, indicated that the problem with Article VII lies not in its terms but in enforcing it, because while it says that "genocide does not count as a political crime in terms of extradition law," requests "for extradition for racially motivated killings during the Nazi era have in several cases been rejected on the ground that the acts in question constituted political crimes."[58] According to the Federal Republic's government, it could "only be assumed that the countries concerned feel entitled on the strength of Article VII (2) of the Convention to refuse such requests because the extradition obligation is, in their view, subject to national law, which may place a special interpretation on the concept of a political crime." The German government felt, quite correctly it would seem, that "the approach is questionable considering the unequivocal wording of Article VII (1) of the Convention."[59]

The Impact of Article VII on U.S. Extradition Treaties and Policy

The terms of Article VII did not attract much attention in the United States until the early 1970s. At hearings on the convention in 1970 and 1971, members of the Committee on Foreign Relations questioned Nixon administration spokesmen and others about various implications of the article. One of their main concerns was whether or not Article VII would require the United States either to amend existing extradition treaties if they did not cover genocide or to conclude new treaties. Although the drafters did not seem to think that Article VII would require either course of action, some critics of the convention in the United States wondered whether it would. It was as though some critics suspected that Article VII itself constituted an extradition treaty, and that if it did not constitute such a treaty in itself, it required the negotiation of new treaties, or the amendment of existing treaties, to cover genocide. Senator Sam Ervin, Jr., was one of the leading opponents of ratification to raise these issues. At the 1970 hearings he conceded that ratification of the convention would not nullify or alter existing U.S. extradition treaties, but he maintained that, as a whole, it would have an impact on extradition law and practice. Senator Frank Church elicited this response from Ervin on these issues:

SENATOR CHURCH: As I recall, both the State Department witness and the Justice Department witness were in agreement that our obligation to extradite under the treaty is limited by the treaty's terms only to those countries with which we have established extradition treaties.

SENATOR ERVIN: That is true about the immediate extradition. But under Article V we have contracted to enact the necessary legislation to give effect to the provisions of the convention, and the convention [in Article VI] provides that a man is to be tried in the court of the nation in whose territory the alleged act of genocide occurred. So if we don't have a treaty now we are obligated to pass a law to provide for delivering him over to that nation. And neither the State Department with assistance of the Department of Justice can erase that provision in the treaty or destroy its plain meaning.[60]

The State and Justice department officials Ervin was criticizing were George Aldrich and William Rehnquist. Clearly, Aldrich read the "plain meaning" of Article VII differently from Ervin:

SENATOR CHURCH: Would this convention, if ratified, impose an obligation on the United States to enter into extradition treaties with all of the signatories to this convention?

MR. ALDRICH: No, Mr. Chairman, it would not. The convention clearly states that extradition shall be in accordance with the laws and treaties in force. The conclusion of extradition treaties is a discretionary matter between the States concerned, and we would only conclude extradition treaties on the basis that we would have concluded them in the past, that is, when it was in the national interest to do so.[61]

Ambassador Rita Hauser also elaborated on the obligations that Article VII would impose on the United States, taking into account the legislative history of the article, and argued that the only "substantive change" that Article VII seemed to make in extradition law was to say that no country would be able to refuse to extradite in cases of genocide on the ground that it is a political offense. But she could see no reason why such a provision should be objectionable.[62] The Nixon administration proposed to deal with the matter in domestic implementing legislation, and, when conditions permitted, in the process of negotiating new extradition treaties or amendments to existing ones.[63]

In any event, the plans of the administration revealed no alarming upheavals in extradition law. In the first place, George Aldrich pointed out that no person could be extradited on charges of genocide until there was in existence an extradition treaty with the requesting state that made genocide an extraditable offense. The Nixon administration did not propose to change this policy, nor did it even propose to negotiate such treaties, or amendments to existing treaties, until the domestic implementing legislation making genocide a crime had been enacted. Aldrich emphasized that one of the principal factors that the United States takes into account in negotiating extradition treaties with any country is whether or not there is in existence a judicial process in that country that affords a person a fair trial. Since judicial systems can change over time, safeguards are built into extradition treaties, including a requirement that requesting states must "produce sufficient evidence to persuade both a U.S. court and the executive that the person sought would be held for trial under U.S. law if the offense had been committed here." Aldrich indicated that this requirement would be retained in future treaties.[64]

Similarly, at hearings in 1970 and 1971 Aldrich and others who testified saw no reasons to be concerned that the terms of Article VII put anyone in danger of double jeopardy. In response to a direct question on the matter, former Supreme Court justice Arthur Goldberg argued that extradition of a person to stand trial abroad on the same charge after having been tried in U.S. courts would not only be against the prevailing policy of the United States, it would be unconstitutional as well under the double jeopardy clause of the Constitution. He argued that this was well-established law in the United States.[65] Aldrich also testified that the double jeopardy provisions of extradition treaties would prevent extradition of Americans actually in the process of trial or who had been tried. But he thought that there was a situation not covered by this standard provision that the administration expected to deal with by a special provision in the implementing legislation for the convention, namely, where a request is made for extradition of an American *before* criminal proceedings have begun in the United States. The administration expected to "reserve discretion to initiate proceedings" rather than extradite. As Aldrich put it: "In other words, if a *prima facie* case of genocide were made out against an American national, and as a practical matter he could be tried in the United States, we could elect to try him in our courts and refuse extradition." The administration had come to think that this "special protection" was justified because the convention itself precluded "the refusal of extradition on the ground that the offense is political."[66] A section of draft implementing legislation submitted by the administration in fact indicated that it was the "sense of the Congress" that in negotiating extradition treaties the executive branch should "reserve for the United States the right to refuse extradition" in various circumstances, including when it "intended to exercise its jurisdiction"; and, to deal with the double jeopardy problem, when the person whose extradition is sought "has already been or is at the time of the request being prosecuted for such offense."[67]

Aldrich provided extensive commentary on Article VII and the intentions of the Nixon administration regarding the domestic implementing legislation in order to "allay any apprehensions that ratification of the Genocide Convention might force at some time in the future the United States to extradite Americans for trial abroad on trumped up charges of genocide."[68] But as so often occurred in debate over ratification, the critics' apprehensions could not be allayed, no matter how reasonable and exhaustive the testimony they were provided. Aldrich was neither the first nor the last representative of an administration whose good intentions did not achieve positive results. Another main concern of the critics of Article VII was precisely the issue that Aldrich hoped to demonstrate could be satisfactorily addressed in implementing legislation—would the article require the United States to extradite its own nationals?

Does Article VII Require Extradition of U.S. Nationals?

At first glance, it may seem strange that the question of whether or not Article VII of the convention would require the United States to extradite its own nationals ever arose in the debate over ratification, or at least that it was ever treated as such an important issue. Unlike some countries, the United States does extradite its own nationals. It has been the policy of the United States not to extradite in the absence of an extradition treaty with the requesting state, and one of the considerations taken into account in negotiating such treaties, as noted above, is the existence within the other country of a judicial system that affords the accused a fair trial. But the United States does extradite its own nationals. Why, then, should questions about this practice be raised in the debate over ratification of the Genocide Convention?

The most serious problem that many critics of the convention perceived to arise from the provisions of Article VII was that American citizens might be arbitrarily accused of committing genocide in a foreign land. They could be arbitrarily accused of committing other crimes as well, but the possibility that such allegations could be made involving *genocide* has always stimulated great apprehension about the effects of ratifying the convention. The issue acquired greater significance in view of the conviction of some senators, such as Sam Ervin, Jr., and John Sherman Cooper, that Article VII, combined with other articles in the convention, would have a large impact on U.S. extradition law and policy. Specifically, would the United States be required to extradite its own nationals to a country that might not have a judicial system that meets U.S. standards?

This issue was especially troublesome to Senator Cooper, who concentrated almost exclusively on the provisions of Articles VI and VII in his questioning of witnesses during the 1970 and 1971 hearings. He raised the hypothetical possibility of another state requesting the extradition of a U.S. national *who had returned to the United States* for a trial on charges of genocide or related crimes.[69] Cooper recognized, of course, that if an American were apprehended abroad and charged with committing such crimes, there was relatively little the U.S. government could do on his or her behalf, except perhaps to use diplomatic channels to attempt to protect the interests of, or secure the release of, the accused. And he recognized that Americans could be charged with committing such crimes abroad and brought to trial even if the United States did not ratify the convention. Nonetheless, he thought it important to establish whether or not the United States should commit itself to extradite *American citizens in the*

United States who are charged with having committed genocide abroad if the law of the requesting country provides insufficient substantive and procedural guarantees.[70] His questioning of George Aldrich of the State Department at the 1970 hearings was quite typical of his approach to these issues:

SENATOR COOPER: Let me ask this direct question. . . . Is your interpretation of this convention that should an American citizen commit a crime of genocide in Russia or any other country and is there, subject to their legal processes, that he shall be tried there? . . .

MR. ALDRICH: He certainly would be tried there, yes, sir.

SENATOR COOPER: Suppose that citizen has come back to the United States. Do you contend that he shall be extradited to Russia or some other country and be tried?

MR. ALDRICH: If they present a prima facie case, and we should decide we did not wish to prosecute him here, then he would be extradited.

SENATOR COOPER: If he is tried in the United States, of course, he is entitled to the due process of the Constitution. For example, he is protected by the writ of habeas corpus. He has all the rights under the Constitution?

MR. ALDRICH: Yes, sir.

SENATOR COOPER: If he should be extradited to country X, the contracting party, he would be tried under their laws?

MR. ALDRICH: Yes, sir.

SENATOR COOPER: Whatever they may be.[71]

The concern about Americans being extradited abroad to stand trial on charges of genocide without adequate procedural and substantive guarantees arose on other occasions. Some critics of the convention obviously saw this as a *policy* issue of profound importance for the United States, especially during the early 1970s when the Vietnam War was still raging. The position was clearly stated by Eberhard Deutsch, who represented the ABA at the 1971 Senate hearings.

SENATOR CHURCH: The treaty provides that extradition would lie only in the case of the crime being committed in the territory of the state.

MR. DEUTSCH: No question about it.

SENATOR CHURCH: What we are facing here, then, is not some extraordinary or revolutionary presentation that has been considered for the first time, but simply the extension of principles that we have long adopted in various extradition treaties, applying those principles to genocide. We apply them to murder; we apply them to other crimes. Now should we apply them to genocide?

MR. DEUTSCH: I agree fully. I say we are taking frightful chances in that regard, constitutional chances, by submitting our Armed Forces, for instance, to that type of situation subject to a charge of genocide because they have acted under orders of their military commanders in doing this, that or the other, and subjecting them to trial in those areas. We are going to regret Nuremberg.

SENATOR CHURCH: I could agree with you there. That is a different question. I think that departed considerably from the precedent of Anglo-Saxon law. That is, however, a different subject.

MR. DEUTSCH: Let me say this, sir. I certainly don't want to express an opinion as to guilt or innocence in the so-called mass murders in the villages in Vietnam, but if I were a member of this body, I would never bring myself to vote that those men now in the United States are subject to extradition to Vietnam because they committed genocide in that country.

That is a matter of constitutional policy rather than of constitutional law.[72]

In brief, for Deutsch, the question was "whether we want to make a treaty permitting that sort of thing."[73]

During the early 1970s representatives of the Nixon administration and others such as Senator Frank Church who were favorably inclined toward ratification of the convention recognized the problems that both Cooper and Deutsch called attention to, and they offered in response three arguments. In the first place, they maintained that similar problems existed regarding all crimes Americans were charged with committing abroad, not just genocide. In brief, an American charged with committing murder abroad might be tried under circumstances that did not afford him the sorts of procedural and substantive guarantees that exist in the United States. Why should the lack of such guarantees in the case of genocide constitute such a special problem? Second, they argued that Article VII did not itself constitute an extradition treaty, and that the article only required the extradition of persons in accordance with "laws and treaties in force." Hence, the United States would continue to apply its own law regarding extradition and continue to conclude the type of extradition treaties it wished to conclude with the countries it decided to conclude them with. Third, they believed that the kinds of issues Senator Cooper and Eberhard Deutsch raised could be addressed in the implementing legislation the

United States would enact in accordance with Article V of the convention.[74] Most parties to the convention have dealt with such problems through their domestic implementing legislation. In fact, only two parties have ratified with statements relative to Article VII. The Philippines indicated that it did "not undertake to give effect" to the terms of Article VII until its congress had "enacted the necessary legislation defining and punishing the crime of genocide, which legislation . . . cannot have retroactive effect."[75] Venezuela's statement indicates that "notice is given that the laws in force in Venezuela do not permit the extradition of Venezuelan nationals."[76] It is not altogether clear from these statements whether or not the Philippines and Venezuela intended them as reservations or declarations. The British government, however, has interpreted them as reservations and objected to them by simply stating that it does not accept them.[77]

In general, the practice of the parties to the convention suggests several possibilities in regard to their interpretations of Article VII. Most of the parties—if not all—have understood the article to say that they would apply their laws and treaties in force should they receive any request for extradition. This is, after all, the plain meaning of the language in the second paragraph of Article VII. All the parties have, of course, recognized that, for purposes of extradition, genocide is not a "political" crime, although this statement must be qualified in view of the German government's comments noted above. But beyond that, most of the parties would follow the dictates of their laws and treaties in force. Perhaps some of these states have seen a need to include specific provisions in their domestic implementing legislation that pertain to extradition. Perhaps not; we know that some states have not adopted any specific implementing legislation. Perhaps some parties have proceeded to conclude new treaties or amend existing treaties to cover genocide. Finally, only two parties have seen a need to make a reservation to Article VII. But even then their reservations actually seem unobjectionable. Venezuela's reservation, for example, simply puts everyone on "notice" that it does not extradite its own nationals, a practice that is not unique to Venezuela.

During the 1970s Nixon administration spokesmen argued that the United States could address—and should address—any problems arising out of Article VII in the implementing legislation Congress would enact. Senator Cooper, however, favored a reservation that stated "that a U.S. Citizen in the United States charged with having committed an act outside the United States in violation of the treaty provisions shall not be subject to extradition unless the Secretary of State determines such person is guaranteed all the constitutional rights of an accused under our Federal laws."[78]

Since this reservation specifically referred to a U.S. citizen "in the United States charged with having committed an act outside the United States," it did not cover a U.S. citizen in another country, whether or not that country was the site of the alleged violation of the convention.

Senator Cooper's reservation was tabled by the Committee on Foreign Relations by a close vote of seven to six that cut across party lines.[79] Generally, the committee members who were opposed to the reservation believed that the matters it addressed could be handled in domestic implementing legislation.[80] In contrast, members who supported it thought that a reservation would be stronger and more appropriate, and, perhaps above all, politically advantageous. As Senator William Spong, Jr. (D., Virginia), observed: "Even if such a statement is deemed unnecessary, as some argue, approval of the convention by the Senate without it may buttress the fears of some that our citizens will be subject to extradition on specious charges to countries with judicial systems alien or inferior to ours. There may be sufficient protections against this threat in the convention and the implementing legislation to be enacted, but I believe this assurance should be spelled out in the resolution of ratification."[81]

Spong indicated that "if the same, or a similar reservation" were offered in the Senate when the convention was debated on the floor, he would vote for it.[82] However, no resolution of ratification was debated in either 1970 or 1971.

In keeping with the decision of the Committee on Foreign Relations not to include Senator Cooper's reservation in a resolution of ratification, and to deal with any matters that involved the extradition provisions of Article VII in the implementing legislation, draft legislation submitted by the Nixon administration included a section that expressed the "sense of the Congress" that when negotiating extradition treaties the executive branch should reserve for the United States the right to refuse extradition of a U.S. national to a foreign country for trial on charges of genocide when (1) the United States is competent to try the accused, (2) it intends to exercise jurisdiction, or (3) where the person whose extradition is sought has already been tried or is in the process of being tried.[83]

The U.S. Understanding regarding Extradition

During the 1980s, especially after President Reagan endorsed ratification of the convention, the Committee on Foreign Relations changed its approach to the issue of extradition under Article VII. Rather than taking the position that any problems regarding extradition could be addressed in the implementing legislation, the committee decided, in 1985, to include an understanding pertaining to extradition in the Lugar-Helms-Hatch Sovereignty Package. In fact, as we have seen, the understanding was designed to apply both to extradition and to problems thought to emanate from the terms of Article VI discussed earlier. The part of the understanding that specifically addresses extradition states that "the pledge to grant extradition in accordance with a state's laws and treaties in force found in Article VII extends only to acts which are criminal under the laws of both the requesting and requested state."[84]

This understanding was interpreted by the Committee on Foreign Relations as merely stating an important element of current U.S. law on the subject of extradition.[85] Hence, from the committee's viewpoint, labeling it an understanding was appropriate. As a statement of current law, the understanding seems to be like the "notice" given by Venezuela that it does not extradite its own nationals. By its understanding, the United States put everyone on notice that it does not extradite anyone unless the acts they are accused of committing are criminal in both the United States and the requesting state. This is current U.S. practice, according to the committee report. But since genocide is branded a crime under the convention, and would therefore be regarded as a crime in any state that has ratified it, it is not clear why the committee thought that the understanding was necessary, unless they had intended to say that the United States would not extradite anyone on charges of genocide to a country that has not ratified the convention. But it remains unclear if the understanding would actually prevent extradition of a person to a nonparty state in all circumstances.

Be that as it may, the committee indicated in its 1985 report to the Senate that it did not interpret Article VII as requiring the United States to make any major changes in its extradition law. To the contrary, the committee had understood the article "as saying that extradition would be governed by municipal law and treaties in force among the parties,"[86] which indicates that the committee finally came around to understanding Article VII in the same way that the bulk of the other parties apparently understand it—in accordance with the plain meaning of its words. So far as U.S. law is concerned, the United States does not extradite in the absence of a bilateral extradition treaty with the requesting state. It is debatable whether this policy has much to commend it. Scholars such as Cherif Bassiouni have argued that the State Department's practice of "clinging to bilateral treaties as the only basis for extradition" lacks merit since multilateral treaties are as binding as bilateral ones. Bassiouni nevertheless recognizes that such is the existing practice.[87]

Most of the extradition treaties the United States has already concluded list the crimes for which extradition can be granted. None lists genocide as an extraditable offense.[88] In recent years the United States has been revising some of its extradition treaties, and the new policy has been not to list the crimes for which extradition can be granted. Listing the crimes has the great disadvantage of making it very difficult to adapt to changes in the legal situation in different countries, because in order to add crimes to the list it is necessary to adopt protocols or amendments to the treaties. The process of securing approval of protocols or amendments can be very time-consuming and seems like a very inefficient way of conducting foreign relations under modern conditions. Hence, the new policy that has been applied in some recent extradition treaties has been to state that any crime which carries a penalty of more than one year's imprisonment in both countries is an extraditable offense. Of special related concern has been to revise or clarify traditional provisions related to political offenses, which, as noted, are normally not extraditable offenses. The newer treaties specifically exclude certain crimes of violence, typically those committed by terrorists, from the scope of the political offense exception.[89]

In its 1985 report to the Senate, the Committee on Foreign Relations noted that the United States had recently concluded treaties with several countries (Costa Rica, Ireland, Italy, Jamaica, Sweden, and Thailand) that allowed extradition under the new so-called double criminality provision.[90] Since then, it has negotiated and concluded a supplementary treaty with the Federal Republic of Germany (June 1987)[91] and a protocol amending the existing treaty with Canada (January 1988).[92] Since the committee expected that the U.S. implementing legislation for the Genocide Convention would prescribe more than one year's imprisonment for committing genocide, and that the penalty would be at least as much in the other countries, the committee noted that the combined effect of the extradition treaties and Article VII of the convention would make the crime of genocide extraditable in all cases except those involving Thailand, which has not ratified the convention.[93] But what if Thailand should adopt legislation making genocide a crime in a manner that is entirely consistent with the convention and still not become a party to it? Under those conditions, would the United States be obliged to extradite under the terms of its extradition treaty with Thailand? If so, the understanding in the Sovereignty Package regarding Article VII, if it was intended to say that the United States would not extradite to nonparty states, would not achieve its objective with respect to Thailand.

Chapter 9 The International Court of Justice

Mr. President, the myth of the day is that the World Court reservation to the Genocide Convention will strengthen America's position in ratifying this treaty. Nothing could be further from the truth.

In many ways it is the ultimate irony of a debate heavy on the evils of Communist despots that those decrying these evils would tie America's hands behind our back in attempting to bring these despots before the bar of justice.—Senator William Proxmire, remarks on Senate floor, April 1986

We come now to Article IX, arguably one of the most important articles of the Genocide Convention, at least in regard to the rule-supervisory measures that are prescribed in that instrument. The article relates to the International Court of Justice and constitutes what is called, in international law terms, a compromissory clause. Such clauses have been included in many international agreements, multilateral as well as bilateral, in which the parties agree to submit disputes to the ICJ, or some other forum, for settlement. Whenever the court exercises jurisdiction in such cases, it does so under Article 36 (1) of its statute; that is, in accordance with a treaty provision that recognizes its competence to deal with the case. Typically, the disputes that the parties agree to submit for settlement concern the "interpretation" and "application" of the treaties or conventions in question.[1] Article IX of the Genocide Convention is somewhat more broadly framed. It states:

> Disputes between the Contracting Parties relating to the interpretation, application or fulfillment of the present Convention, including those relating to the responsibility of a State for genocide or for any of the other acts enumerated in Article III [conspiracy, incitement, attempt, and complicity to commit genocide], shall be submitted to the International Court of Justice at the request of any of the parties to the dispute.

The United States ratified the convention with a reservation to this article which states:

> That with reference to Article IX of the Convention, before any dispute to which the United States is a party may be submitted to the jurisdiction of the International Court of Justice under this article, the specific consent of the United States is required in each case.[2]

This reservation deserves attention for two reasons. In the first place, it is important because of its policy implications. Research by John Gamble and Dana Fischer has shown that the acceptance of compromissory clauses providing for the resolution of disputes by the ICJ is the best single predictor of state "support" for the court, and the United States has traditionally ranked high in this respect.[3] In fact, the United States has already ratified many treaties and conventions that contain clauses providing for the resolution of disputes by the ICJ without making reservations to those clauses. One study prepared for the Senate Committee on Foreign Relations during the early 1980s listed forty such multilateral conventions and other international agreements.[4] Another study compiled a list of seventy treaties and conventions, bilateral as well as multilateral.[5] The U.S. reservation to Article IX of the Genocide Convention therefore signifies a departure from past practice. Whether or not it signifies a permanent change in policy remains to be seen. Regardless of the outcome, the reservation can only serve to undermine efforts to strengthen the role of the ICJ at a time when it is widely perceived to be underused. Recent work by various international legal scholars has suggested that compromissory clauses are a more important source of the court's jurisdiction than are declarations made accepting its general compulsory jurisdiction under Article 36 (2) of its statute.[6]

Second, the U.S. reservation deserves attention because of its legal implications. Obviously, the reservation modifies the legal effects of Article IX. Given its terms, it is even reasonable to suppose that it was intended to cover any unanticipated problems that might arise as a result of ratification inasmuch as it aims to prevent the court from resolving any dispute involving the United States without its specific consent. The reservation to Article IX could presumably be invoked in any dispute that another party to the convention might wish to make about the U.S. interpretations of those provisions. The reservation could therefore be considered the most important provision of the entire Lugar-Helms-Hatch Sovereignty Package because it has the most far-reaching implications.

In this chapter we shall explore the rationale and implications of the U.S. reservation to Article IX. What considerations gave rise to its adoption?

What arguments were advanced for and against its adoption, and how cogent were they? Was the reservation necessary? Is it desirable? Will it achieve its purposes? Since the convention is a multilateral treaty that has already been ratified by about a hundred states, the practice of these other states regarding Article IX is, for reasons we have already noted, relevant to assessing the acceptability of the U.S. reservation, and we shall therefore want to examine what the practice of these other states has been. Let us look first, however, at the terms of Article IX itself, specifically at the sorts of disputes that the ICJ is given competence to resolve.

The Role of the ICJ Under Article IX of the Convention

Throughout the negotiations on the Genocide Convention, most drafters seemed to agree that the ICJ should be designated as one of the main rule-supervisory organs of the convention. In fact, during the earliest stages of the drafting process, in the Ad Hoc Committee of the ECOSOC, Platon Morozov, the Soviet representative, voiced the only opposition to a role for the court.[7] His position was consistent with the staunch pro-sovereignty line that he took on every important issue during the negotiations. With respect to Article IX, Morozov was especially concerned that "the establishment of international jurisdiction for cases of genocide would constitute intervention in the internal affairs of States and be a violation of their sovereignty."[8] As we shall see later in this chapter, under President Mikhail Gorbachev the Soviets have staged a dramatic about-face on this issue, and, in March 1989, even withdrew their long-standing reservation to Article IX of the Genocide Convention.

The Soviets did not prevail on this issue, however, when the convention was drafted in 1948. They could not persuade the Ad Hoc Committee of the ECOSOC to delete a compromissory clause from the draft convention; nor could they later persuade the Sixth Committee of the General Assembly to do so. As a result, Article IX was adopted over strenuous Soviet objections. It is considered by many commentators to be one of the most important articles of the convention. This is not surprising, because the article deals with two very important matters: (1) the resolution of various types of disputes by the ICJ, and (2) the responsibility of states for the commission of genocide and related acts. Let us examine each of these matters separately.

The Resolution of Disputes

All early drafts of the Genocide Convention included an article on the resolution of disputes by the ICJ. They differed from each other, however, on the sorts of disputes that could be submitted to the court. The draft conventions prepared by the UN Secretariat and the Ad Hoc Committee of the ECOSOC covered only disputes concerning the "interpretation or application" of the convention, both drafts stating that such disputes "shall be submitted" to the court.[9] Article IX, in contrast, is broader in terms of the sorts of disputes that can be resolved by the ICJ, but more equivocal on the issue of the conditions under which the court can exercise jurisdiction in resolving such disputes.

With regard to the sorts of disputes that the court can resolve, Article IX refers to those involving the "interpretation, application, or fulfillment" of the convention, "including those relating to the responsibility of a State for genocide." While the drafters apparently felt that the meaning of "interpretation" was clear enough, they experienced some difficulty with "application" and "fulfillment." The word "fulfillment" was not used in the drafts of Article IX prepared by the UN Secretariat and the Ad Hoc Committee of the ECOSOC, so its addition in the Sixth Committee of the General Assembly suggests that the drafters thought it conveyed a different idea from the word "application." The issue gave rise to some discussion. To the drafters, "application" seemed to mean the conditions or circumstances under which the convention should apply.[10] "Fulfillment" seemed to have been understood to relate to the matter of compliance or noncompliance with the terms of the convention.[11] The term is therefore especially important in view of the fact that it is followed by the clause relating to state responsibility for genocide, to which we shall return in a moment.

In regard to the issue of the conditions under which the ICJ can exercise jurisdiction, Article IX states that disputes between parties to the convention "shall be submitted" to the court "at the request of any of the parties to the dispute." The qualifying clause "at the request of any of the parties to the dispute" was inserted in the article by the Sixth Committee of the General Assembly on the urging of the delegations of the United Kingdom and Belgium. These delegations were motivated to propose the clause because, as they put it, the "Court's jurisdiction was compulsory only for the limited number of states which had recognized it under Article 36 of its statute."[12] Hence, in their view, inserting the clause in Article IX would effectively "impose upon all States party to the convention the obligation to refer all disputes relating to cases of genocide to the international court."[13] The clause, although adopted, did not achieve this objective, however, because it does not impose on the parties an obligation to refer disputes to the ICJ. To the contrary, according to Article IX any party to a dispute concerning the interpretation, application, or fulfillment of the convention can exercise discretion in deciding whether or not to submit the dispute to the court. In other words, it is a matter of choice, of the policy a party wishes to pursue with regard to using the court. Should one or more of the parties choose to submit a dispute to the court, the other(s) would be obliged to accept its jurisdiction and abide by its judgment—assuming, of course, that reservations to Article IX do not prevent the court from exercising jurisdiction.

The policy options that parties to the convention can exercise with regard to Article IX are not unusual. Indeed, when compared with the content of compromissory clauses in some other treaties or conventions, the terms of Article IX give more emphasis to the role of the ICJ. Clauses in many other treaties specify that disputes among parties that cannot be resolved by negotiations or some other means, including arbitration, can be taken to the court. In short, these other clauses stress the well-known preference of states for settling disputes by nonjudicial as opposed to judicial means, and actually call upon states to resort to judicial means only when nonjudicial ones fail. In comparison, then, the terms of Article IX seem stronger than those of the usual compromissory clause. Still, the article allows the parties to exercise considerable discretion in deciding whether or not to take a dispute to the ICJ, which has important practical consequences.

As we have seen, especially in chapters 3 and 5, many of the most important words and concepts of the convention are not defined and might well benefit from authoritative interpretation by the ICJ. Among these essential terms are "mental harm," a "part" of a group, and the "intent" element in the commission of genocide, all important concepts from Article II of the convention. However, no dispute over the meaning of these words has ever been brought to the court under Article IX. As we shall see later, there have been differences of opinion regarding reservations to Article IX itself, but even these have not resulted in a dispute—at least the states involved in the disagreements have not considered them disputes—requiring an ICJ ruling. More serious, perhaps, has been the failure of the parties to bring cases to the ICJ concerning the second main issue dealt with by Article IX, the responsibility of states for genocide.

States' Responsibility for Genocide

The Sixth Committee of the General Assembly inserted the clause on states' responsibility for genocide in Article IX. The UN Secretariat and the Ad Hoc Committee of the ECOSOC had both ignored the subject. The clause was controversial for two reasons. First, some delegations were concerned that "it would make it possible for an unfriendly State to charge, on vague and unsubstantial allegations, that another State was responsible for genocide within its territory."[14] The Indian delegate introduced this argument in the Sixth Committee, apparently in a defensive strategy to defeat a proposal introduced by the Pakistani delegation. Throughout the negotiations on the convention in the Sixth Committee, the Pakistani delegation lobbied aggressively in favor of an article on cultural genocide. A draft article on the subject covered such acts as "forced and systematic exile of individuals representing the culture of a group." Provisions such as this could arguably have made the convention applicable to the kinds of atrocities that occurred during the breakup of India and the creation of Pakistan.[15] Since the Pakistani proposal had not been finally disposed of at the time Article IX was being debated, the Indian delegation evidently wanted to prevent the adoption of the clause on states' responsibility out of fear that, should the cultural genocide provisions be adopted, Pakistan could bring a case before the ICJ charging India with genocide. As usual, the drafters sought a compromise that would address the main concerns of the most interested parties. In this case they resolved the controversy by eventually rejecting the Pakistani proposals on cultural genocide but retaining the clause on states' responsibility. India, as a result, made a reservation to Article IX when it ratified the convention.

The second reason why the clause on states' responsibility was controversial concerned the kind of responsibility that was envisaged. Was it to be civil or criminal or both? The British and Belgian representatives, the main proponents of the clause, stated that "the responsibility envisaged by [their joint proposal] was the international responsibility of States following a violation of the convention," which is "civil responsibility, not criminal responsibility."[16] Indeed, these representatives were acutely aware of the "enormous practical difficulties of bringing rulers and heads of state to justice, except perhaps at the end of a war."[17] They believed that in time of peace it would be "virtually impossible to exercise any effective international or national jurisdiction over rulers or heads of State," and for that reason they thought it was necessary to be able to refer acts of genocide to the ICJ.[18] This argument was sufficient to carry the clause, but by only a narrow margin.[19] Some delegations, such as that of the United States, supported the clause but believed that it should be made clear that the sort of responsibility envisaged by Article IX was civil, not criminal. In fact, the United States made a statement to this effect in the Sixth Committee.[20]

In accord with this statement, President Truman, when he transmitted the convention to the Senate in 1949, proposed that the United States ratify with an understanding that the states' responsibility clause of Article IX referred to civil responsibility. The subcommittee of the Committee on Foreign Relations that held hearings on the convention in 1950 included such an understanding in its draft resolution of ratification.[21] In the years since then, however, the understanding has not been included in the proposed resolutions of ratification. Nor was one included in the Lugar-Helms-Hatch Sovereignty Package. Some international legal scholars have argued that such an understanding would be unnecessary and that it is obvious that the states' responsibility clause refers to civil responsibility. Usually responsibility involves a question of compensation, though some scholars have argued that the full definition of civil responsibility remains unclear.[22]

The parties to the convention have been reluctant to bring disputes regarding states' responsibility for genocide to the ICJ. Despite numerous allegations of genocide in the post–World War II period, only one case involving the convention has ever been brought to the ICJ, and that one was short-lived and actually withdrawn by the parties and settled out of court. Ironically, the parties to the case were India and Pakistan, although the issue was not cultural genocide committed at the time Pakistan came into existence in the late 1940s, but India's intention to try Pakistani prisoners captured during the war over the creation of Bangladesh during the early 1970s. India threatened to try the prisoners for various crimes, including genocide, committed during that violent struggle. In May 1973, in an apparent attempt to prevent the trials and secure the repatriation of the prisoners, Pakistan filed an application with the ICJ instituting proceedings against India with respect to the situation and seeking interim measures of protection. This dispute never proceeded to a discussion of the merits of the case and was settled out of court, with India repatriating the prisoners.[23]

In more recent years efforts have been made to bring a case to the ICJ concerning the genocide that occurred in Cambodia during the 1970s. Cambodia ratified the Genocide Convention in October 1950. Since 1975, when the Khmer Rouge came to power, a huge amount of documentation supporting claims of genocide has been amassed by at least two organizations: the Cambodian Documentation Commission, headed by David Hawks, and the Cambodian Genocide Project, headed by Gregory Stanton. The Khmer Rouge government was removed from power by a Vietnamese-backed invasion of Cambodia in 1978, but elements of that government continued to represent Cambodia in the United Nations as part of a coalition of various factions.[24]

In the opinion of some legal experts, including Gregory Stanton[25] and

Hurst Hannum,[26] the evidence of genocide in this case provides a basis upon which another party to the convention could invoke Article IX and bring a claim against the Khmer Rouge before the ICJ. Most parties, including Cambodia, ratified the convention without making a reservation to Article IX that would complicate bringing a case to the court. In fact, both Stanton and Hannum have argued that there are few, if any, technical problems to overcome in initiating a case against the Khmer Rouge. But efforts to persuade another party to the convention to take up the case have been to no avail. The Australian government at one point indicated some interest but later declined, citing a concern that taking up the case might imply recognition of the government that represented Cambodia in the United Nations.[27] These official concerns strain credibility. For whatever reasons, the Australian government has no interest in starting proceedings against Cambodia. Nor, of course, have any other parties found it in their interest to do so. To its credit, the Australian government at least considered the possibility.

The same lack of determination, or political will, on the part of states to make an issue out of allegations of genocide and invoke Article IX has also been evident in their apparent unwillingness to discuss the allegations in the political organs of the United Nations. Article VIII of the convention states that the parties may call upon the "competent organs" of the United Nations to take "appropriate" action for the suppression of genocide and related crimes. Although the "competent organs" are not specified, the drafters probably had in mind the General Assembly and Security Council. But other organs, and even subsidiary bodies of other organs, such as the Economic and Social Council and its Commission on Human Rights or subcommissions thereof, may also be considered competent to deal with such matters. This presumption seems reasonable in light of the fact that the precise terms of Article VIII emerged as a compromise between two different viewpoints. Some drafters thought that the article was superfluous and should be deleted because it was obvious that any member state could call upon the political organs of the UN to take action in cases of genocide.[28] Others wanted a more specific article—one that would have required that all cases "likely to create a threat to the peace" must be taken to the Security Council.[29] As adopted, Article VIII reflects the middle ground between these two extremes: it expressly recognizes the right of parties to call upon the organs of the UN to take action in cases of genocide, but it allows flexibility in choosing the organ to which cases are brought.

Whether or not Article VIII is superfluous, the political organs of the United Nations—or more precisely, the representatives of the member states in the political organs—have not been hospitable to the airing of allegations of genocide. The numerous instances of alleged genocide since World War II have either not been discussed or have been discussed only in a broader context of human rights violations, which seem less foreboding. To be sure, there are always exceptions to a rule, and the case of Cambodia provides at least a partial exception. In 1978 Australia, Canada, Norway, the United Kingdom, and the United States brought charges to the UN Commission on Human Rights against the Khmer Rouge government for massive violations of human rights. The commission referred the matter to its Subcommission on Prevention of Discrimination and Protection of Minorities, which in turn appointed a rapporteur to study the allegations. Although the rapporteur concluded that the case represented the worst case of human rights violations since World War II, nothing came of his report.[30] Many governments denounce the gross violations of human rights that occurred, but discussion of such episodes is always a "sensitive" or "delicate" matter, giving rise to charges and countercharges of interference in the internal affairs of states.

Reservations to Article IX

While the failure of the parties to the Genocide Convention to use the ICJ under Article IX may be due mainly to a lack of political will, reservations that some parties have made to the article also make recourse to the court unlikely, if not impossible. Some states—including now even the United States—have apparently used reservations to Article IX as a way of insulating themselves from becoming involved in a dispute before the ICJ regarding the interpretation, application, or fulfillment of the convention. Of all the articles in the convention, Article IX has always been the main target of reservations. This fact alone is powerful testimony to how important the article has been perceived to be. As the data in table 9.1 show, by the end of 1989 nineteen parties (or 18.6 percent of the total) had ratified the convention with a reservation to Article IX.

As would be expected, the data show variations in the practice of the different geographical groups in formulating their reservations to Article IX. The East European states (six of the eleven, or 54.5 percent) had made more reservations to the article than had any of the other geographical groups. But in the past the figure was much higher. As recently as the end of 1988, ten of the eleven states in the East European group (90.9 percent) had made reservations to Article IX. The exception was Yugoslavia, which

Table 9.1 Ratifications, Reservations, and Objections to Reservations to Article IX of the Genocide Convention as of the End of 1989

Area	No. parties	No. reservations	(%)	No. parties that object to reservations	(%)
Africa[1]	18	3	(16.7)	0	(0)
Americas[2]	24	3	(12.5)	2[a]	(8.3)
Asia & Pacific[3]	30[b]	6	(20.0)	2[b]	(6.7)
Eastern Europe[4]	11	6[c]	(54.5)	0	(0)
Western Europe[5]	19	1	(5.3)	5	(26.3)
TOTALS	102	19	(18.6)	9	(8.8)

Source: compiled from data contained in the UN publication *Multilateral Treaties Deposited with the Secretary-General* (status as at 31 December 1989) ST/LEG/SER. E/8, pp. 97–105 (1990).

[a] This figure does not include Cuba, which objected to the Soviet bloc reservations when it ratified the convention in March 1953 but withdrew its objection in January 1982.

[b] The Republic of China (Taiwan) is not counted among the parties; nor is it counted among those that objected to reservations to Article IX. The 1951 ratification of "the Taiwan local authorities" was denounced by the PRC when it ratified the convention in April 1983. At that time, the PRC entered a reservation to Article IX.

[c] As discussed in the text, in March and April 1989, the USSR, Byelorussian SSR, and Ukrainian SSR withdrew long-standing reservations to Article IX. In December 1989 Hungary also withdrew its reservation.

[1] Africa: Algeria, Burkina Fasso, Egypt, Ethiopia, Gabon, Gambia, Ghana, Lesotho, Liberia, Mali, Morocco, Mozambique, Rwanda, Senegal, Tanzania, Togo, Tunisia, Zaire.

[2] Americas: Antigua and Barbuda, Argentina, Bahamas, Barbados, Brazil, Canada, Chile, Colombia, Costa Rica, Cuba, Ecuador, El Salvador, Guatemala, Haiti, Honduras, Jamaica, Mexico, Nicaragua, Panama, Peru, St. Vincent and the Grenadines, USA, Uruguay, Venezuela.

[3] Asia and Pacific: Afghanistan, Australia, Burma, Cambodia, China, Democratic Yemen, Fiji, India, Iran, Iraq, Israel, Jordan, Laos, Lebanon, Libya, Maldives, Mongolia, Nepal, New Zealand, North Korea, Pakistan, Papua New Guinea, the Philippines, South Korea, Saudi Arabia, Sri Lanka, Syria, Tonga, Vietnam, Yemen.

[4] Eastern Europe: Albania, Bulgaria, Byelorussian SSR, Czechoslovakia, German Democratic Republic, Hungary, Poland, Romania, Ukrainian SSR, USSR, Yugoslavia.

[5] Western Europe: Austria, Belgium, Cyprus, Denmark, Finland, France, Federal Republic of Germany, Greece, Iceland, Ireland, Italy, Luxembourg, Monaco, the Netherlands, Norway, Spain, Sweden, Turkey, United Kingdom.

ratified the convention in August 1950 with no reservations whatsoever.[31] Its delegation to the United Nations when the convention was drafted in 1948 exhibited some independence during the negotiations, though it supported the Soviet position on most issues.

In contrast to the East European group, the tendency among all other geographical groups has been to ratify the convention without reservations to Article IX. As table 9.1 shows, the West European, American, and African groups have been especially "supportive" of the ICJ in this respect. By the end of 1989, only one West European (Spain),[32] three American (Argentine, USA, and Venezuela),[33] and three African states (Algeria, Morocco, Rwanda)[34] had ratified the convention with a reservation to Article IX. The favorable disposition of the West European states in particular toward the ICJ is also shown by the fact that they have been much more likely than any other geographical group to object to the reservations of other states. Five of the nineteen West European parties (26.3 percent) to the convention have made such objections. We shall return to this point.

In general, the data in table 9.1 are consistent with the findings of Gamble and Fischer's study of state support for the ICJ.[35] A major exception, of course, is the United States, which is among the American states having made a reservation to Article IX even though it has traditionally accepted compromissory clauses of that sort. But there is nothing unusual in the fact that a very large proportion of the Soviet bloc had also made reservations, or that the West European states showed up as strong supporters of the court. What is really interesting is the major change brought about by developments in 1988. In a major, wide-ranging address to the UN General Assembly in December 1988, President Mikhail Gorbachev of the Soviet Union spoke at length about human rights and about what his country was doing and intended to do in that field domestically and internationally. So far as international measures are concerned, he said, "We intend to expand the Soviet Union's participation in the controlling mechanisms of human rights under the aegis of the UN, and within the framework of the European process. We think that the jurisdiction of the International Court in the Hague with regard to the interpretation and application of agreements on human rights must be binding on all states."[36]

Soon thereafter, in February 1989, the Presidium of the Supreme Soviet adopted a decree whereby the Soviet Union withdrew reservations to compromissory clauses that it had previously made and accepted the jurisdiction of the ICJ with respect to the interpretation and application of six conventions, including the Genocide Convention.[37] Foreign Minister Eduard Shevardnadze officially notified the United Nations of this decision in a letter transmitted by the Soviet ambassador to the United Nations in March 1989. Shevardnadze indicated that

> in taking this decision [to withdraw the reservations], the Soviet Union was guided by the desire to strengthen the international legal order,

> which upholds the primacy of law in political affairs. In advocating the primacy of international law, we take the position that international legal norms and obligations of States take precedence over their domestic enactments. Naturally, this approach also presupposes the comprehensive use of all means of peaceful settlement of disputes, including active use of the potential of the International Court of Justice.[38]

In his letter Shevardnadze also stressed that the withdrawal of the reservations to the six human rights conventions was part of an ongoing, larger process of considering the question of withdrawing reservations to compromissory clauses in other conventions. The Soviet Union was now taking the position that the role of the ICJ in world affairs should be enhanced, and it had decided to begin this process of enhancement with human rights agreements because of the "importance of the further promotion of co-operation among States in the humanitarian sphere."[39] Ukrainian SSR and Byelorussian SSR, federated republics of the Soviet Union that ratified the conventions in their own right, followed suit and withdrew their reservations. Hungary also withdrew its reservation in 1989. At the time of this writing (1990) the other members of the East European group have not withdrawn their reservations to Article IX.

The new Soviet policy reflects quite a different attitude from the one expressed by Soviet representatives when the convention was being drafted, and should they take further steps to enhance the role of the ICJ in world affairs, it could very well herald a fundamental change in the traditional Soviet theory of international law. The withdrawal of the reservation to Article IX does not, of course, mean that the Soviets would actually take a case to the court in accordance with that article. More than three-quarters of the parties of the convention have ratified without a reservation to Article IX, and none has yet invoked the article. Why should the Soviets be expected to do so? Nonetheless, the change in attitude is significant, and the Soviets are now in a position to invoke the article; at the same time they have exposed themselves to the possibility that another party to the convention could invoke the article against them. It is noteworthy that this occurred about the same time that the United States was breaking with its past practice and ratifying the convention with a reservation to Article IX.

The Purpose of the Reservations to Article IX

Generally, the purpose of reservations is to either exclude or modify in some way(s) the legal effects of certain provisions of a treaty. The reservations that have been made to Article IX of the Genocide Convention do both, though only a few of them suggest an intent to completely deprive the article of its legal effects. Algeria's reservation (1963), for example, states that it "does not consider itself bound" by Article IX.[40] Spain (1968) and Rwanda (1975) made similar reservations.[41] While these states could accept the jurisdiction of the court by a special agreement in any case, their reservations suggest that they would likely be unreceptive to such an appeal.

Most of the reservations to Article IX modify its legal effects, though these reservations have the same *practical* effect as the reservations of Algeria, Rwanda, and Spain. The Soviet Union's reservation, which it withdrew in March 1989, was typical of these reservations:

> The Soviet Union does not consider as binding upon itself the provisions of article IX which provides that disputes between the Contracting Parties with regard to the interpretation, application, and implementation of the present Convention shall be referred for examination to the International Court at the request of any party to the dispute, and declares that, as regards the International Court's jurisdiction in respect of disputes concerning the interpretation, application, and implementation of the Convention, the Soviet Union will, as hitherto, maintain the position that in each particular case the agreement of all parties to the dispute is essential for the submission of any particular dispute to the International Court for decision.[42]

This reservation modified the effects of Article IX because it meant—or was intended to mean—that the Soviet Union could not be brought before the ICJ by any other parties without its consent. Several other states, India and Morocco, for example, made similar reservations.[43] The Lugar-Helms-Hatch Sovereignty Package contains a reservation, quoted at the beginning of this chapter, that does the same thing the Soviet reservation did. In fact, it may do more, since the U.S. reservation explicitly mentions "specific" consent, a word that Senator Helms and others insisted be included so that in no case could consent be implied.[44] While those who believe that the United States should accept Article IX's dispute resolution procedures are dismayed by the reservation, some individuals or groups favored an even more restrictive reservation. Phyllis Schlafly of the Eagle Forum favored a reservation that would have stated that "the United States does not accept the jurisdiction of the World Court or of any international penal tribunal, and the President is hereby prohibited from accepting such jurisdiction under executive agreement."[45]

Whatever the precise wording of the reservations to Article IX, the fact that they were made at a very early stage in the existence of the convention became an issue of great importance. These early reservations led to the celebrated 1951 advisory opinion of the ICJ, *Reservations to the Convention on the Prevention and Punishment of the Crime of Genocide.*[46] While this opinion is familiar to specialists in international law and politics, it is known best for its implications for the subsequent development of the law of treaties, particularly with regard to reservations,[47] and hardly ever in terms of its implications for the Genocide Convention itself. Moreover, the opinion's implications rarely entered the debate over ratification in the United States; and when they were discussed, it is far from certain that they were understood. Let us review the main issues raised in the case and the principal elements of the court's opinion.

The 1951 Advisory Opinion of the ICJ

The considerations that led the UN General Assembly to ask the ICJ for an advisory opinion on reservations to the Genocide Convention had what could be considered the basic elements of a dispute.[48] Upon ratification, some states, particularly Australia and Ecuador, objected to the reservations made by other states, notably to the reservations made to Article IX by some members of the Soviet bloc (Bulgaria, Poland, and Romania, all of which ratified the convention in 1950). It is arguable that it would have been better if the objections had been brought to the court as a dispute under Article IX of the convention; that is, as a dispute concerning the interpretation or even the application of the convention. But the convention had not yet entered into force. The secretary general of the United Nations, the designated depository of the instruments of ratification, therefore faced a dilemma. How should his office deal with the reservations and the objections to them? He turned to the General Assembly for its "approval and advice."[49] Before the assembly decided to request the advisory opinion of the court, sufficient ratifications had been deposited for the convention to enter into force.[50] Nonetheless, the issue was not brought to the court by a party under Article IX of the convention. Rather, the assembly took the issue to court under Article 96 of the UN Charter, which authorizes the General Assembly and the Security Council to request advisory opinions of the ICJ on any legal question.

Two questions of practical significance were put to the court: first, could a state ratifying the convention with a reservation become a party if the reservation were objected to by one or more parties but not by others; and, second, if such a state could be a party, what would be the effect of its reservation as between it and a state accepting the reservation versus one objecting to it? The court was sharply divided in its response to these questions, voting seven to five.[51] One of the five dissenting judges, Alejandro Alvarez, filed a separate opinion that was quite different in substance from the other four. Thus, as summarized in table 9.2, three different points of view were expressed on the issues addressed by the court.

At one extreme, a minority of four judges, whose world order perspective could best be described as favoring a decentralized, state sovereignty system, defended the traditional unanimity rule with regard to reservations to conventions. They were of the opinion that states should be free to make reservations, which other states could either accept or reject. If another party objected, the reserving state would have to choose between either withdrawing its reservation and becoming a party to the convention or maintaining the reservation and not becoming a party. As table 9.2 shows, these judges hoped for universal acceptance of the principles affirmed in the Genocide Convention, but they did not think that achieving that goal was

Table 9.2 Summary of Positions in the 1951 ICJ Advisory Opinion

Philosophy or issue	Judge Alvarez	Majority	Minority
World order perspective	New international order	Legitimacy of old order but flexible rules	State sovereignty
Reservations	None permitted; convention deals with social issue	Permitted if compatible with "object and purpose"	Traditional unanimity rule; consent of other parties required
Convention coverage	Universality would occur eventually	Premium on universality	Universality desired
Integrity of provisions	Implied emphasis on integrity of convention's provisions	Compromise on integrity of convention's provisions	Priority on integrity of convention's provisions
Judicial role	Judicial activism	Modified judicial activism	Judicial self-restraint

Source: Compiled from *Reports of Judgments, Advisory Opinions and Orders* [Advisory Opinion, *Reservations to the Convention on the Prevention and Punishment of the Crime of Genocide*], pp. 15–69 (1951).

worth any price—in particular, it was not worth sacrificing the integrity of the convention's provisions.[52] One could summarize the perspective of these judges on their own roles as being decidedly in favor of judicial self-restraint. They saw the issue of the acceptability of reservations as a political matter that was to be resolved by the parties themselves, not by judicial intervention.

At the opposite extreme, the Chilean jurist Alejandro Alvarez, who also dissented in the opinion but for fundamentally different reasons, advocated an abandonment of traditional rules in favor of a wholly new outlook. In his opinion, international law must adapt to changes in the international system, and that system was undergoing profound changes. World War II, which Alvarez called the "last social cataclysm," made absolute state sovereignty a relic of the past. In fact, he believed that the court could play a role in ushering in a new international order. According to Alvarez, no reservations to the Genocide Convention should be considered acceptable, because the convention formed, in a manner of speaking, a part of a new "constitution" for the world at large. Like the other dissenting judges, Alvarez's position implied an emphasis on the integrity of the convention's provisions, although he thought that integrity would be preserved by what he called "psychological factors" (that is, by states finding themselves in an "awkward position in international society" if they failed to ratify conventions such as the Genocide Convention), rather than through the requirement of treaty law.[53] Unlike the other dissenting judges, however, Alvarez was decidedly oriented toward judicial activism. In his view, the court could itself throw out the traditional unanimity rule on reservations through its own reading of developing trends in the international political order.

The majority on the court sought a compromise between the two extremes and enunciated a completely new doctrine regarding the acceptability of reservations. They embraced elements of both points of view, recognizing the advantages of the minority's traditionalism but favoring the "more flexible application" of traditional principles endorsed by Alvarez. They wanted to concentrate more on the widespread acceptance of the convention and less on the integrity of its provisions. But they did not believe that any and every reservation should be permissible. Rather, the compatibility of a reservation with the "object and purpose" of the convention should be the test of its acceptability. The majority was of the opinion that a state objecting to another's reservation on the ground of its incompatibility with the object and purpose of the convention can "in fact consider that the reserving State is not a party to the Convention." On the other hand, if another state accepts the reservation, it "can in fact consider that the reserving State is a party to the Convention."[54] The perspective of the majority on their own judicial roles might thus be characterized as a modified judicial activism. To them, the question of whether or not states could ratify the convention with reservations was a matter that fell essentially within the political arena. Yet they established a test for the acceptability of reservations that could potentially have led to a need for judicial intervention in resolving disputes. In fact, it was through judicial activism that the majority could fashion a new outlook on reservations.

The compromise came as a shock to most UN members. As Michla Pomerance has observed, most apparently expected the court to defend tradition—that is, to embrace the minority's position. But even the sharpest critics came to agree that the majority opinion should be accepted as applying to the Genocide Convention. Eventually, the court's new doctrine was accepted even for general application, as signified by its being enshrined in the reservation provisions of the Vienna Convention on the Law of Treaties of 1969, which is now regarded as embodying the most widely accepted rules of treaty law.[55]

The Impact of the Court's Opinion

What impact did the court's opinion have on the Genocide Convention? The data presented in table 9.3 provide some insight into this question. The table shows the deposit of instruments of ratification of the Genocide Convention from the first one in July 1949 through the end of 1989. It also shows, for each of the time periods indicated, the number of reservations made to Article IX and the number of objections to those reservations. The first period extends from the convention's adoption to November 16, 1950, the date on which the General Assembly requested the ICJ's advisory opinion. The second period covers only the months between the request for the advisory opinion and the date on which it was issued, May 28, 1951. The third period begins the use of five-year intervals, though the first few months of 1951 were included in the second period. The data were grouped in this way to see if they showed any immediate impact of the court's opinion.

Table 9.3 shows that most ratifications of the Genocide Convention occurred during the first decade of its existence. Well over half (63) of the parties to the convention had already ratified it by the end of 1960. The table shows a steady stream of ratifications since 1960, though not at a very high rate given the rapid increase in UN membership. Using the membership of the United Nations (159) as it moves into the 1990s as a yardstick,

Table 9.3 Chronology of Ratifications of the Genocide Convention, Reservations to Article IX, and Objections to Reservations

Periods	No. ratifications	No. reservations	No. objections
1. Up to 11/1950	25	4	4
2. 12/1950–5/1951	2	1	3
3. 6/1951–12/1955	21	1[c]	4[a, b]
4. 1/1956–12/1960	15	4	0[a]
5. 1/1961–12/1965	3	1	0
6. 1/1966–12/1970	7	2	2
7. 1/1971–12/1975	7	2	1
8. 1/1976–12/1980	4	0	0
9. 1/1981–12/1985	12	2	1
10. 1/1986–12/1989	6	2	3
TOTALS	102	19	18

Source: Compiled from data contained in the UN publication *Multilateral Treaties Deposited with the Secretary-General* (status as at 31 December 1989) ST/LEG/SER. E/8, pp. 97–105 (1990).

[a] Does not include objections made during this period by Republic of China (Taiwan). The PRC denounced the Taiwan ratification of July 1951 when it ratified in April 1983.

[b] Does not include an objection made by Cuba when it ratified in March 1953. The objection was withdrawn in January 1982.

[c] The USSR, Byelorussian SSR, Ukrainian SSR, and Hungary withdrew the reservations they had made during this period and are therefore not included here.

slightly less than two-thirds of its members have ratified the convention. Therefore, if the ICJ's opinion opened the way for more states to ratify the convention than otherwise would have, it did not stimulate the sort of universality of acceptance that might have been anticipated over the long term. This suggests that the willingness of the court's majority to compromise the integrity of the convention's provisions in the hope of achieving universality of acceptance has been to no avail.

As table 9.3 also shows, most of the reservations to Article IX (originally a total of fourteen, but now ten owing to the fact that four of them were withdrawn) were made before the end of 1960. Four of these reservations were made during the first period, and, as we discussed earlier, were actually the reason the court was asked for an advisory opinion regarding their acceptability. One state, Czechoslovakia, even made its reservation to Article IX between the time the General Assembly requested the advisory opinion and the date it was issued, though this action was probably already in progress by the time the assembly voted to make the request. What is most interesting is that of the twenty-one states ratifying the convention in the period immediately following the issuance of the advisory opinion (period 3 in table 9.3), five of them—all Soviet bloc members, including the USSR—made reservations to Article IX. Since then, states have continued to ratify the convention with slightly varying frequencies, but over the long run approximately 20 percent of the parties have made reservations to Article IX. Of course, this trend could now be reversed by the long-term impact of the withdrawal of the Soviet Union's reservation.

Finally, table 9.3 shows the number of objections that have been made to Article IX reservations. The figures in this column refer to the total number of objections (in the form of formal statements) made to the reservations. The total does not agree with the total number of parties that have made objections (table 9.1) because some parties have objected to Article IX reservations on more than one occasion. In fact, by comparing tables 9.1 and 9.3, we can see that nine parties to the convention (table 9.1) have made eighteen objections (table 9.3) to reservations to Article IX. States have more often than not objected to the reservations of serveral states in one statement. It is also noteworthy that there has been a marked decline in the number of objections. Most objections were made by the end of 1955 (eleven of the eighteen).

Objections to Reservations to Article IX

The substance of the objections to the Article IX reservations reveals the impact of the ICJ's advisory opinion on the Genocide Convention. The object-and-purpose test implies, of course, that a reservation could be incompatible with the convention. If a party to the convention should find the reservation of another party incompatible, it could object. The reserving state might then either withdraw its reservation or maintain it. If it were to maintain the reservation, the objecting state could consider the reserving state not to be a party to the convention. What matters in the case of an objection, then, is how the objecting state views the status of the one making the reservation. Does the objecting state consider the reserving state not a party to the convention? Or does it object to the reservation but still consider the state a party to the convention? Because not all parties to the convention would necessarily object to the same reservations, the effect of the object-and-purpose test could be to convert a multilateral treaty into a series of bilateral agreements with varying terms. In practice, in the case of the Genocide Convention, some states have objected to reservations of some parties while others have not. In addition, some states have objected to reservations of some parties but not to the reservations of others. And few objecting states have made clear whether they consider the reserving states parties to the convention. Indeed, a potentially deleterious impact of the ICJ's opinion is evident in the practice of parties to the Genocide Convention, the very instrument that was to be the beneficiary of the new and enlightened doctrine of the object-and-purpose test.

As the record clearly shows, some states simply abandoned the practice of objecting to reservations. This was true of Australia and Ecuador, the two states whose objections had been a major factor in the General Assembly's decision to request the advisory opinion in the first place.[56] Others, including Belgium, Brazil, Norway, and Sri Lanka, have objected to the reservations of some states, such as those of Soviet bloc members, but not (at least officially) to those of others.[57] Among these states, the objection made by Brazil in 1952 is unique, for it states expressly that Brazil "considers the said reservations as incompatible with the object and purpose of the Convention," but it "reserves the right to draw any such legal consequences as it may deem fit from its formal objection to the . . . reservations."[58] None of these states' objections indicate whether or not they consider the states whose reservations they reject to be parties to the convention.

The United Kingdom has indicated that it does "not accept" Article IX reservations; on two occasions it stated further that a reservation to Article IX "is not the kind of reservation which intending parties to the Convention have the right to make." These statements leave open the question of whether or not the British government considers the states that have made such reservations parties to the convention. Nonetheless, the British government is distinguished as a sort of reservations watchdog, making objections on five occasions—in 1970, 1975, 1983, 1987, and 1989—in the process objecting to all Article IX reservations, those of friend and foe alike.[59] There was some speculation in the Senate about whether or not the British government would object to the terms of the Lugar-Helms-Hatch Sovereignty Package, particularly to the Article IX reservation.[60] In fact, Britain followed through and carried along other European states that objected to the reservation as well.

In contrast to these rather diplomatic objections, Greece ratified the convention in December 1954, declaring that "we have not accepted and do not accept any reservation which has already been made or which may hereafter be made by the countries signatory to this instrument or by countries which have acceded or may hereafter accede thereto."[61] The

Greek government could hardly be accused of discriminating among states on the basis of their political bloc. Taken literally, the objection would apply to every reservation made in the past and contemplated in the future, including every provision of the Lugar-Helms-Hatch Sovereignty Package. The Greek objection is the only one consistent with the views expressed by Alejandro Alvarez when the ICJ issued its advisory opinion on reservations to the convention. But the Greek objection may itself be susceptible to the charge that it is incompatible with the object and purpose of the convention because it does not seem to consider, as the majority of the ICJ maintained, that some reservations might be compatible with the object and purpose of the convention.

Of all the states objecting to reservations, only the Netherlands has done so with precision and clarity. Upon ratifying the convention in June 1966, the Netherlands objected to all reservations that had been made to Article IX, declaring that it "considers the reservations . . . to be incompatible with the object and purpose of the Convention." It then stated that it "does not deem any State which has made or which will make such reservation a party to the Convention." The objection was entirely consistent with the ICJ's opinion and surely meant that the Netherlands would not consider the United States a party to the Genocide Convention if it ever ratified with a reservation to Article IX. In fact, along with other European parties, the Netherlands objected to the U.S. reservation to Article IX, specifying that because of the reservation it does not consider the United States a party to the convention. It went on to say that in the event the United States should withdraw its reservation, it would then be in treaty relationship with the Netherlands. Consistent with this position, the Netherlands withdrew its objection when the reservations of the USSR, Byelorussian SSR, and Ukrainian SSR were withdrawn,[62] and will presumably do the same with regard to Hungary.

However commendable we find the Netherlands's objection in form and substance, it too reflects the problems that arise as a result of the object-and-purpose test: the Netherlands has simply made the objection, it has not carried it any further. In particular, it has not elevated its disagreement to the level of a dispute. This is in part—and perhaps mainly—due to a lack of political will, and in this respect the Netherlands is not alone. But it is also in part a legal problem. Since no one forces the issue, states use Article IX reservations to protect themselves from undesired ICJ intrusion into their affairs. In fact, some parties evidently assume that they can make a reservation to Article IX if they wish, and that by doing so they cannot be required to appear before the ICJ without their consent. Under the doctrine of reciprocity, the reservations can be invoked against the reserving states by parties that have not made reservations, but the reserving states may consider that a small price to pay for the protection they gain.

In the absence of an actual case involving the Genocide Convention, it cannot be said with certainty that the assumptions that seem to lie behind Article IX reservations are without foundation. But it also cannot be said that they are beyond challenge. Such reservations might be deemed incompatible with the object and purpose of the convention for several reasons. It may even be reasonable to suggest that the ICJ could itself resolve the issue if it were asked to adjudicate a dispute between two of the parties. Although none of the parties has forced the issue upon the court, the following considerations suggest that reservations to Article IX are incompatible with the object and purpose of the convention: the rationale of the drafters of the convention in adopting the article; the specific tasks assigned the ICJ under the article; the reasoning of most judges on the ICJ when it issued its advisory opinion, including the majority and Judge Alvarez; and the fact that quite a few parties to the convention consider reservations to the article to be incompatible with its object and purpose.

The U.S. Reservation to Article IX

Since virtually every word of the Genocide Convention was carefully scrutinized over the years that it was under consideration in the U.S. Senate, it is not surprising that Article IX was always a matter of concern. The provisions of the article were discussed extensively at the 1950 hearings. At that time everyone seemed to recognize that Article IX would "override" or "bypass" the Connally reservation, the so-called self-judging reservation to Article 36 (2) of the ICJ's statute that was made by the United States in 1946.[63] According to the Connally reservation, the United States excluded from the compulsory jurisdiction of the court matters that fell "essentially within the domestic jurisdiction" of the United States *as determined by the United States.*[64] In the debate over ratification of the convention in 1950, it was understood that the Connally reservation would be inapplicable in all cases arising under Article IX; in those cases, the ICJ would be acting in accordance with Article 36 (1) of its statute; that is, dealing with a matter "specially provided for" in a convention in force. Hence, if the United States ratified the Genocide Convention without excluding the application of Article IX, it would be obligated to go to court should another party initiate a case, and it would furthermore be obligated to accept the court's finding.

These facts did not trouble any of the representatives of the Truman administration who testified in favor of ratification of the convention at the 1950 hearings. However, they were troubling to some senators and other critics of the convention, notably the representatives of the ABA. As a result, the subcommittee of the Senate Committee on Foreign Relations that held the hearings in 1950 gave some consideration to drafting a reservation to Article IX that the committee as a whole could recommend to the Senate.[65] But the committee failed to recommend ratification, largely because of the ABA's opposition, so nothing ever came of the proposed reservation.

At various hearings that were held during the 1970s, the terms of Article IX were again carefully examined. Senator Sam Ervin, Jr., the arch-critic of the convention during the 1970s, repeatedly called attention to the fact that Article IX would effectively "bypass" the Connally reservation.[66] ABA representatives Eberhard Deutsch and Alfred Schweppe also noted the importance of Article IX. They were concerned that under the article the ICJ could provide authoritative interpretations of the convention's terms, and that the court's interpretations might be different from those in a series of understandings being proposed by the Committee on Foreign Relations during the 1970s. As Deutsch and Schweppe correctly pointed out, it was the ICJ, and not the Senate, that was ultimately competent to determine the meaning of words and phrases in the convention.[67]

Despite these often-repeated concerns, throughout the 1970s the Committee on Foreign Relations recommended the convention's ratification *without* a reservation to Article IX. In fact, in its reports to the Senate, usually prepared by Senator Frank Church, the committee argued that the article posed no serious problems so far as the United States was concerned, that it was even a "stock provision" that could be found in many multilateral treaties and conventions ratified by the United States. The committee also pointed out that the communist bloc states had ratified the convention with a reservation to Article IX, and that in accordance with the doctrine of reciprocity the United States would be able to "invoke [those reservations] in its own behalf in cases brought by members of the bloc." As late as September 1984 the committee stated:

> The committee does not envisage any real difficulties resulting from article IX. No disputes arising from alleged violations of the Genocide Convention have been decided by the Court to date. This is not to say, of course, that the United States might not be someday charged with nonfulfillment of the treaty by another signatory and might even be found in default of its treaty obligation—though this is hard to con-

ceive—but as a practical matter that is where it would end. The court has no enforcement powers. It is also well to recall that only states party to the Statute can bring cases before the World Court—not individuals or groups. In the Committee's view, the fears expressed about the role of a moribund court in genocide matters appear very far-fetched.[68]

By July 1985 the Committee on Foreign Relations, under new leadership, had completely reversed its position and now insisted on a reservation to Article IX. When formal debate on the resolution of ratification opened on the Senate floor in February 1986, Senator Robert Dole (R., Kansas), majority leader at the time, said that "if there was a successful effort made to knock down the world court reservation," it was his "intention to move to something else."[69] The threat was sufficient to lead opponents of the reservation to drop their opposition, and as a result, it was included in the Lugar-Helms-Hatch Sovereignty Package. What led to this abrupt and significant change of attitude? Why should the ICJ be perceived as moribund in September 1984 and a major threat to the United States by July 1985?

The Origins and Rationale of the Reservation

The chief architect of the U.S. reservation to Article IX was Senator Jesse Helms. Claiming inspiration from the late Senator Sam Ervin, Jr., Helms introduced a proposal regarding Article IX in the Senate Committee on Foreign Relations in September 1984, shortly after President Reagan endorsed ratification of the convention. The president's endorsement came only a few weeks before the 1984 presidential election, though the administration claimed to have had the convention under intensive interdepartmental review for about three years. The fact that the endorsement was made in a speech to the B'nai B'rith provoked tremendous cynicism, especially among Senate Democrats.[70] Helms, too, was apparently caught by surprise and seemed confused, as his initial proposal that culminated in the reservation to Article IX showed.

Initially, Helms had proposed the addition of an understanding to the package of understandings that had been proposed by the Committee on Foreign Relations on several occasions during the 1970s. It stated that the U.S. government understood and construed Article IX of the convention "in accordance with the 1946 declaration" (the Connally reservation) it had made in "submitting to the jurisdiction of the International Court of Justice pursuant to article 36 (2) of the statute of the Court."[71] Helms insisted that his proposal merely upheld the law of the United States by being consistent with the Connally reservation to the ICJ's statute, and upheld international law by being consistent with Article 2 (7) of the UN Charter, which barred the organization's involvement in matters that fell within the domestic jurisdiction of states.[72] In other words, Helms claimed to be proposing a pure understanding, and not a reservation. In fact, he spoke warmly of President Reagan's endorsement of the convention, indicating that he too favored ratification "consistent with the U.S. Constitution."[73] He insisted that his understanding with regard to Article IX, together with an additional understanding that eventually became the "constitutional reservation" in the Sovereignty Package (discussed in chapter 6), would not "take away from the importance or operation of the Genocide Convention but . . . would protect [the United States] from unforeseen mischief in the future."[74]

Considering the distinction between an understanding and a reservation, it appears that the problem with Helms's proposal was precisely that it could have been regarded as a reservation by other parties to the convention. In fact, neither of his claims could withstand critical examination, especially the claim that his understanding was consistent with the Connally reservation to Article 36 (2) of the ICJ's statute. It has always been understood—by senators, representatives of the ABA, and representatives of various administrations—that ratification of the Genocide Convention without a reservation to Article IX would "bypass" the Connally reservation. This is because, in resolving a dispute under Article IX of the convention, the ICJ would be exercising jurisdiction under Article 36 (1) of its statute, that is, regarding a matter specially provided for in a convention in force.

Regardless of what Senator Helms claimed, it is important to note that in 1984 the Reagan administration opposed the adoption of his proposed understanding. Davis Robinson, legal adviser to the Department of State, and Theodore Olson, assistant attorney general, testified for the administration in 1984. Robinson argued as follows:

> While we certainly understand Senator Helms' concern, we do have difficulties with this proposal. First of all, from our perspective, the fundamental purpose of the Genocide Convention is to define genocide as a matter of international concern. That is to say that the international community is seeking to define genocide as a matter which no longer can be considered solely a question of domestic interest. Thus, it would appear to us to be somewhat inconsistent with the convention to suggest that some forms of genocide may not be proper concerns of the international community.[75]

But this was not Robinson's only concern. He pointed out that the so-called understanding appeared to be "in reality" a reservation, and if it were,

> other parties to the convention might argue that such a reservation, if it is one, is incompatible with the object and purpose of the Genocide Convention. For example, the United Kingdom, Australia and the Netherlands have already objected on such grounds to reservations to article IX made by other states in their adherence to the Genocide Convention. Thus, some states might consider such a reservation inconsistent with international law and indeed consider us as not in treaty relations with them.[76]

Finally, Robinson was concerned about the policy implications of a reservation to Article IX, noting that the United States had already ratified a large number of treaties and other agreements with similar clauses. In brief, in 1984 the Reagan administration opposed Senator Helms's proposal on two grounds: it would be bad policy, and it would set a bad precedent.[77]

But Helms was persistent. On the one hand, it became increasingly apparent that the word "understanding" would not be appropriate for what he had in mind. On the other hand, it seemed too extreme to label the proposal a reservation because that might suggest the United States was emulating the Soviet bloc's practice with regard to Article IX. The word "proviso" was considered as an alternative, but that only added to the confusion. What, precisely, was a proviso, and how did it differ from an understanding or a reservation? When it became obvious that reservation was the only appropriate label for Helms's proposal, he suggested (hoping to avoid the appearance of following the Soviet Union's lead in the matter) that the "Indian formula" might serve as a model.[78] But India's reservation modified the legal effects of Article IX just as much as the Soviet Union's, though in different language.[79] There was no way out of this dilemma but to adopt a statement called a reservation that would have the same effects as all the others, including those of the Soviet bloc.

By 1985 the Reagan administration had capitulated to the most outspoken critics of the convention. A major factor in this regard was Senator Richard Lugar's position. He wrote a letter to the administration, ostensibly in his personal capacity but looking very much like an official committee document in the opinion of Senator Christopher Dodd, in which he reiterated his publicly stated views that he would support ratification only with a reservation to Article IX.[80] Since he was the chairman of the Committee on Foreign Relations (though he was actually behind Senator Helms in seniority on the committee), the administration had to take his views into account. In fact, the administration changed its position abruptly and with apparent eagerness. Assistant Secretary of State Elliott Abrams enthusiastically explained and defended this significant change in policy at the March 1985 Senate hearings:[81] the administration had not *proposed* a reservation; rather, it would *support* a reservation proposed by others for practical and prudential reasons.

According to Abrams, the practical reason was political—the necessity of agreeing to a reservation in order to get the Senate's advice and consent to the convention's ratification. All previous efforts to secure ratification had been futile, and the administration seemed to have concluded that it should pay any price to resolve the matter once and for all.[82] In fact, for Abrams the justification for ratifying the convention was political, pure and simple. As he put it:

> It is very strange and does no credit to us that 35-odd years after the United States helped draw up the Genocide Convention to put the nations of the world on record in their abhorrence of a crime that occurred, to try to bind them to passing domestic legislation with regard to it, that the United States is not a party and has been unable to ratify. It opens us to attacks. It makes it more difficult for us to respond not only to those attacks, but to other very difficult situations such as Cambodia where one would wish to refer to the terms of the Genocide Convention. And that is to say that it is useful to us in world political terms to ratify the convention, and it hurts us not to.[83]

Others, including Ambassador Jeanne Kirkpatrick, claimed to have come to the same conclusion regarding the political benefits that might flow from ratification. As she noted in a statement submitted to the Committee on Foreign Relations in 1984:

> I believe that the Senate's ratification of the Convention will enhance the standing of the United States in the United Nations and other international organizations. The Soviets and others hostile to the United States have long focused on the United States' failure to ratify the Convention as a part of their anti-American propaganda. It is contrary to our national interest to provide fuel to this campaign by failing to reaffirm clearly and unequivocally U.S. support for the important objectives of this Convention.[84]

In 1981, however, neither Ambassador Kirkpatrick nor any of her aides testified in favor of ratification when Senator Charles Percy held hearings on the convention in the Committee on Foreign Relations. In fact, in 1981 the Reagan administration had shown a distinct lack of interest in the convention, and some of its most important allies in the Senate, like Senator

Strom Thurmond, had expressed a strong desire to have President Reagan withdraw the convention from the Senate (see chapter 6).[85] Thurmond maintained his opposition to the end, voting against the Lugar-Helms-Hatch Sovereignty Package and then working to delay the passage of the implementing legislation, the Proxmire Act.

The prudential reason that Abrams advanced for supporting a reservation to Article IX was the ICJ's handling of *Nicaragua* v. *United States*.[86] The court had not yet handed down its judgment in the case at the time the Senate held its hearings in 1985. Nonetheless, the very fact that it had declared that it had jurisdiction in the case, despite the strong protest of the United States, was sufficient to convince influential senators such as Lugar, and some people in the executive branch as well, that a reservation to Article IX would be prudent. Put another way, *Nicaragua* indicated that the court was not moribund, as the Committee on Foreign Relations had confidently asserted as late as September 1984. In fact, Lugar noted in his opening statement at the committee's March 1985 hearings that *Nicaragua* demonstrated how the ICJ could "be used for blatant political attacks or that it would allow itself to be used for such attacks." Hence, he would support ratification of the Genocide Convention *only* with a reservation to Article IX.[87] His position was crucial to the outcome. On most issues the Committee on Foreign Relations was split nine to eight, almost strictly along party lines, with Senator Edward Zorinsky (D., Nebraska) voting with the Republicans, and Senator Charles Mathias voting with the Democrats.[88]

The Article IX reservation became a key provision of the Lugar-Helms-Hatch Sovereignty Package, and its adoption represents a break with past U.S. policy. Other parties to the Genocide Convention could object to the U.S. reservation on the ground that it is incompatible with the object and purpose of the convention, and even declare, as the Netherlands already has, that they do not recognize the United States as a party to the convention because of the reservation. And any of the other parties could, in accordance with the doctrine of reciprocity, invoke the U.S. reservation should it ever attempt to bring a case of genocide against them before the ICJ. This effectively guts the U.S. ratification.

Perhaps more important, relations between the United States and the ICJ in the wake of *Nicaragua* have cast doubt upon the soundness of the reasoning of senators who thought that the provisions of the Sovereignty Package were so comprehensive that they addressed all possible future problems. Senator Orrin Hatch, for example, argued on the Senate floor that it was better to ratify the convention with the Sovereignty Package than to reject it altogether. As Hatch saw it, the convention would inevitably "rise again" if it were rejected, and there was "no guarantee that a future president and a future Senate [would] not approve an unencumbered convention."[89] The Sovereignty Package so encumbered the convention that it was reduced to a "mere symbol of opposition to genocide, a crime which every civilized society and freedom-loving people abhors."[90] The Senate hearings and reports stressed the binding nature of all the conditions specified in the Sovereignty Package. The Committee of Foreign Relations even claimed to have been assured by the Reagan administration that all the conditions of ratification would be stated in the instrument of ratification when it was deposited at the United Nations.[91] They wanted absolutely no future misunderstandings about the Senate's intentions in giving its advice and consent to ratification. The administration followed through on its pledge; the instrument of ratification contains all the conditions specified in the Sovereignty Package except the declaration regarding the adoption of domestic legislation, which was purely a domestic procedural matter.[92]

But could the Senate actually impose all of these conditions, including the reservation to Article IX, indefinitely into the future? The Reagan administration, as we know, willingly accepted the conditions as the necessary political price it had to pay to get ratification. But what about any future administration? The U.S. response to the ICJ's handling of *Nicaragua* provides some insight into this question. Even before the court handed down its judgment in that case, perhaps in anticipation of an unfavorable judgment, the administration launched a campaign to discredit the court. After the judgment, in October 1985, the Reagan administration withdrew the 1946 U.S. declaration accepting the compulsory jurisdiction of the court under Article 36 (2) of its statute. In accordance with the six-month notification period, the termination became effective in April 1986.[93] The administration attempted to minimize the significance of its action, claiming that the declaration was not a treaty and that terminating acceptance of the court's compulsory jurisdiction did "not expose the United States to new commitments and obligations." The administration also announced that the United States and Italy had agreed to take a dispute concerning an American-owned commercial enterprise to the court,[94] presumably proving that the administration was not opposed in principle to going to the court and would indeed use the court for resolving disputes in some instances.

Nonetheless, the declaration accepting the compulsory jurisdiction of the ICJ had been mandated by Senate action in 1946, though the legislative history of that declaration made it clear that the president was authorized to terminate it with six months' notice.[95] The legislative history of the Sovereignty Package does not expressly grant such authority to the president. It may even be argued that the Senate intended to deny the president such authority. But will the Senate's intentions bind a future president? Or might the Sovereignty Package be withdrawn at a later date? Some opponents of ratification, such as Senator Steven Symms, were not as certain as Senator Orrin Hatch and others that the Sovereignty Package would be binding on future administrations.[96] While withdrawing the package in whole or in part would arguably *increase* the United States's "exposure" to new commitments and obligations, it is not at all clear that it would be impermissible. It might merely result in a political dispute of relatively minor proportions, as with the Reagan administration's action regarding the compulsory jurisdiction of the court in response to *Nicaragua*.

Senators Mark Hatfield (R., Oregon) and Daniel P. Moynihan (D., New York) denounced President Reagan's action regarding the ICJ and introduced an amendment to pending legislation that would have terminated U.S. financial contributions to international organizations until the court's compulsory jurisdiction was restored. This strange proposal, which its sponsors undoubtedly realized had no chance of passage, was rejected by a large margin—twenty-one in favor, seventy-four against, and five not voting. Although the amendment was supported almost exclusively by Democrats, it is noteworthy that Senator Barry Goldwater voted in favor of it. He did not indicate why he supported it. We can note, however, that Goldwater had brought suit against President Carter for terminating a treaty relationship with Taiwan on his own authority, and perhaps he felt that Reagan's action on the declaration regarding the compulsory jurisdiction of the ICJ also constituted an abuse of executive authority in the exercise of the treaty-making power.[97] In any event, the overwhelming rejection of the Hatfield-Moynihan amendment indicated that defending the ICJ in light of *Nicaragua* was not popular. But does this experience suggest that a different president at a different time could withdraw the reservation to Article IX—or any other provision of the Sovereignty Package—on his own authority?

Perceptions of the Reservation

The opponents and proponents of the Article IX reservation were sharply divided on its desirability for reasons of policy as well as law. As a matter of policy, some critics were concerned about the image of the United States that a reservation concerning Article IX would project. From their point of view, it seemed manifestly undesirable for the United States to take the same position on Article IX as virtually the entire Soviet bloc. Since the objection was raised mostly by liberals, there was a strong element of sarcasm in it. In fact, the liberals seemed to delight in the opportunity the administration had presented them to score at least a minor point when they were surely headed for defeat in opposing the reservation. Senator John Kerry, for example, asked Reagan administration representatives at the 1985 Senate hearings why the United States should not stand with its allies and others that had ratified the convention without a reservation to Article IX: "Does it not bother you as a matter of public policy as representatives of the Government of the United States of America that you are espousing that we join in reservation with those Communist nations and those nations against our allies from Canada, Italy and many others in what I think . . . just nullifies the effect of this?"[98]

In reply, Elliott Abrams tried to minimize the significance of the reservation, stating that he did "not think that the utility of the Convention lies in the ICJ."[99] Then, when pushed to reply to the question, Abrams put the blame for the reservation on the ICJ itself! He said, "It does bother me, and it bothers me that we are driven to do this by an outrageous assertion of jurisdiction by the International Court of Justice, which makes it necessary for us to agree that some protection of the United States is wise and sensible."[100]

Senators who strongly favored the reservation also tended to minimize its significance. Like Abrams, they simply denied that Article IX is an integral part of the convention, pointing out that many parties had made reservations to the article anyway. In general, they deemphasized the significance of the reservation, insisting that it would probably not be necessary for the United States to invoke it often. Senator Lugar, for example, in the report the Committee on Foreign Relations submitted to the Senate, stated that the committee did "not anticipate that the United States will rely on this reservation frequently, if at all"; nor did he think that "its use will be controversial." Rather, according to Lugar, the committee believed that the "types of cases where it will be appropriate to withhold specific consent to ICJ jurisdiction will be plain to all." What Lugar failed to explain, however, was why, if the reservation was truly insignificant, the "Committee expect[ed] the President to consult with Committee members when deciding whether to accept or decline jurisdiction"?[101] More than anything, this attitude reflected the strong feelings that some committee members had about the ICJ at the time of ratification. It reflects as well the assertiveness the Senate has evidenced from time to time when it has exercised its constitutional mandate by giving its advice and consent to ratification of treaties and conventions.

The reservation to Article IX was also carefully scrutinized for its legal implications. Senator Charles Mathias, for example, suggested that allies of the United States and others might object to the reservation on the ground that it is incompatible with the object and purpose of the convention. He also noted that in 1984 the Reagan administration had opposed a reservation to Article IX because under the doctrine of reciprocity another party could invoke a U.S. reservation in a proceeding before the ICJ brought by the United States. Hence, Mathias was concerned that the United States could lose more than it gained by ratifying the convention with a reservation to Article IX—it could make it impossible for the United States to make an issue of an alleged violation of the convention such as the Cambodian case.[102]

Senator Christopher Dodd also was concerned about the legal impact of a reservation to Article IX, particularly an open-ended reservation such as Senator Helms was proposing, on the ground that it could completely undermine the convention's effectiveness. Dodd proposed to amend Helms's version of the reservation to state that the United States would submit to ICJ jurisdiction in cases brought by another party which had not made a reservation to Article IX.[103] Such a reservation would, of course, have eliminated as possible claimants against the United States the entire East European bloc at the time the United States ratified. But from the point of view of senators who favored a reservation, the problem with Dodd's proposal was that the United States still would have been exposed to claims brought against it by other adversaries and potential adversaries, and who was to say that the friends of today would not be the enemies of tomorrow? *Nicaragua* had itself demonstrated how problems of this sort could arise. One of the bases of the ICJ's jurisdiction in that case was a compromissory clause in a treaty between Nicaragua and the United States concluded long before the Sandinista government had come to power.[104] Dodd's proposal was therefore unacceptable precisely because it would have failed to adequately insulate the United States from being brought to court against its wishes. In other words, it would have failed to prevent another *Nicaragua*. The Committee on Foreign Relations rejected Dodd's amendment by a vote of eight in favor and nine against.[105]

The proponents of the reservation took issue with the legal concerns of critics such as Kerry, Dodd, and Mathias. They denied that their attitude was hostile to the development of international law, as the critics implied or explicitly charged. Furthermore, they were highly skeptical that the United

States would ever call upon the ICJ to resolve a dispute concerning the convention once it became a party. On this matter, proponents of the reservation expressed a strangely protective attitude toward the court. Senator Lugar even suggested that it could be burdensome to expect the court to deal with a case concerning the Genocide Convention. In his opinion, such a case would be too controversial, and any court ruling would likely be ignored, thus not only failing to "enhance the standing of the ICJ" but actually undermining it. As the report of the Committee on Foreign Relations stated, there are "other, better suited international fora where pressures against offending states can be brought to bear." Presumably this statement referred to political forums, but they were not specified. In any event, according to Lugar, what the committee did "not want to see is the ICJ asked to engage in a futile exercise."[106]

Senator Jesse Helms, in contrast, was considerably more straightforward in his concerns. For him, the convention as a whole posed problems almost too numerous to mention, and he was always concerned with "protecting the sovereignty of the American people and of this Nation."[107] On this subject, at the 1985 hearings, he had this to say: "Now, this is part of the problem. I am not sure anybody understands what is afoot here. Probably I do not. But just speaking as one Senator, I do not intend to sit silently when the sovereignty of this country is under assault, whether you agree that it is or not, because time passes and people move on."[108]

Later, in comments on the Senate floor just before voting *against* the Sovereignty Package, even though he was its chief architect, Helms's comments revealed the enormous gulf that separated him from proponents of ratification such as Senator William Proxmire. He said,

> Mr. President, the vote which the Senate is about to conduct upon the so-called Genocide Convention is, at most symbolic. Thanks to the eight provisos—or reservations—that some of us insisted should be a part of the instrument, the sovereignty of our Nation and the freedom of our people have been protected against assault by the World Court.
>
> In other words, the treaty has been defanged in terms of the dangerous defects in its original version. . . .
>
> So, Mr. President, this Genocide Convention upon which we are about to vote is purely symbolic. We might as well be voting on a simple resolution to condemn genocide—which every civilized person does.
>
> My vote against the treaty is likewise symbolic. Even in its present form, harmless as it now is, this treaty has the remote potential of an entangling alliance. So I shall vote against it for that reason—and also as a

> postscript of gratitude to a great American, Sam Ervin, who long ago took the time to make me aware of the great constitutional implications of this treaty in its original form.[109]

As for U.S. allies that might object to an Article IX reservation in particular, Helms fell back on a unilateralist, staunch pro-sovereignty position. As he stated, if our allies condemn us "for protecting the sovereignty of the United States of America and the people thereof, then good, I want to see what the substance of their condemnation is."[110]

Chapter 10 Conclusion

We have waited too long to delay further. The convention is not perfect, but that is hardly reason to reject it. As a nation which enshrines human dignity and freedom as a God-given right in its constitution, we must correct our anomalous position on this basic rights issue. The time to debate is over. The time to act is now.—Senator Robert Dole, Senate floor debate, February 1986

The Senate's adoption of a resolution of ratification for the Genocide Convention in February 1986 closed an important chapter in the long and bitter struggle over ratification that had occurred since President Truman requested the Senate's advice and consent to ratification in June 1950. It resolved the issue of whether or not the United States *should* ratify the convention. The passage of the Proxmire Act in the closing days of the One Hundredth Congress in October 1988 brought to a close a second chapter. It opened the way for the United States to deposit its instrument of ratification at the United Nations and at long last officially become a party to the convention. President Reagan's action in depositing the U.S. instrument of ratification in November 1988 closed the third, and final, chapter in the ratification process. According to Article XIII, the Genocide Convention became legally binding on the United States in February 1989, ninety days after the United States deposited its instrument of ratification. Why such prolonged debate? Was it all worth the effort? Does the experience in dealing with the Genocide Convention provide any insight into what we might expect if the ratification of similar treaties should come under active consideration in the Senate?

As we have seen throughout this book, many issues were raised in the debate over ratification of the Genocide Convention. Some of these issues concerned the rule on genocide. Others concerned the rule-supervisory measures. With regard to the rule, everyone agrees—and the Genocide Convention makes it clear—that genocide is a crime committed against groups of human beings. Indeed, Raphael Lemkin coined the word "genocide" to apply to situations in which individuals become the victims of crimes not for any reason peculiar to them but simply because they are members of certain types of groups. He had observed this phenomenon in Europe during the 1930s as the Nazis began their persecution of the Jews, Poles, Gypsies, and other groups that would culminate in the Holocaust. But this is perhaps the only important principle affirmed in the convention on which everyone was in agreement. Other components of the rule were exceedingly controversial, and for almost forty years the proponents and opponents of ratification fought over their meaning and implications.

In chapters 3, 4, and 5, we discussed how various aspects of Article II of the convention, the basic article that sets forth the rule on genocide, became the subject of extensive debate. For example, the article defines the crime of genocide in terms of an "intent to destroy, in whole or in part," national, ethnic, racial, or religious groups. In its ordinary meaning, the phrase says that the intent could be to destroy one or more of the protected groups either in whole or in part. Commentators on the convention, as well as virtually all of the proponents and opponents of ratification in the United States, generally agreed with this interpretation. However, opponents of ratification made an issue out of what constitutes a part of a group. If single individuals could be understood to constitute a part of a group, and thus become victims of genocide, could the convention be considered applicable to racial lynchings?

Specific genocidal acts stipulated in Article II were also perceived as raising the possibility that the convention could have an impact on race relations within the United States. For example, the article stipulates that inflicting "mental harm" on members of a group could constitute genocide, and opponents of ratification wondered if segregation laws might be seen as inflicting "mental harm" on black people. In fact, as far back as the 1950 Senate hearings there has been concern that ratification of the Genocide Convention by the United States would make it a tool in the civil rights struggle.

Other acts considered genocidal under the terms of Article II created different problems. Even the very obvious genocidal technique of "killing members of groups" became controversial in light of the fact that Article I brands genocide a crime whether committed in times of war or peace. During the 1970s this fact raised the question of whether or not American soldiers fighting in the Vietnam War would be exposed to charges of committing genocide if the United States ratified the convention.

Finally, Article II was controversial because of a perceived loophole in its definition of genocide that could have had a deleterious impact on the enforcement of the convention. This loophole was allegedly created when the drafters decided not to extend protection to political groups as such. As we have seen, Article II defines the crime of genocide as involving the destruction of national, ethnic, racial, or religious groups. The drafters settled on these groups after lengthy debate. In fact, the issue of what groups should be designated as objects of protection under the terms of Article II was the subject of the most extensive debate during the drafting process. In the main, the drafters decided to extend protection only to what they considered "stable" groups, and political groups as such did not qualify under this standard. Many critics of the convention in the United States have argued that its failure to protect political groups has made it inapplicable where it is most needed—that is, to totalitarian states, especially the Soviet Union, where groups such as national groups could be liquidated under the guise of political reasons having to do with state security.

Other issues that arose in the struggle over ratification concerned the measures that it prescribes to ensure compliance with its terms. The measures include the adoption of domestic implementing legislation, the creation of an international criminal court, and the submission of disputes concerning the interpretation, application, or fulfillment of the convention to the International Court of Justice for settlement. As discussed in chapters 6, 7, 8, and 9, the question of whether or not the United States should agree to these rule-supervisory measures arose frequently in the debate over ratification.

In retrospect, during the four decades the Genocide Convention was under consideration in the United States, virtually every word in it was scrutinized for its implications, real or imagined. Although the potential impact that ratification might have for race relations within the United States was a factor in this debate, it would be erroneous to conclude that the basis for opposition to ratification was simply racism against blacks. It is true that some of the most outspoken opponents of ratification, such as Senator Sam Ervin, Jr., introduced arguments that implied a deep concern for the racial factor. But there have also been comments from fringe group representatives, such as Liberty Lobby's Trisha Katson, that bordered on anti-Semitism. There was also a strong anti-Sovietism in the debate, particularly in connection with the so-called political group exemption. However, none of these factors taken alone explains the intensity of the debate on the convention as a whole.

In broader terms, we could say that the disagreements that arose in the debate over ratification reflected profound differences of opinion regarding the relative benefits and costs of an internationalist as opposed to a unilateralist foreign policy stance on human rights issues, and the racial and anti-Soviet issues were elements of these broader concerns. Many of the strongest proponents of ratification, such as Senator William Proxmire, argued along lines that reflected a firm internationalist stance. Generally, they advanced the view that human rights are a legitimate matter of international concern and that the United States should play a leading role in the field. Accordingly, it would be "good" foreign policy for the United States to ratify international human rights instruments, and particularly the Genocide Convention, which many proponents of ratification saw as a moral imperative.

The most outspoken opponents of ratification, in contrast, especially Senators Sam Ervin, Jr., and Jesse Helms, more often than not argued a strong unilateralist position. They took issue with the most fundamental assumptions of the proponents regarding the wisdom of accepting international obligations such as that embodied in the Genocide Convention, and, indeed, were prepared to defend the broadest possible conception of national sovereignty at all costs. They also fought against ratification on practical grounds, expressing a profound pessimism about the potential impact of ratification on preventing the crime of genocide. The opponents claimed to abhor genocide as much as the proponents of ratification did, but they insisted that the Genocide Convention will not prevent its occurrence or lead to the punishment of any of its perpetrators. While the proponents argued that ratification was important symbolically, the opponents emphasized the negative legal implications of ratification.

Was all this debate worth the effort? To those who have perceived—and do perceive—the ratification of the Genocide Convention as an important symbolic act, the debate may have been worth the effort. When so many other states in the world—principal allies as well as adversaries of the United States—had already ratified the convention, it seemed dishonorable that the United States did not also ratify. To its proponents, ratification at least allowed the United States to claim to be on the side of virtue. Moreover, symbolic acts can in the long run produce desirable results. Despite the difficulties that we know have attended the enforcement of the Genocide Convention, there is always the chance that it will be invoked in the future, and the United States could play an important role in this regard.

Those who see the ratification of the convention primarily in legal terms, however, might answer the question differently. As we have seen, most of the issues that arose regarding both the rule and the rule-supervisory measures dealt with in the convention were addressed in the resolution of ratification, the Lugar-Helms-Hatch Sovereignty Package; where appropriate, they were also addressed in the implementing legislation, the Proxmire Act. When compared with the instruments of ratification of all other parties to the Genocide Convention, the Sovereignty Package is unique in its content and breadth of coverage. Some might even say that it makes a mockery of the convention. After all, no other party to the convention has ratified with so many reservations or understandings. In fact, the only provision of the Sovereignty Package that resembles the practice of other parties is the reservation to Article IX, the compromissory clause regarding the role of the ICJ in settling disputes regarding the interpretation, application, and fulfillment of the convention. Almost one-quarter of the parties to the convention have ratified it with a reservation to Article IX, apparently perceiving such a reservation as insulation from any unforeseen problems that they did not anticipate before ratification.

The United States also intended the Article IX reservation to be a protective device. In the past the United States had usually accepted compromissory clauses such as Article IX when ratifying multilateral as well as bilateral treaties. However, the ICJ's handling of the case brought by Nicaragua against the United States in 1984 led to a demand for a break with this past policy, and specifically to the adoption of the reservation to Article IX of the Genocide Convention. The U.S. reservation, championed mainly by Senator Jesse Helms, actually has the same effects as the reservations that virtually the entire Soviet bloc made upon ratification. Ironically, only a few months after President Reagan deposited the Sovereignty Package at the United Nations, the Soviet Union withdrew its reservation to Article IX, breaking with its long-standing practice of making such reservations. But unlike the majority of the other parties to the Genocide Convention, the U.S. Sovereignty Package does not rely only on the Article IX reservation as a protective device. The Sovereignty Package goes considerably further: it also contains the so-called constitutional reservation, which affirms the supremacy of the U.S. Constitution over the convention, and five understandings that pertain to various aspects of the rule and rule-supervisory mechanisms dealt with in the convention. The breadth of coverage of the Sovereignty Package suggests that the United States wanted to address every conceivable problem that might arise as a result of ratification in the instrument of ratification itself. It remains to be seen if this strategy will achieve the desired results. There are two main reasons to be doubtful.

In the first place, while reservations to the Genocide Convention are allowed, there are limitations regarding the types of reservations that any party can make. In particular, any reservation that violates the object and purpose of the convention is not permissible. Since the convention is a multilateral treaty, other parties to it have a voice in determining the acceptability of the U.S. conditions as spelled out in the Lugar-Helms-Hatch Sovereignty Package. It could be expected that other parties would make such determinations at least in part, and perhaps mainly, on the basis of political considerations—the sort of relationship that they have or hope to have and maintain with the United States. Although objections have already been lodged by some European parties to the convention, it may be that many of the other parties will not object to the U.S. conditions—and a few of these conditions are actually unobjectionable. The understanding regarding the international criminal court, for example, in which the United States asserts that acceptance of the jurisdiction of such a court must be effected by the conclusion of a treaty to which the Senate gives its advice and consent, was intended more as a statement about the domestic political system of the United States in general, and the relationship between the executive and the legislative branches in the exercise of the treaty-making power in particular, than anything else. Other parties would also find it difficult to build a case for objecting to the U.S. understanding regarding extradition, or to its assertion of jurisdiction for its own courts to try persons who commit genocide on the basis of either the nationality or territorial principles. In fact, this latter understanding provides a good example of how the fanaticism of the opponents of ratification led to the endorsement of exceedingly narrow interpretations of the terms of the convention. For this reason, it could hardly be interpreted as violative of the object and purpose of the convention.

Nonetheless, as we have discussed throughout this book, other parties to the convention would have good reasons for objecting to parts of the Sovereignty Package. Some of its provisions—for example, the understandings regarding intent and the meaning of mental harm—seem to carve out exceptions for the United States. Thus, even if the statements are called understandings, and are not technically designed to exclude or vary the legal effect of provisions of the convention as would reservations, they could be understood by other parties as being reservations that may be incompatible with the object and purpose of the convention. The considerations that gave rise to the adoption of these understandings—mainly domestic racial considerations—would lend credibility to the viewpoint of those who object. In other instances, like the Article IX reservation, some parties have already objected to its terms, and a few would not even consider the United States a party to the convention because of it. Beyond that, the so-called constitutional reservation, combined with all of the provisions of the Sovereignty Package as a whole, has already led some parties to suspect that the United States did not ratify the convention in good faith. As some senators oriented toward a strong internationalist posture argued, some provisions of the Sovereignty Package gave rise to suspicions that the United States had something to hide. This concern gets at the question of policy—of whether or not the Sovereignty Package, even if found to be legally unobjectionable, might still be considered objectionable on policy grounds. After all, even the Soviet Union, whose alleged genocidal policies figured so prominently in the debate over ratification of the convention, is now a party to it with no reservations whatever. Could not the United States have done the same?

Even if other parties to the convention should fail to object to the Sovereignty Package in whole or in part, in the long run it might still not achieve the objectives of its principal authors. The main architects of the package, especially Senators Jesse Helms and Orrin Hatch, were thinking of the future. They would clearly have preferred for the United States never to become a party to the convention. But President Reagan's endorsement of the convention in 1984 dramatically changed the conditions under which the debate over ratification would henceforth be conducted. After his endorsement, only the most extreme fringe elements could continue to oppose ratification. Helms, Hatch, and the few other outspoken critics of the convention in the Senate were left with no practical alternative but to work for ratification under conditions that would reduce the convention to nothing more than a symbol of opposition to genocide. The Sovereignty Package was intended to accomplish that objective. But presidents can break international agreements on their own authority, and on some occasions they have done so. Moreover, they can apparently disregard, and even withdraw, conditions that the Senate imposes when it gives its advice and consent to ratification of a treaty. Beyond that, there is always the possibility that changing circumstances can fundamentally change policy, and in the future a different Congress might well be open to a different approach to international cooperative action on genocide and related human rights abuses. In such circumstances the Sovereignty Package, or specific provisions of it, could be withdrawn.

The one major concern that could not be addressed in the Sovereignty Package was the so-called political group exemption in Article II of the convention. This issue, unlike the other issues discussed above, which concerned words, phrases, or articles *contained* in the convention, arose because the word "political" was *deleted* from the article during the drafting stage. This created a loophole in the definition of genocide that critics claimed could be exploited by totalitarian states, especially the Soviet Union, which would be able to persecute any of the protected groups while claiming that their actions were directed against political enemies, and not at protected groups as such. The critics therefore attempted to persuade the Senate to amend Article II of the convention to insert the word "political" before adopting the resolution of ratification. This strategy having failed, they pushed for the adoption of a sense of the Senate resolution—which passed—that calls for the United States to work toward the adoption of an amendment by the United Nations.

The idea of amending the Genocide Convention to extend its coverage to political groups carries more disadvantages than advantages. In the first place, the proposal reflects a profound misunderstanding of the motives of the drafters in deleting the word "political" from Article II. As we have seen, the drafters were motivated to extend protection only to stable groups. Moreover, they wanted to draft a convention that would be acceptable to the largest possible number of states, and they were concerned that some states would decline to ratify the convention if political groups were protected. It is arguable that their reasons are as valid today as they were when the convention was drafted. As adopted, the Genocide Convention would apply to the genocide committed against the Jews, Poles, Gypsies, and other groups during World War II, and to the genocide committed against the Armenians during World War I. An amendment of Article II to cover political groups would probably make the convention applicable in other situations as well, including some that the critics want it to apply to, such as Afghanistan and Cambodia; but it could also make it applicable in precisely the kinds of situations they would not want it to apply to, for example, the Vietnam War. All things considered, the so-called political group exemption would be better dealt with through the adoption of a protocol to the convention that states could ratify if they wished, or through the drafting of a new, separate treaty or convention on what some have called the crime of politicide.

What lessons can be drawn from the U.S. experience with the Genocide Convention? One that seems especially important is that opponents of ratification were virtually always on the offensive and proponents were on the defensive. Indeed, it would be no exaggeration to say that the opponents of ratification were able to control the debate at virtually every stage, from the 1950 hearings to the adoption of the resolution of ratification in 1986, and even through the adoption of the implementing legislation in 1988. The Lugar-Helms-Hatch Sovereignty Package is not inappropriately labeled. The critics were able to manipulate the most important symbols—the flag and the Constitution—to their advantage. Even if their arguments against ratification might have seemed—and indeed were—irrational at times, they had an intimidating quality, leaving the proponents of ratification with little choice but to accept the conditions of ratification that the opponents wanted to impose. President Reagan's endorsement of ratification was very important in this respect, for it eliminated any possibility that a senator who voted in favor of ratification could be accused of being soft on flag and country.

The opponents of ratification were exceedingly resourceful: as one argument was laid to rest, another rose to take its place. The arguments were generally couched in legal language, often giving them the appearance of being highly sophisticated in content, but they were as much political as they were legal, and perhaps more so. As I suggested earlier, the arguments used by the proponents and opponents of ratification reflected different visions of what they perceived to be good foreign policy for the United States, and even different visions of world order. The debate largely involved matters of preference. The ability of the opponents of ratification to control the debate was crucial to their success. Those who favor the ratification of other controversial human rights treaties have much to learn from this experience with the Genocide Convention. It is important to devise strategies that enable proponents of ratification of other human rights treaties to be on the offensive rather than on the defensive.

The importance of devising effective strategies is doubly important in view of the second main lesson that comes out of this experience with the Genocide Convention. Brickerism did not end with the defeat of the Bricker Amendment to the Constitution. To the contrary, it lingers on as an effective force even if it may not represent the majority view, or even that of a significant minority. The Lugar-Helms-Hatch Sovereignty Package has the stamp of the Bricker Amendment all over it, especially in its so-called constitutional reservation and the understanding regarding the acceptance of the jurisdiction of an international criminal court by a treaty alone. While it could be maintained that the convention itself contemplates the use of a treaty or convention for the creation of an international criminal court, and that the U.S. understanding is therefore superfluous and of no great consequence, it remains important because of the attitude it reflects. In a word, the Sovereignty Package *amounts* to a Bricker Amendment. It achieves through a resolution of ratification what Bricker tried to achieve through a constitutional amendment. Those who carry on Bricker's legacy could use similar strategies in the future when presidents request approval of controversial treaties. To be sure, Bricker's constitutional amendment would have had more lasting effects than would a resolution of ratification, which, as we have seen, might be withdrawn in the future. But a resolution of ratification could still be effective because of its political significance. The forces against the U.S. acceptance of formal international obligations in this field remain powerful and are likely to persist into the future.

Appendix A Convention on the Prevention and Punishment of the Crime of Genocide

(UN GAOR Res. 260A (III) 9 December 1948)

Text of the Convention

THE CONTRACTING PARTIES,

HAVING CONSIDERED the declaration made by the General Assembly of the United Nations in its resolution 96 (I) dated 11 December 1946 that genocide is a crime under international law, contrary to the spirit and aims of the United Nations and condemned by the civilized world;

RECOGNIZING that at all periods of history genocide has inflicted great losses on humanity; and

BEING CONVINCED that, in order to liberate mankind from such an odious scourge, international co-operation is required:

HEREBY AGREE AS HEREINAFTER PROVIDED:

Article I

The Contracting Parties confirm that genocide, whether committed in time of peace or in time of war, is a crime under international law which they undertake to prevent and to punish.

Article II

In the present Convention, genocide means any of the following acts committed with intent to destroy, in whole or in part, a national, ethnical, racial, or religious group, as such:

(*a*) Killing members of the group;
(*b*) Causing serious bodily or mental harm to members of the group;
(*c*) Deliberately inflicting on the group conditions of life calculated to bring about its physical destruction in whole or in part;
(*d*) Imposing measures intended to prevent births within the group;
(*e*) Forcibly transferring children of the group to another group.

Article III

The following acts shall be punishable:

(*a*) Genocide;
(*b*) Conspiracy to commit genocide;
(*c*) Direct and public incitement to commit genocide;
(*d*) Attempt to commit genocide;
(*e*) Complicity in genocide.

Article IV

Persons committing genocide or any of the other acts enumerated in Article III shall be punished, whether they are constitutionally responsible rulers, public officials, or private individuals.

Article V

The Contracting Parties undertake to enact, in accordance with their respective Constitutions, the necessary legislation to give effect to the provisions of the present Convention and, in particular, to provide effective penalties for persons guilty of genocide or of any of the other acts enumerated in Article III.

Article VI

Persons charged with genocide or any of the other acts enumerated in Article III shall be tried by a competent tribunal of the State in the territory of which the act was committed, or by such international penal tribunal as may have jurisdiction with respect to those Contracting Parties which shall have accepted its jurisdiction.

Article VII

Genocide and the other acts enumerated in Article III shall not be considered as political crimes for the purpose of extradition.

The Contracting Parties pledge themselves in such cases to grant extradition in accordance with their laws and treaties in force.

Article VIII

Any Contracting Party may call upon the competent organs of the United Nations to take such action under the Charter of the United Nations as they consider appropriate for the prevention and suppression of acts of genocide or any of the other acts enumerated in Article III.

Article IX

Disputes between the Contracting Parties relating to the interpretation, application, or fulfillment of the present Convention, including those relating to the responsibility of a State for genocide or for any of the other acts enumerated in Article III, shall be submitted to the International Court of Justice at the request of any of the parties to the dispute.

Article X

The present Convention, of which the Chinese, English, French, Russian, and Spanish texts are equally authentic, shall bear the date of 9 December 1948.

Article XI

The present Convention shall be open until 31 December 1949 for signature on behalf of any Member of the United Nations and of any nonmember State to which an invitation to sign has been addressed by the General Assembly.

The present Convention shall be ratified, and the instruments of ratification shall be deposited with the Secretary-General of the United Nations.

After 1 January 1950 the present Convention may be acceded to on behalf of any Member of the United Nations and of any nonmember State which has received an invitation as aforesaid.

Instruments of accession shall be deposited with the Secretary-General of the United Nations.

Article XII

Any Contracting Party may at any time, by notification addressed to the Secretary-General of the United Nations, extend the application of the present Convention to all or any of the territories for the conduct of whose foreign relations that Contracting Party is responsible.

Article XIII

On the day when the first twenty instruments of ratification or accession have been deposited, the Secretary-General shall draw up a *procès-verbal* and transmit a copy thereof to each Member of the United Nations and to each of the nonmember States contemplated in Article XI.

The present Convention shall come into force on the ninetieth day following the date of deposit of the twentieth instrument of ratification or accession.

Any ratification or accession effected subsequent to the latter date shall become effective on the ninetieth day following the deposit of the instrument of ratification or accession.

Article XIV

The present Convention shall remain in effect for a period of ten years as from the date of its coming into force.

It shall thereafter remain in force for successive periods of five years for such Contracting Parties as have not denounced it at least six months before the expiration of the current period.

Denunciation shall be effected by a written notification addressed to the Secretary-General of the United Nations.

Article XV

If, as a result of denunciations, the number of Parties to the present Convention should become less than sixteen, the Convention shall cease to be in force as from the date on which the last of these denunciations shall become effective.

Article XVI

A request for the revision of the present Convention may be made at any time by any Contracting Party by means of a notification in writing addressed to the Secretary-General.

The General Assembly shall decide upon the steps, if any, to be taken in respect of such request.

Article XVII

The Secretary-General of the United Nations shall notify all Members of the United Nations and the nonmember States contemplated in Article XI of the following:

(*a*) Signatures, ratifications, and accessions received in accordance with Article XI;
(*b*) Notifications received in accordance with Article XII;
(*c*) The date upon which the present Convention comes into force in accordance with Article XIII;
(*d*) Denunciations received in accordance with Article XIV;
(*e*) The abrogation of the Convention in accordance with Article XV;
(*f*) Notifications received in accordance with Article XVI.

Article XVIII

The original of the present Convention shall be deposited in the archives of the United Nations.

A certified copy of the Convention shall be transmitted to each Member of the United Nations and to each of the nonmember States contemplated in Article XI.

Article XIX

The present Convention shall be registered by the Secretary-General of the United Nations on the date of its coming into force.

Appendix B Resolution of Ratification Proposed 1970, 1971, 1973, 1976, and 1984

(S. EXEC. REP. 50, 98th Cong., 2d sess. 21–22 [1984])

Resolved (*two-thirds of the Senators present concurring therein*), That the Senate advise and consent to the ratification of the International Convention on the Prevention and Punishment of the Crime of Genocide, adopted unanimously by the General Assembly of the United Nations in Paris on December 9, 1948, and signed on behalf of the United States on December 11, 1948 (Executive O, Eighty-first Congress, first session), subject to the following understandings and declaration:

1. That the United States Government understands and construes the words "intent to destroy, in whole or in part, a national, ethnical, racial, or religious group as such" appearing in Article II, to mean the intent to destroy a national, ethnical, racial, or religious group by the acts specified in Article II in such manner as to affect a substantial part of the group concerned.
2. That the United States Government understands and construes the words "mental harm" appearing in Article II (b) of this Convention to mean permanent impairment of mental faculties.
3. That the United States Government understands and construes Article VI of the Convention in accordance with the agreed language of the Report of the Legal Committee of the United Nations General Assembly that nothing in Article VI shall affect the right of any State to bring to trial before its own tribunals any of its nationals for acts committed outside the State.
4. That the United States Government declares that it will not deposit its instrument of ratification until after the implementing legislation referred to in Article V has been enacted.

Appendix C Resolution of Ratification (Lugar-Helms-Hatch Sovereignty Package)

Adopted February 19, 1986

(S. EXEC. REP. 2, 99th Cong., 1st sess. 26–27 [1985])

Resolved (*two-thirds of the Senators present concurring therein*), That the Senate advise and consent to the ratification of the International Convention on the Prevention and Punishment of the Crime of Genocide, adopted unanimously by the General Assembly of the United Nations in Paris on December 9, 1948 (Executive O, Eighty-first Congress, first session), *Provided that:*

I. The Senate's advice and consent is subject to the following reservations:

(1) That with reference to Article IX of the Convention, before any dispute to which the United States is a party may be submitted to the jurisdiction of the International Court of Justice under this article, the specific consent of the United States is required in each case.

(2) That nothing in the Convention requires or authorizes legislation or other action by the United States of America prohibited by the Constitution of the United States as interpreted by the United States.

II. The Senate's advice and consent is subject to the following understandings, which shall apply to the obligations of the United States under this Convention:

(1) That the term "intent to destroy, in whole or in part, a national, ethnical, racial, or religious group as such" appearing in Article II means the specific intent to destroy, in whole or in substantial part, a national, ethnical, racial, or religious group as such by the acts specified in Article II.

(2) That the term "mental harm" in Article II (b) means permanent impairment of mental faculties through drugs, torture, or similar techniques.

(3) That the pledge to grant extradition in accordance with a state's laws and treaties in force found in Article VII extends only to acts which are criminal under the laws of both the requesting and the requested state and nothing in Article VI affects the right of any state to bring to trial before its own tribunals any of its nationals for acts committed outside a state.

(4) That acts in the course of armed conflicts committed without the specific intent required by Article II are not sufficient to constitute genocide as defined by this Convention.

(5) That with regard to the reference to an international penal tribunal in Article VI of the Convention, the United States declares that it reserves the

right to effect its participation in any such tribunal only by a treaty entered into specifically for that purpose with the advice and consent of the Senate.

III. The Senate's advice and consent is subject to the following declaration: That the President will not deposit the instrument of ratification until after the implementing legislation referred to in Article V has been enacted.

Appendix D The Genocide Convention Implementation Act of 1988 (the Proxmire Act)

Title 18—Crimes and Criminal Procedure

Part I—Crimes Chapter 50A—Genocide

Sec.
1091. Genocide.
1092. Exclusive remedies.
1093. Definitions.

§ 1091. Genocide

(a) BASIC OFFENSE—Whoever, in time of peace or in time of war, in a circumstance described in subsection (d) and with the specific intent to destroy, in whole or in substantial part, a national, ethnic, racial, or religious group as such—
- (1) kills members of that group;
- (2) causes serious bodily injury to members of that group;
- (3) causes permanent impairment of the mental faculties of members of the group through drugs, torture, or similar techniques;
- (4) subjects the group to conditions of life that are intended to cause the physical destruction of the group in whole or in part;
- (5) imposes measures intended to prevent births within the group; or
- (6) transfers by force children of the group to another group; or attempts to do so, shall be punished as provided in subsection (b).

(b) PUNISHMENT FOR BASIC OFFENSE—The punishment for an offense under subsection (a) is—
- (1) in the case of an offense under subsection (a) (1), a fine of not more than $1,000,000 and imprisonment for life; and
- (2) a fine of not more than $1,000,000 or imprisonment for not more than twenty years, or both, in any other case.

(c) INCITEMENT OFFENSE—Whoever in a circumstance described in subsection (d) directly and publicly incites another to violate subsection (a) shall be fined not more than $500,000 or imprisoned not more than five years, or both.

(d) REQUIRED CIRCUMSTANCE FOR OFFENSE—The circumstance referred to in subsections (a) and (c) is that—
- (1) the offense is committed within the United States; or
- (2) the alleged offender is a national of the United States (as defined in section 101 of the Immigration and Nationality Act [8 U.S.C. 1101]).

(e) NON-APPLICABILITY OF CERTAIN LIMITATIONS—Notwithstanding section 3282 of this title, in the case of an offense under subsection (a) (1), an indictment may be found, or an information instituted, at any time without limitation.

§ 1092. Exclusive remedies

Nothing in this chapter shall be construed as precluding the application of State or local laws to the conduct proscribed by this chapter, nor shall anything in this chapter be construed as creating any substantive or procedural right enforceable by law by any party in any proceeding.

§ 1093. Definitions

As used in this chapter—

(1) the term "children" means the plural and means individuals who have not attained the age of eighteen years;

(2) the term "ethnic group" means a set of individuals whose identity as such is distinctive in terms of common cultural traditions or heritage;

(3) the term "incites" means to urge another to engage imminently in conduct in circumstances under which there is a substantial likelihood of imminently causing such conduct;

(4) the term "members" means the plural;

(5) the term "national" group means a set of individuals whose identity as such is distinctive in terms of nationality or national origins;

(6) the term "racial" group means a set of individuals whose identity as such is distinctive in terms of physical characteristics or biological descent;

(7) the term "religious group" means a set of individuals whose identity as such is distinctive in terms of common religious creed, beliefs, doctrines, practices, or rituals; and

(8) the term "substantial part" means a part of a group of such numerical significance that the destruction or loss of that part would cause the destruction of the group as a viable entity within the nation of which such a group is a part.

Notes

Chapter 1 Introduction

1 For the text of the Genocide Convention, see appendix A.

2 For a table of parties to the convention as of the end of 1989, see MULTILATERAL TREATIES DEPOSITED WITH THE SECRETARY-GENERAL (Status as at 31 December 1989) ST/LEG/SER. E/8 97–98 (1990).

3 132 CONG. REC. S1377 (daily ed., Feb. 19, 1986).

4 For the text of the resolution of ratification, see appendix C.

5 For the text of the legislation, see appendix D. The legislation passed the Senate on October 14, 1988. See 134 CONG. REC. S16107–17, S16231–32, S16266–69 (daily ed., Oct. 14, 1988). The legislation had passed the House of Representatives on April 25. For background on the bill, see S. REP. NO. 333, 100th Cong., 2d sess. 1–3 (1988).

6 See MULTILATERAL TREATIES DEPOSITED WITH THE SECRETARY-GENERAL, *supra* note 2, at 101.

7 According to Articles XI and XIII of the convention, the United States would become a party by "accession." However, throughout this book I will use the more commonly used term "ratification." The legal effect of becoming a party by accession or ratification is the same.

8 See generally L. KUPER, THE PREVENTION OF GENOCIDE (1985); and I. CHARNY, HOW CAN WE COMMIT THE UNTHINKABLE? GENOCIDE: THE HUMAN CANCER (1982).

9 For discussion of this recommendation, see the report authored by Ben Whitaker, UN Economic and Social Council, *Revised and Updated Report on the Question of the Prevention and Punishment of the Crime of Genocide*, 42–44 UN Doc. E/CN.4/Sub.2/1985/6 (1985).

10 ICJ, REPORTS OF JUDGMENTS, ADVISORY OPINIONS AND ORDERS [Advisory Opinion, *Reservations to the Convention on the Prevention and Punishment of the Crime of Genocide*] 15–69 (1951).

11 2 RESTATEMENT OF THE FOREIGN RELATIONS LAW OF THE UNITED STATES (1987). According to section 701, the United States is bound by the international customary law of human rights (p. 153). In section 702, genocide is

recognized as a violation of customary international human rights law (pp. 161–63).

12 For general discussion and summary of the advantages and disadvantages of ratification, see 132 CONG. REC. S1253–77 (daily ed., Feb. 18, 1986); the 1985 hearings conducted by Senator Orrin Hatch, chairman of the Subcommittee on the Constitution of the Senate Committee of the Judiciary, *Hearing Before the Subcomm. on the Constitution of the Senate Comm. on the Judiciary*, 99th Cong., lst sess. (1985). See also F. BOYLE, DEFENDING CIVIL RESISTANCE UNDER INTERNATIONAL LAW 291–312.

13 D. FORSYTHE, HUMAN RIGHTS AND U.S. FOREIGN POLICY: CONGRESS RECONSIDERED (1988).

14 See generally C. CRABB and P. HOLT, INVITATION TO STRUGGLE: CONGRESS, THE PRESIDENT, AND FOREIGN POLICY 13–16 (1989); M. GOLDSTEIN, AMERICA'S FOREIGN POLICY: DRIFT OR DECISION 348–50 (1984); L. HENKIN, FOREIGN AFFAIRS AND THE CONSTITUTION 129–71 (1972); J. ROURKE, CONGRESS AND THE PRESIDENCY AND FOREIGN POLICYMAKING 272–83 (1983).

15 For the text of the resolution of ratification proposed during those years and in 1984, see appendix B.

16 *Hearing on the Genocide Convention Before the Senate Comm. on Foreign Relations*, 99th Cong., 1st sess. 100 (1985).

17 Of the six senators who did not vote, two Republicans (Durenberger and Mathias) and two Democrats (Glenn and Mitchell) were reported in favor of ratification; two Democrats (Exon and Inouye) were reported absent because of illness. See 132 CONG. REC. S1377 (daily ed., Feb. 21, 1986).

18 Message from the President of the United States, *Four Treaties Pertaining to Human Rights*, 95th Cong., 2d sess. (Executives C, D, E, and F) (1978).

19 *Hearing on Constitutional Issues Relating to the Proposed Genocide Convention Before the Subcomm. on the Constitution of the Senate Comm. on the Judiciary*, 99th Cong., 1st sess. (1985).

20 For the text of the Vienna Convention see L. HENKIN et al., INTERNATIONAL LAW: CASES AND MATERIALS (BASIC DOCUMENTS SUPPLEMENT) 264 (1980).

21 *Hearing on the Genocide Convention before a Subcomm. of the Senate Comm. on Foreign Relations*, 92d Cong., 1st sess. 106–7 (1971).

22 *Ibid.*, at 106.

23 See MULTILATERAL TREATIES DEPOSITED WITH THE SECRETARY-GENERAL, *supra* note 2, at 102–4.

24 H. JACOBSON, NETWORKS OF INTERDEPENDENCE (1984).

25 *Ibid.*, at 83.

26 *Ibid.*

27 *Ibid.*

28 *Ibid.*

Chapter 2 Development of the Rule on Genocide

1 R. Lemkin, Axis Rule in Occupied Europe 79 (1944).
2 *Ibid.*
3 *Ibid.*
4 *Ibid.* See also M. Lippman, *The Drafting of the 1948 Convention on the Prevention and Punishment of the Crime of Genocide*, 3 Boston U. Int'l L. J. 2–3 (1984).
5 *Ibid.*, at 91.
6 *Ibid.*
7 Current Biography 336 (1950).
8 *Ibid.*, at 337.
9 The Secretariat's draft convention is reproduced in N. Robinson, The Genocide Convention: A Commentary 122—30 (1960).
10 2 Executive Sessions of the Senate Foreign Relations Committee, Historical Series 645 (1976).
11 *Ibid.*
12 *Ibid.*
13 *Ibid.*, at 645–46.
14 Current Biography 337 (1950).
15 *Hearing on the Genocide Convention Before the Senate Comm. on Foreign Relations*, 99th Cong., 1st sess. 132–46 (1985) [hereinafter cited as *1985 Senate Hearings*].
16 *Ibid.*, at 132.
17 *Ibid.*, at 137.
18 *Ibid.*, at 116.
19 Perlman, *The Genocide Convention*, 30 Neb. L. R. 1–2 (1950); see also testimony of Ambassador Rita Hauser, *Hearings on the Genocide Convention Before a Subcomm. of the Senate Comm. on Foreign Relations*, 91st Cong., 2d sess. 39 (1970).
20 In Rwanda, Hutus are alleged to have slaughtered Tutsis; and in Burundi, Tutsis are accused of having slaughtered Hutus. See L. Kuper, The Pity of It All 170–208 (1977); T. Melady, Burundi: The Tragic Years (1974).
21 Genocide in Paraguay (R. Arens, ed., 1976).
22 Emerson, *The Fate of Human Rights in the Third World*, 27 World Politics (1975); K. Chaudhuri, Genocide in Bangladesh (1972); L. Kuper, The Prevention of Genocide 44–61 (1985); Paust and Blaustein, *War Crimes Jurisdiction and Due Process: The Bangladesh Experience*, 11 Vand. J. Trans. L. (1978).
23 *Hearing on the Genocide Convention Before a Subcomm. of the Senate Comm. on Foreign Relations*, 92d Cong., 1st sess. 53 (1971) [hereinafter cited as *1971 Senate Hearings*].
24 Robinson, *supra* note 9, at 18–19.

25 *Ibid.*, at 22; see also Lippman, *supra* note 4, at 20–25.
26 *Supra* note 9.
27 3 UN ESCOR, Doc. E/447–623, at 139–40 (1948).
28 *Ibid.*, at 141.
29 *Ibid.*, at 143.
30 *Ibid.*, at 141–42.
31 *Ibid.*, at 145.
32 *Ibid.*, at 146.
33 *Ibid.*, at 147.
34 *Report of the Ad Hoc Committee on Genocide*, 3 UN ESCOR Supp. 6, UN Doc. E/794 (1948) [hereinafter cited as *Report of the Ad Hoc Committee on Genocide.*]
35 3 UN GAOR C.6 (78th mtg) at 145 (1948).
36 3 UN GAOR C.6 (80th mtg) at 170 (1948).
37 3 UN GAOR C.6 (79th mtg) at 153–61 (1948).
38 The matter was debated in the Ad Hoc Committee of the ECOSOC (*Report of the Ad Hoc Committee on Genocide*, *supra* note 34, at 9) and in the Sixth Committee (3 UN GAOR C.6 [92d mtg] at 303–4, [95th mtg] at 340, 358, and [128th mtg] at 660 [1948]).
39 *1971 Senate Hearings*, *supra* note 23, at 17–18, 100.
40 *1985 Senate Hearings*, *supra* note 15, at 14–15.
41 R. Woetzel, The Nuremberg Trials in International Law 96 (1962).
42 See testimony of Ambassador Richard Gardner in *Hearings on the Genocide Convention Before a Subcomm. of the Senate Comm. on Foreign Relations*, 91st Cong., 2d sess. 116–17 (1970).
43 *Hearing on the Genocide Convention Before the Senate Comm. on Foreign Relations*, 97th Cong., 1st sess. 25 (1981).

Chapter 3 The Intent to Destroy Groups

1 Bryant, Comment, *Part I: Substantive Scope of the Convention*, 16 Harv. Int'l L. J. 686, 692 (1975).
2 N. Robinson, The Genocide Convention: A Commentary 63 (1960); emphasis mine.
3 UN Economic and Social Council, *Revised and Updated Report on the Question of the Prevention and Punishment of the Crime of Genocide Prepared by Mr. B. Whitaker*, 25–26 UN Doc. E/CN.4/Sub.2/1985/6 (1985) [hereinafter cited as *Revised and Updated Report on Genocide*]; emphasis mine.
4 3 UN GAOR C.6 (73d mtg) at 97 (1948).
5 *Ibid.*, at 92–97.
6 *Ibid.*, at 96.
7 *Ibid.*, at 97.
8 *Ibid.*, at 96.
9 *Ibid.*, at 97.

10 See *Hearings on the Genocide Convention Before a Subcomm. of the Senate Comm. on Foreign Relations*, 81st Cong., 2d sess. 12 (1950) [hereinafter cited as *1950 Senate Hearings*]; emphasis mine.

11 *Ibid.*, at 4.

12 *Ibid.*, at 201–2.

13 *Ibid.*, at 204–5.

14 *Ibid.*, at 205.

15 The ABA House of Delegates voted to oppose ratification of the convention in September 1949. In February 1970, an attempt to reverse the 1949 decision failed by the close margin of 126 to 130. By 1972 every section of the ABA that had specialized competence on the matter had come out in favor of ratification, and at a meeting in February 1976, the House of Delegates endorsed ratification with the "understandings" and the "declaration" proposed by the Senate Committee on Foreign Relations (see appendix B). See Phillips, *The Genocide Convention: Its Effects on Our Legal System*, 35 A.B.A.J. 623 (1949); Phillips and Deutsch, *Pitfalls of the Genocide Convention*, 56 A.B.A.J. 641 (1970); Bitker, *Genocide Revisited*, 56 A.B.A.J. 71 (1970); Goldberg and Gardner, *Time to Act on the Genocide Convention*, 58 A.B.A.J. 141 (1972); and Resolution, 62 A.B.A.J. 475–76 (1976).

16 Other groups, especially the Liberty Lobby, replaced the ABA as critics of the convention. At the 1981 Senate hearings, the representatives of Liberty Lobby were the most outspoken. In fact, they attacked the ABA for reversing its position on ratification. *Hearing on the Genocide Convention Before the Senate Comm. on Foreign Relations*, 97th Cong., 1st sess. 78–99 (1981) [hereinafter cited as *1981 Senate Hearings*].

17 Three different drafts of an executive report were prepared in 1950, but none was ever released because the Foreign Relations Committee decided not to report the convention to the Senate. The drafts were published in 1976 in 2 EXECUTIVE SESSIONS OF THE SENATE FOREIGN RELATIONS COMMITTEE, HISTORICAL SERIES 781–805 (1976); emphasis mine.

18 See understanding no. 1 in appendix B.

19 See understanding no. 1 in appendix C.

20 2 EXECUTIVE SESSIONS OF THE SENATE FOREIGN RELATIONS COMMITTEE, HISTORICAL SERIES, *supra* note 17, at 369–70.

21 *Ibid.*, at 370.

22 *Ibid.*

23 *Ibid.*

24 *Ibid.*

25 S. EXEC. REP. 23, 94th Cong., 2d sess. 6 (1976); emphasis on *entire* mine.

26 *Hearing Before a Subcomm. of the Senate Comm. on Foreign Relations*, 92d Cong., 1st sess. 55–56 (1971) [hereinafter cited as *1971 Senate Hearings*].

27 *1950 Senate Hearings*, *supra* note 10, at 249.

28 See section 1093 (8) of the Proxmire Act in appendix D.

29 S. REP. NO. 333, 100th Cong., 2d sess. 9, 10–11 (1988).
30 *Ibid.*, at 5.
31 *Ibid.*, at 9.
32 *Ibid.*
33 *Hearing on the Genocide Convention Before the Senate Comm. on Foreign Relations*, 99th Cong., 1st sess. 16 (1985) [hereinafter cited as *1985 Senate Hearings*].
34 *Ibid.*
35 GENOCIDE IN PARAGUAY (R. ARENS, ed., 1976).
36 *Ibid.*, at 8–16, 141.
37 For a partial record of the proceedings, see AGAINST THE CRIME OF SILENCE: PROCEEDINGS OF THE INTERNATIONAL WAR CRIMES TRIBUNAL (J. DUFFETT, ed., 1970).
38 J.-P. Sartre, ON GENOCIDE 57–58 (1968).
39 *Ibid.*, at 58; emphasis mine.
40 *Ibid.*, at 79.
41 *Ibid.*, at 78–79.
42 G. LEWY, AMERICA IN VIETNAM 301–4 (1978).
43 Bassiouni, *International Law and the Holocaust*, 9 CAL. W. L. REV. 274 (1979).
44 *Ibid.*, at 275.
45 Bedau, *Genocide in Vietnam?*, in PHILOSOPHY, MORALITY AND INTERNATIONAL AFFAIRS 46 (V. HELD et al., eds., 1974). See also Falk, *Six Legal Dimensions of the United States Involvement in the Vietnam War*, in 2 THE VIETNAM WAR AND INTERNATIONAL LAW 216 (R. FALK, ed., 1969).
46 Bryant, *supra* note 1, and accompanying text.
47 S. EXEC. REP. NO. 23, *supra* note 25, at 6.
48 See section 1091 (a) of the Proxmire Act in appendix D.
49 For a table of parties to the Genocide Convention, and a list of their reservations as well as objections to those reservations, see MULTILATERAL TREATIES DEPOSITED WITH THE SECRETARY-GENERAL (Status as at 31 December 1989) ST/LEG/SER. E/8 97–105 (1990).
50 See K. CHAUDHURI, GENOCIDE IN BANGLADESH (1972); L. KUPER, THE PREVENTION OF GENOCIDE 44–61 (1985).
51 L. KUPER, THE PITY OF IT ALL 197–208; for the views of a former U.S. ambassador to Burundi, see T. MELADY, BURUNDI: THE TRAGIC YEARS (1974).
52 GENOCIDE IN PARAGUAY, *supra* note 35, at 38.
53 *Ibid.*
54 S. DAVIS, VICTIMS OF THE MIRACLE: DEVELOPMENT AND THE INDIANS OF BRAZIL 167–68 (1977).
55 Genocide Act 1969, ch. 12, 40 HALSBURY'S STATUTES OF ENGLAND 387–90 (3d ed.).
56 CAN. REV. STAT., 1st Supp. 171–81 (1970).

57 *1985 Senate Hearings*, *supra* note 33, at 4–13.
58 132 CONG. REC. S1274 (daily ed., Feb. 18, 1986).
59 S. EXEC. REP. NO. 2, 99th Cong., 1st sess. 16–17 (1985).
60 *Ibid.*, at 15.
61 *Supra* note 49, at 101.
62 See, for example, comments of Senator Symms in 132 CONG. REC., *supra* note 58, at S1284–88. See also "additional views" of Senators Pell, Biden, Sarbanes, Cranston, Mathias, Dodd, Eagleton, and Kerry in S. EXEC. REP. NO. 2, *supra* note 59, at 28–33.

Chapter 4 Protected Groups and Political Groups

1 *Report of the Ad Hoc Committee on Genocide*, 3 UN ESCOR Supp. 6, UN Doc. E/794, at 6 (1948) [hereinafter cited as *Report of the Ad Hoc Committee on Genocide*].
2 3 UN GAOR C.6 (75th mtg) at 116–17 (1948).
3 *Report of the Ad Hoc Committee on Genocide*, *supra* note 1, at 3.
4 Note #2 above, at 115–17.
5 *Ibid.*, at 117.
6 3 UN GAOR C.6 (74th mtg) at 98, and (75th mtg) at 115–16 (1948).
7 In principle, drafting international agreements always entails a choice between mere enumeration and detailed definitions. For a discussion of the relative advantages and disadvantages of each approach, see A. ROBERTSON, HUMAN RIGHTS IN EUROPE 17–18 (1963).
8 UN Economic and Social Council, *Study of the Question of the Prevention and Punishment of the Crime of Genocide* 45, 140–53 UN Doc. E/CN.4/Sub.2/416 (1978) [hereinafter cited as *Study of the Question of the Prevention and Punishment of the Crime of Genocide*].
9 CAN. REV. STAT., 1st Supp. 171–81 (1970).
10 Genocide Act 1969, ch. 12, 40 HALSBURY'S STATUTES OF ENGLAND 387–90 (3d ed.).
11 See appendix D.
12 *Supra* note 9.
13 *See* 3 UN GAOR C.6 (69th–74th mtgs) at 54–109 (1948).
14 *Report of the Ad Hoc Committee on Genocide*, *supra* note 1, at 5.
15 *Ibid.*, at 6.
16 For examples of this sort of testimony, see *Hearings on the Genocide Convention Before a Subcomm. of the Senate Comm. on Foreign Relations*, 91st Cong., 2d sess. 183 (1970) [hereinafter cited as *1970 Senate Hearings*]; and *Hearings on the Genocide Convention Before the Senate Comm. on Foreign Relations*, 95th Cong., 1st sess. 83–85 (1977) [hereinafter cited as *1977 Senate Hearings*].
17 3 UN GAOR C.6 (69th mtg) at 54–62 (1948).
18 3 UN GAOR C.6 (75th mtg) at 114–115 (1948).

19 3 UN GAOR C.6 (74th mtg) at 100 (1948).
20 3 UN GAOR C.6 (69th mtg) at 58 (1948).
21 *Ibid.*
22 Transcript of the debate setting forth the position of the U.S. representative can be found at 3 UN GAOR C.6 (74th mtg) at 101–3 (1948).
23 *Ibid.*, at 100.
24 *Ibid.*, at 101.
25 3 UN GAOR C.6 (128th mtg) at 659–61 (1948).
26 *Ibid.*
27 *Ibid.*, at 661–62.
28 3 UN GAOR C.6 (49th mtg) at 407 (1948).
29 See *supra* text accompanying note 21.
30 132 CONG. REC. S1355 (daily ed., Feb. 19, 1986).
31 *Ibid.*
32 *Ibid.*, at S1356.
33 *Ibid.*
34 *Ibid.*, at S1357; emphasis mine.
35 *Ibid.*, at S1361–62.
36 *Ibid.*, at S1379–80.
37 *Ibid.*, at S1379.
38 132 CONG. REC. S1613 (daily ed., Feb. 25, 1986).
39 132 CONG. REC. S1372 (daily ed., Feb. 19, 1986).
40 On this point, see also Rosenthal, *Legal and Political Considerations of the United States' Ratification of the Genocide Convention*, 3 ANTIOCH L. J. 117, 122–24, 142 (1985). Rosenthal suggests that anti-Sovietism was one of the three main "doctrinal rationales" embraced by opponents of ratification, the two others being antiglobalism and neopositivism. *Ibid.*, at 118–19, 133–42.
41 *Hearings on the Genocide Convention Before a Subcomm. of the Senate Comm. on Foreign Relations*, 81st Cong., 2d sess. 194 (1950) [hereinafter cited as *1950 Senate Hearings*].
42 *Hearings on the Genocide Convention Before a Subcomm. of the Senate Comm. on Foreign Relations*, 92d Cong., 1st sess. 54 (1971) [hereinafter cited as *1971 Senate Hearings*].
43 *Ibid.*, at 19.
44 *Ibid.*
45 *Ibid.*, at 114–15.
46 *Ibid.*, at 115.
47 *Ibid.*
48 See generally A. DALLIN, THE SOVIET UNION AT THE UNITED NATIONS (1962).
49 See *supra* text accompanying notes 27–29.
50 See understanding no. 5 in appendix C.
51 *1950 Senate Hearings*, *supra* note 41, at 217–18.

52 *Ibid.*

53 43 AM. J. INT'L L. 732–38 (1949).

54 *1971 Senate Hearings, supra* note 42, at 54–55.

55 See *Hearings on the Genocide Convention Before the Senate Comm. on Foreign Relations*, 97th Cong., 1st sess. 78–111 (1981) [hereinafter cited as *1981 Senate Hearings*].

56 See *supra* note 36.

57 132 CONG. REC. S1379 (daily ed., Feb. 19, 1986).

58 See *Study of the Question of the Prevention and Punishment of the Crime of Genocide, supra* note 8, at 114–17.

59 See UN Economic and Social Council, *Revised and Updated Report on the Question of the Prevention and Punishment of the Crime of Genocide* 18–19, UN Doc. E/CN.4/Sub.2/1985/6 (1985).

60 132 CONG. REC. S1254 (daily ed., Feb. 18, 1986).

61 3 UN GAOR C.6 (75th mtg) at 118 (1948).

62 *Ibid.*, at 117–18.

63 *Ibid.*, at 124.

64 *Ibid.*, at 124–25, 133.

65 See N. ROBINSON, THE GENOCIDE CONVENTION: A COMMENTARY 58 (1960).

66 P. Drost, The Crime of State: Genocide 83 (1959).

67 *1950 Senate Hearings, supra* note 41, at 261.

68 *Ibid.*, at 261–62.

69 The Ukrainian Congress Committee, for example, strongly supported ratification in 1950 and in the 1970s. See *1970 Senate Hearings*, at 165–74.

70 132 CONG. REC. S7919–21 (daily ed., June 19, 1986).

71 *Genocides and Politicides Since 1945: Evidence and Anticipation*, 13 INTERNET ON THE HOLOCAUST AND GENOCIDE (1987).

72 *Ibid.*, at 1.

73 *Ibid.*, at 4.

74 *Ibid.* See also Harff and Gurr, *Toward Empirical Theory of Genocides and Politicides: Identification and Measurement of Cases since 1945*, 32 INT'L STUD. Q. 359–71 (1988).

75 See L. KUPER, THE PREVENTION OF GENOCIDE 130–32 (1985); J. BARRON and A. PAUL, MURDER OF A GENTLE LAND: THE UNTOLD STORY OF COMMUNIST GENOCIDE IN CAMBODIA (1977); F. PONCHAUD, CAMBODIA YEAR ZERO (1978); L. KUPER, GENOCIDE: ITS POLITICAL USES IN THE TWENTIETH CENTURY 154–60 (1981).

76 See *Kampuchea*, 11 HUM. RTS. INTERNET REP., at 166 (1987).

77 *Cambodia Case*, 71 A.B.A.J. 31 (1985); *Update: Justice and Genocide*, 14 STUDENT LAWYER 12 (1986).

78 See KUPER, GENOCIDE: ITS POLITICAL USES IN THE TWENTIETH CENTURY,

supra note 75, at 138–60; AMNESTY INTERNATIONAL, POLITICAL KILLINGS BY GOVERNMENTS (1983).

79 Edwards, *Contributions of the Genocide Convention to the Development of International Law*, 8 OHIO N. U. L. REV. 300, 302 (1981).

80 K. GLASER and S. POSSONY, VICTIMS OF POLITICS 39 (1979).

81 L. KUPER, *supra* note 75, at 138.

82 132 CONG. REC. S1614 (daily ed., Feb. 25, 1986).

83 Paust, *Aggression Against Authority: The Crime of Oppression, Politicide and Other Crimes Against Human Rights*, 18 CASE W. RES. J. INT'L L. 294 (1986).

84 *Ibid.*

85 *Ibid.*, at 304–6.

Chapter 5 Genocidal Acts and Techniques

1 Lemkin, *Genocide Is a Crime under International Law*, 41 AM. J. INT'L L. 147 (1947).

2 3 UN GAOR C.6 (78th mtg) at 143–45 (1948).

3 *Report of the Ad Hoc Committee on Genocide*, 3 UN ESCOR Supp. 6, UN Doc. E/794, at 6–7 (1948) [hereinafter cited as *Report of the Ad Hoc Committee on Genocide*].

4 The Secretariat's draft convention is reproduced in N. ROBINSON, THE GENOCIDE CONVENTION: A COMMENTARY 122–30 (1960).

5 3 UN GAOR C.6 (83d mtg) at 193–205 (1948); 3 UN GAOR Plenary (178th mtg) at 818–48.

6 *Ibid.*, at 193.

7 *Ibid.*, at 194–205.

8 UN Economic and Social Council, *Study of the Question of the Prevention and Punishment of the Crime of Genocide* 45, 160–63 UN Doc. E/CN.4/Sub.2/416 (1978) [hereinafter cited as *Study of the Question of the Prevention and Punishment of the Crime of Genocide*]; R. WOETZEL, THE NUREMBERG TRIALS IN INTERNATIONAL LAW 245–72 (1962).

9 3 UN GAOR C.6 (81st mtg) (1948).

10 *Hearing on the Genocide Convention Before a Subcomm. of the Senate Comm. on Foreign Relations*, 92d Cong., 1st sess. 53 (1971) [hereinafter cited as *1971 Senate Hearings*].

11 *Hearings on the Genocide Convention Before a Subcomm. of the Senate Comm. on Foreign Relations*, 91st Cong., 2d sess. 204 (1970) [hereinafter cited as *1970 Senate Hearings*]; emphasis mine.

12 *Ibid.*, at 12.

13 See, for example, the testimony of John Norton Moore at *Hearing on Constitutional Issues Relating to Proposed Genocide Convention Before the Subcomm. on the Constitution of the Senate Comm. on the Judiciary*, 99th Cong., 1st sess. 4–5 (1985) [hereinafter cited as *1985 Hatch Hearings*].

14 *1971 Senate Hearings*, *supra* note 10, at 84–85.

15 G. Von Glahn, Law Among Nations 775–76 (1986); Woetzel, *supra* note 8, at 118–21.

16 *Report of the Ad Hoc Committee on Genocide*, *supra* note 3, at 9–10.

17 3 UN GAOR C.6 (92d mtg) at 302, 313 (1948).

18 UN Economic and Social Council, *Revised and Updated Report on the Question of the Prevention and Punishment of the Crime of Genocide Prepared by Mr. B. Whitaker*, 25–26 UN Doc. E/CN.4/Sub.2/1985/6 (1985) [hereinafter cited as *Revised and Updated Report on Genocide*].

19 *Ibid.*, at 26.

20 *1970 Senate Hearings*, *supra* note 11, at 19–20; see also testimony of Ambassador Rita Hauser at 74–75, and of Professor Richard Gardner at 111. See also testimony of Ambassador Arthur Goldberg in *1971 Senate Hearings*, *supra* note 10, at 118–19.

21 *Hearings on the Genocide Convention Before the Senate Comm. on Foreign Relations*, 95th Cong., 1st sess. 4 (1977) [hereinafter cited as *1977 Senate Hearings*].

22 See appendix B.

23 See understanding no. 4 in appendix C.

24 132 Cong. Rec. S1274 (daily ed., Feb. 18, 1986).

25 *Ibid.*, at S1275.

26 *Ibid.* For the indictment see The Palestine Arab Delegation, An Indictment of Israeli Political and Military Leaders for Genocide, Crimes against Humanity and War Crimes Against the Palestinians in the West Bank and Gaza (1983).

27 S. Exec. Rep. No. 2, 99th Cong., 1st sess. 32 (1985); emphasis mine.

28 *Report of the Ad Hoc Committee on Genocide*, *supra* note 3, at 6.

29 *Ibid.*

30 3 UN GAOR C.6 (81st mtg) at 177–79 (1948).

31 *Ibid.*

32 *Ibid.*

33 N. Robinson, *supra* note 4, at 57–65.

34 Perlman, *The Genocide Convention*, 30 Neb. L. R. 7 (1950).

35 Bryant, Comment, *Part I: Substantive Scope of the Convention*, 16 Harv. Int'l L. J. 693–96 (1975); Gorove, *The Problem of "Mental Harm" in the Genocide Convention*, Washington U. L. Q. 174–87 (1951).

36 *Hearings on the Genocide Convention Before a Subcomm. of the Senate Comm. on Foreign Relations*, 81st Cong., 2d sess. 217 (1950) [hereinafter cited as *1950 Senate Hearings*].

37 *Ibid.*, at 263–64.

38 *Ibid.*, at 255.

39 2 Executive Sessions of the Senate Foreign Relations Committee, Historical Series 373 (1976).

40 *Ibid.*, at 652–53.
41 *Ibid.*, at 651–54.
42 *1970 Senate Hearings*, *supra* note 11, at 12–14.
43 See understanding no. 2 in appendix B.
44 *1970 Senate Hearings*, *supra* note 11, at 44.
45 *Ibid.*, at 201–2.
46 *Ibid.*
47 120 CONG. REC. S2202–4 (1974).
48 *1971 Senate Hearings*, *supra* note 10, at 18–19.
49 Reference here is to section 1092 (a) (3) of the proposed legislation. See S. EXEC. REP. NO. 23, 94th Cong., 2d sess. 35–36 (1976).
50 See understanding no. 2 in appendix C.
51 See section 1091 (a) (3) of the Proxmire Act in appendix D.
52 S. EXEC. REP. NO. 2, 99th Cong., 1st sess. 23 (1985).
53 *Ibid.*
54 *Ibid.*
55 *Hearing on the Genocide Convention Before the Senate Comm. on Foreign Relations*, 99th Cong., 1st sess. 17 (1985) [hereinafter cited as *1985 Senate Hearings*].
56 *Ibid.*
57 *Ibid.*
58 See MULTILATERAL TREATIES DEPOSITED WITH THE SECRETARY-GENERAL (Status as at 31 December 1989) ST/LEG/SER. E/8 98–105 (1990).
59 BRYANT, *supra* note 35, at 695.
60 ROBINSON, *supra* note 4, at 64–65.
61 Falk, "Responding to Severe Violations" 226, in ENHANCING GLOBAL HUMAN RIGHTS (J. DOMINGUEZ, ed., 1979).
62 *1970 Senate Hearings*, *supra* note 11, at 202; emphasis mine.
63 *Ibid.*, at 193.
64 *Ibid.*, at 221.
65 *1971 Senate Hearings*, *supra* note 10, at 12–13.
66 *Ibid.*, at 91.
67 *Hearings on the Genocide Convention Before the Senate Comm. on Foreign Relations*, 95th Cong., 1st sess. 55 (1977) [hereinafter cited as *1977 Senate Hearings*].
68 *Ibid.*
69 *Hearing on the Genocide Convention Before the Senate Comm. on Foreign Relations*, 98th Cong., 2d sess. 51–52 (1984) [hereinafter cited as *1984 Senate Hearings*].
70 *Ibid.*, at 52–61.
71 *1970 Senate Hearings*, *supra* note 11, at 147–65.
72 *Ibid.*, at 148–49.
73 *Ibid.*, at 18–19.

74 R. Weisbord, Genocide? Birth Control and the Black American (1975).
75 *Ibid.*, at 178.
76 *Ibid.*, at 158–74.
77 *Ibid.*, at 170, 178.
78 *Ibid.*, at 182.
79 *Ibid.*
80 S. Exec. Rep. No. 6, 92d Cong., 1st sess. 12 (1971).
81 *Ibid.*
82 3 UN GAOR C.6 (82d mtg) at 189–90 (1948).
83 *Ibid.*, at 190.
84 *Ibid.*, at 189.
85 *Ibid.*, at 184.
86 *1970 Senate Hearings*, *supra* note 11, at 138–39.

Chapter 6 Domestic Implementing Legislation

1 Kunz, Ed. Comment, *The United Nations Convention on Genocide*, 43 Am. J. Int'l L. 738–46 (1949).
2 See generally F. Boyle, Defending Civil Resistance Under International Law 304–5 (1987); G. Von Glahn, Law Among Nations 45–48 (1986); T. Buergenthal and H. Maier, Public International Law in a Nutshell 91–114 (1985).
3 *Report of the Ad Hoc Committee on Genocide*, 3 UN ESCOR Supp. 6, UN Doc. E/794, at 10 (1948) [hereinafter cited as *Report of the Ad Hoc Committee on Genocide*].
4 *Ibid.*
5 *Ibid.*
6 *Ibid.*
7 3 UN GAOR C.6 (93d mtg) at 326 (1948).
8 *Ibid.*
9 UN Economic and Social Council, *Study of the Question of the Prevention and Punishment of the Crime of Genocide* 45 UN Doc. E/CN.4/Sub.2/416 (1978) [hereinafter cited as *Study of the Question of the Prevention and Punishment of the Crime of Genocide*].
10 *Ibid.*, at 184.
11 *Ibid.*
12 Kunz, *supra* note 1, at 744.
13 W. Jones, *The Genocide Convention and Its Relation to the U.S.* 25 S. Cal. L. Rev. 436–37 (1952).
14 *Ibid.*
15 *Study of the Question of the Prevention and Punishment of the Crime of Genocide*, *supra* note 9, at 46–47.

16 N. Robinson, The Genocide Convention: A Commentary 74–79 (1960).
17 P. Drost, The Crime of State: Genocide 100 (1959).
18 *Ibid.*
19 Kunz, *supra* note 1, at 744.
20 *Study of the Question of the Prevention and Punishment of the Crime of Genocide*, *supra* note 9, at 142.
21 *Ibid.*
22 *Ibid.*, at 141.
23 *Ibid.*
24 *Ibid.*
25 See for example, the legislation of the United Kingdom (Genocide Act 1969, ch. 12, 40 Halsbury's Statutes of England 387–90 [3d ed.]) and Canada (Can. Rev. Stat. Supp. 1, 171–81 [1970]).
26 *Study of the Question of the Prevention and Punishment of the Crime of Genocide*, *supra* note 9, at 144–45.
27 *Ibid.*, at 161.
28 *Ibid.*, at 146–47.
29 *Ibid.*, at 149–50.
30 In the early 1970s several states (Cyprus, Malawi, and Kuwait) claimed to have adopted legislation on genocide even though they were not parties to the convention. Since then, Cyprus (1982) ratified the convention, but Malawi and Kuwait had not done so by the end of 1988. See ibid., at 151–53.
31 See aba, The Convention on the Prevention and Punishment of the Crime of Genocide (an independent appraisal and brief statement of the grounds of opposition to reversal of the position taken by the American Bar Association in 1949 that "The Convention on Genocide now before the United States Senate be not approved as submitted") January 1970.
32 V. Van Dyke, Human Rights, the United States, and World Community 131–41 (1970).
33 *Hearing Before a Subcomm. of the Senate Comm. on Foreign Relations*, 92d Cong., 1st sess. 137–39 (1971) [hereinafter cited as *1971 Senate Hearings*].
34 Bricker did not want to see the Constitution and the Bill of Rights become "a mere scrap of paper," and he thought ratification of the Genocide Convention would have that effect. *Ibid.*, at 139.
35 Korey, *Human Rights Treaties: Why Is the U.S. Stalling?*, 45 For. Aff. 414 (1967).
36 Van Dyke, *supra* note 32.
37 Boyle, *supra* note 2, at 304–9.
38 N. Hevener Kaufman and D. Whiteman, *Opposition to Human Rights Treaties in the United States Senate: The Legacy of the Bricker Amendment*, 10 Human Rights Q. 309–37 (1988).
39 *Ibid.*, at 331.

40 *Ibid.*
41 *Ibid.*, at 312.
42 *Ibid.*, at 335.
43 See *Hearings on the Genocide Convention Before a Subcomm. of the Senate Comm. on Foreign Relations*, 81st Cong., 2d sess. 13–15, 31–33 (1950) [hereinafter cited as *1950 Senate Hearings*].
44 *Ibid.*, at 31.
45 *Ibid.*
46 *Ibid.*, at 31–33.
47 *Ibid.*
48 *Ibid.*, at 35–36.
49 *Ibid.*, at 35.
50 *Ibid.*, at 36.
51 See reservation no. 2 in appendix C.
52 See BOYLE, *supra* note 2, at 302–3.
53 *Ibid.*, at 304. See also Hevener Kaufman and Whiteman, *supra* note 38, at 312–18; and L. JOHNSON, THE MAKING OF INTERNATIONAL AGREEMENTS: CONGRESS CONFRONTS THE EXECUTIVE 85–91 (1984).
54 *Hearings on the Genocide Convention Before a Subcomm. of the Senate Comm. on Foreign Relations*, 91st Cong., 2d sess. 196–97 (1970) [hereinafter cited as *1970 Senate Hearings*].
55 *Ibid.*, at 156.
56 *Ibid.*, at 157.
57 *Ibid.*
58 *Ibid.*, at 147.
59 Draft legislation was introduced in Congress in 1971 and again in 1976. See S. EXEC. REP. 23, 94th Cong., 2d sess. 9, 33–38 (1976).
60 See statement no. 4 in appendix B.
61 132 CONG. REC. S1275 (daily ed., Feb. 18, 1986).
62 *Hearing Before the Subcomm. on the Constitution of the Senate Comm. on the Judiciary*, 99th Cong., 1st sess. (1985) [hereinafter cited as *1985 Hatch Senate Hearings*].
63 *Hearing on the Genocide Convention before the Senate Comm. on Foreign Relations*, 99th Cong., 1st sess. 1 (1985) [hereinafter cited as *1985 Senate Hearings*].
64 See part III in appendix C.
65 132 CONG. REC. S1274–75 (daily ed., Feb. 18, 1986).
66 *Ibid.*, at S1274.
67 *Ibid.* Hatch was concerned that a future State Department might claim that some provisions of the convention were self-executing, and he thought that the declaration "forestalls a later claim by the executive branch that certain provisions of the convention are self-executing in nature."
68 The Committee on Foreign Relations claimed that the declaration was identi-

cal to the one proposed in previous years. See S. Exec. Rep. No. 2, 99th Cong., 1st sess. 26 (1985).

69 *Ibid.*

70 *1950 Senate Hearings*, *supra* note 43, at 31–35.

71 2 Executive Sessions of the Senate Foreign Relations Committee: Historical Series 361–66 (1976).

72 Special Committee of Lawyers of the President's Commission for the Observance of Human Rights Year 1968, A Report in Support of the Treatymaking Power of the United States in Human Rights Matters 1 (1969).

73 *Ibid.*, at 2–4.

74 2 Executive Sessions of the Senate Foreign Relations Committee, *supra* note 71, at 362–63.

75 *1970 Senate Hearings*, *supra* note 54, at 196–221.

76 See generally Report in Support of the Treatymaking Power, *supra* note 72, at 8–9; L. Henkin, Foreign Affairs and the Constitution 144–48 (1972); G. Von Glahn, Law Among Nations 46–48 (1986); Boyle, *supra* note 2, at 300–301.

77 See Hevener Kaufman and Whiteman, *supra* note 38, at 314–15; see also Johnson, *supra* note 53, at 86, 94–96.

78 *1970 Senate Hearings*, *supra* note 75, at 147–65.

79 S. Exec. Rep. No. 25, 91st Cong., 2d sess. 7 (1970).

80 *Ibid.*

81 *Hearings on the Genocide Convention Before the Senate Comm. on Foreign Relations*, 95th Cong., 1st sess. 22 (1977) [hereinafter cited as *1977 Senate Hearings*].

82 *Ibid.*, at 35.

83 *1985 Hatch Senate Hearings*, *supra* note 62.

84 *Ibid.*, at 22.

85 *Ibid.*, at 23 (question no. 15).

86 *Ibid.*

87 *Ibid.*

88 *Ibid.*, at 91.

89 *Ibid.*, at 67; emphasis mine.

90 *Ibid.*, at 133–34.

91 *Ibid.*, at 2–3.

92 *Hearing on the Genocide Convention Before the Senate Comm. on Foreign Relations*, 99th Cong., 1st sess. 15 (1985) [hereinafter cited as *1985 Senate Hearings*].

93 *Supra* note 48 and accompanying text.

94 *Hearing on the Genocide Convention Before the Senate Comm. on Foreign Relations*, 97th Cong., 1st sess. (1981) [hereinafter cited as *1981 Senate Hearings*].

95 In 1981, Senator Jesse Helms said that he thought the hearings were "an exercise in futility and a waste of time," and assured everyone that the votes were not there for passage. *Ibid.*, at 4.

96 *Ibid.*, at 8.

97 *Hearing on the Genocide Convention Before the Senate Comm. on Foreign Relations*, 98th Cong., 2d sess. (1984) [hereinafter cited as *1984 Senate Hearings*].

98 *Ibid.*, at 1.

99 *Ibid.*, at 36.

100 See reservation no. 2 in appendix C.

101 132 CONG. REC., *supra* note 65.

102 S. EXEC. REP. NO. 2, *supra* note 68, at 19–21.

103 *1985 Hatch Senate Hearings*, *supra* note 62, at 11.

104 See the "additional views" of Senators Pell, Biden, Sarbanes, Cranston, Mathias, Dodd, Eagleton, and Kerry in S. EXEC. REP. NO. 2, *supra* note 68, at 28–34.

105 See MULTILATERAL TREATIES DEPOSITED WITH THE SECRETARY-GENERAL (status as at 31 December 1989) ST/LEG/SER. E/8 97–105 (1990).

106 134 CONG. REC. S16269 (daily ed., Oct. 14, 1988).

107 S. REP. NO. 333, 100th Cong., 2d sess. 7–8 (1988).

108 *Supra* note 20 and accompanying text.

109 See section 1092 of the Proxmire Act in appendix D.

110 S. REP. NO. 333, *supra* note 107, at 8.

111 See section 1091 (a) (1–6) of the Proxmire Act in appendix D.

112 See section 1091 (a) and (d) of the Proxmire Act in appendix D.

113 *Report of the Ad Hoc Committee on Genocide*, *supra* note 3, at 10.

114 *Ibid.*

115 S. EXEC. REP. NO. 2, *supra* note 68, at 8.

116 *Ibid.*, at 7–8.

117 *Ibid.*, at 8.

118 *1985 Hatch Senate Hearings*, *supra* note 62, at 14–15.

119 *1970 Senate Hearings*, *supra* note 75, at 148.

120 See section 1093 (3) of the Proxmire Act in appendix D.

121 S. REP. NO. 333, *supra* note 107, at 10.

122 *Ibid.*, at 5.

123 *Ibid.*, at 14–15.

124 *Supra* note 96 and accompanying text.

125 132 CONG. REC. S1377 (daily ed., Feb. 19, 1986).

126 *Hearing on Legislation to Implement the Genocide Convention Before the Senate Comm. on the Judiciary* (*S. 1851*), 100th Cong., 2d sess. 4 (1989); emphasis mine.

127 S. REP. NO. 333, *supra* note 107, at 14.

128 *Ibid.*, emphasis mine.

129 *Ibid.*, at 15.
130 *Ibid.*, at 9.

Chapter 7 An International Criminal Court

1 *Report of the Ad Hoc Committee on Genocide*, 3 UN ESCOR Supp. 6, UN Doc. E/794, at 11–12 (1948) [hereinafter cited as *Report of the Ad Hoc Committee on Genocide*].
2 3 UN GAOR C.6 (98th mtg) at 379 (1948); 3 UN GAOR C.6 (129th mtg) at 665–70 (1948).
3 UN GAOR Plenary (178th mtg) at 814–15 (1948).
4 3 UN GAOR C.6 (98th mtg) at 379 (1948).
5 *Ibid.*
6 For the text of the instruments of ratification, see MULTILATERAL TREATIES DEPOSITED WITH THE SECRETARY-GENERAL (Status as at 31 December 1989) ST/LEG/SER. E/8 98–101 (1990) [hereinafter cited as MULTILATERAL TREATIES].
7 *Ibid.*, at 100–101.
8 See understanding no. 5 in appendix C.
9 See understanding no. 3 in appendix C.
10 Article IX of the Secretariat's draft convention. The draft can be found in N. ROBINSON, THE GENOCIDE CONVENTION: A COMMENTARY 122–30 (1960).
11 *Ibid.*, draft Article X.
12 *Report of the Ad Hoc Committee on Genocide*, *supra* note 1, at 11–12.
13 3 UN GAOR C.6 (98th–100th mtgs) at 379–407 (1948); see also *Report of the Ad Hoc Committee on Genocide*, *supra* note 1, at 11.
14 3 UN GAOR C.6 (129th mtg) at 671–72 (1948).
15 *Ibid.*
16 *Ibid.*, at 665–70; 3 UN GAOR C.6 (130th mtg) at 673–75 (1948).
17 *Ibid.* (130th mtg), at 674–75.
18 B. FERENCZ, 2 AN INTERNATIONAL CRIMINAL COURT 22–23 (1980).
19 *Ibid.*, at 24.
20 *Ibid.*, at 23.
21 The report, entitled *Question of International Criminal Jurisdiction* (Doc. A/CN.4/15, 1950), is reprinted in ibid., at 240–58.
22 *Ibid.*, at 249.
23 *Ibid.*, at 253.
24 *Ibid.*, at 253–54.
25 *Ibid.*, at 256.
26 *Ibid.*, at 256, 257.
27 *Ibid.*, at 257.
28 *Ibid.*

29 Sandstrom's report (Doc. A/CN.4/20, 1950) is reprinted in *ibid.* at 259–64.
30 *Ibid.*, at 260–61.
31 *Ibid.*, at 261.
32 *Ibid.*, at 262.
33 *Ibid.*, at 263.
34 *Ibid.*, at 267; see also 1950 YEARBOOK OF THE UNITED NATIONS 857 (1951).
35 1950 YEARBOOK OF THE UNITED NATIONS 858 (1951).
36 *Ibid.*
37 *Ibid.*, at 858–59. For more general discussion of this line of thought, see H. KELSEN, PEACE THROUGH LAW (Garland ed.) 110–24, (1973); V. Pella, *Towards an International Criminal Court*, 44 AM. J. INT'L L. 37–68 (1950); and J. Bridges, *The Case for an International Court of Criminal Justice and the Formulation of International Criminal Law*, 13 INT. & COMP. L. Q. 1255–81 (1964).
38 *Ibid.*, at 859.
39 *Ibid.*, at 861.
40 1957 YEARBOOK OF THE UNITED NATIONS 376 (1958).
41 1 A TREATISE ON INTERNATIONAL CRIMINAL LAW: CRIMES AND PUNISHMENT 636–75 (C. BASSIOUNI, ed., 1973); see also L. Kutner, *A World Genocide Tribunal—Rampart Against Future Genocide: Proposal for Planetary Preventive Measures Supplementing a Genocide Early Warning System*, 18 VALPARAISO U. L. REV. 375–414 (1984).
42 WORLD FEDERALIST NEWS, vol. 9, no. 1, May 1989; see also H. CON. RES. 66, 101st Cong., 1st sess. (1989).
43 JOHNSON FOUNDATION, THE ESTABLISHMENT OF AN INTERNATIONAL CRIMINAL COURT 5 (1971).
44 *Ibid.*, at 4–8; A TREATISE ON INTERNATIONAL CRIMINAL LAW, *supra* note 41, at 648–53; Bridges, *supra* note 37, at 1266–81; Kelsen, *supra* note 37, at 110–24; J. STONE and R. WOETZEL, TOWARD A FEASIBLE INTERNATIONAL CRIMINAL COURT (1970).
45 See *Hearings on the Genocide Convention Before a Subcomm. of the Senate Comm. on Foreign Relations*, 81st Cong., 2d sess. 247 (1950) [hereinafter cited as *1950 Senate Hearings*].
46 *Ibid.*
47 *Ibid.*, at 24.
48 *Hearings on the Genocide Convention Before a Subcomm. of the Senate Comm. on Foreign Relations*, 91st Cong., 2d sess. 20 (1970) [hereinafter cited as *1970 Senate Hearings*].
49 *Ibid.*, at 42, 88.
50 *Ibid.*, at 204.
51 S. EXEC. REP. NO. 25, 91st Cong., 2d sess. 8 (1970).
52 *Hearing on the Genocide Convention Before a Subcomm. of the Senate Comm. on*

Foreign Relations, 92d Cong., 1st sess. 88 (1971) [hereinafter cited as *1971 Senate Hearings*].

53 *Ibid.*, at 21, 88; emphasis mine.

54 *Ibid.*, at 21.

55 *Hearing on the Genocide Convention Before the Senate Comm. on Foreign Relations*, 99th Cong., 1st sess. (1985) [hereinafter cited as *1985 Senate Hearings*].

56 *Ibid.*, at 19.

57 *Ibid.*, at 20.

58 *Ibid.*

59 *Ibid.*

60 *Ibid.*

61 *Ibid.*, at 178–79.

62 *Ibid.*, at 17.

63 *Ibid.*, at 17–18.

64 132 Cong. Rec. S1275 (daily ed., Feb. 18, 1986).

65 *Ibid.*

66 *Ibid.*

67 C. Crabb and P. Holt, Invitation to Struggle: Congress, The President, and Foreign Policy 13–16 (1989); M. Goldstein, America's Foreign Policy: Drift or Decision 348–50 (1984); L. Johnson, The Making of International Agreements: Congress Confronts the Executive 116–51 (1984).

68 L. Margolis, Executive Agreements and Presidential Power in Foreign Policy 5, 95 (1986).

69 *Ibid.*, at 26.

70 *Ibid.*, at 95–99.

71 L. Henkin, Foreign Affairs and the Constitution 173–87 (1972).

72 *Ibid.*, at 176.

73 Johnson, *supra* note 67, at 26.

74 Margolis, *supra* note 68, at 49.

75 Henkin, *supra* note 71, at 59–65, 184–87; Margolis, *supra* note 68, at 48–62.

76 Goldstein, *supra* note 67, at 349.

77 Margolis, *supra* note 68, at 97.

78 S. Exec. Rep. No. 2, 99th Cong., 1st sess. 25–26 (1985).

79 *Ibid.*, at 32–33.

80 *1985 Senate Hearings*, *supra* note 55, at 20.

81 *Ibid.*, at 179.

Chapter 8 Jurisdiction of Domestic Courts and Extradition

1 See understanding no. 3 in appendix C.

2 3 UN GAOR C.6 (97th mtg) at 363 (1948).

3 3 UN GAOR C.6 (129th mtg) at 671–72 (1948).
4 *Ibid.*
5 *Ibid.*, at 51 of annexes.
6 3 UN GAOR C.6 (131st mtg) at 685 (1948).
7 *Ibid.*
8 *Ibid.*, at 691.
9 *Ibid.*
10 T. Buergenthal and H. Maier, International Law in a Nutshell 170–71 (1985).
11 *Supra* note 6, at 692.
12 3 UN GAOR C.6 (134th mtg) at 716–17 (1948); emphasis mine.
13 *Ibid.*
14 UN Economic and Social Council, *Study of the Question of the Prevention and Punishment of the Crime of Genocide* 57 UN Doc. E/CN.4/Sub.2/416 (1978) [hereinafter cited as *Study of the Question of the Prevention and Punishment of the Crime of Genocide*].
15 *Supra* note 10, at 169–70; emphasis mine. See also J. Paust, *Federal Jurisdiction Over Extraterritorial Acts of Terrorism and Nonimmunity for Foreign Violators of International Law under the FSIA and the Act of State Doctrine*, 23 Va. J. Int'l L. 211–15 (1983).
16 G. Von Glahn, Law Among Nations 282–307 (1986).
17 Article VIII of the Secretariat's draft. The draft is reprinted in N. Robinson, The Genocide Convention: A Commentary 122–30 (1960).
18 *Report of the Ad Hoc Committee on Genocide*, 3 UN ESCOR Supp. 6, UN Doc. E/794, at 12 (1948) [hereinafter cited as *Report of the Ad Hoc Committee on Genocide*].
19 *Ibid.*
20 3 UN GAOR C.6 (97th mtg) at 363 (1948).
21 *Study of the Question of the Prevention and Punishment of the Crime of Genocide*, *supra* note 14, at 54.
22 *Ibid.*, at 52–53.
23 *Ibid.*, at 55–56.
24 See UN Economic and Social Council, *Revised and Updated Report on the Question of the Prevention and Punishment of the Crime of Genocide* 44–45 UN Doc. E/CN.4/Sub.2/1985/6 (1988).
25 See Multilateral Treaties Deposited with the Secretary-General (Status as at 31 December 1989), UN Doc. St/Leg/Ser. E/8 98 (1990).
26 *Ibid.*
27 *Ibid.*, at 100.
28 *Ibid.*
29 *Ibid.*, at 102.
30 *Hearings on the Genocide Convention Before a Subcomm. of the Senate Comm. on*

Foreign Relations, 91st Cong., 2d sess. 117–20 (1970) [hereinafter cited as *1970 Senate Hearings*].

31 *Ibid.*, at 19.

32 *Ibid.*, at 149.

33 *Ibid.*, at 60, 70–72, 117–20.

34 *Ibid.*, at 127.

35 *Ibid.*, at 127–28.

36 *Ibid.*, at 159–62.

37 See section 1092 of the Proxmire Act in appendix D.

38 See understanding no. 3 in appendix B.

39 *1970 Senate Hearings, supra* note 30, at 163.

40 *Ibid.*

41 *Ibid.*

42 See understanding no. 3 in appendix C.

43 See sections 1091 (d) and 1092 of the Proxmire Act in appendix D.

44 *Hearing on the Genocide Convention Before the Subcomm. on the Constitution of the Senate Comm. on the Judiciary*, 99th Cong., 1st sess. 79 (1985) [hereinafter cited as *1985 Hatch Senate Hearings*].

45 *Ibid.*

46 *Hearing on S. 1851 Before the Senate Comm. on the Judiciary*, 100th Cong., 2d sess. 17 (1988) [hereinafter cited as *1988 Judiciary Committee Hearings*].

47 *Ibid.*

48 *Ibid.*, at 25.

49 *Ibid.*, at 17–18.

50 *Ibid.*, at 5.

51 *Report of the Ad Hoc Committee on Genocide, supra* note 18, at 13.

52 3 UN GAOR C.6 (95th mtg) at 337 (1948).

53 3 UN GAOR C.6 (94th mtg) at 329–37 (1948).

54 Draft article VII, *supra* note 17.

55 *Report of the Ad Hoc Committee on Genocide, supra* note 18, at 13; see also 3 UN GAOR C.6 (133d mtg) at 705 (1948).

56 3 UN GAOR C.6 (94th mtg) at 333–37 (1948).

57 3 UN GAOR C.6 (95th mtg) at 337–38 (1948).

58 *Study of the Question of the Prevention and Punishment of the Crime of Genocide, supra* note 14, at 71.

59 *Ibid.*

60 *1970 Senate Hearings, supra* note 30, at 212.

61 *Ibid.*, at 56.

62 *Ibid.*, at 57.

63 *Ibid.*, at 45.

64 *Ibid.*

65 *Hearing on the Genocide Convention Before a Subcomm. of the Senate Comm. on*

Foreign Relations, 92d Cong., 1st sess. 113–14 (1971) [hereinafter cited as *1971 Senate Hearings*].

66 *1970 Senate Hearings, supra* note 30, at 46.

67 Draft legislation was introduced in Congress in 1971 and again in 1976. See S. Exec. Rep. 23, 94th Cong., 2d sess. 9, 37–38 (1976).

68 *1970 Senate Hearings, supra* note 30, at 46.

69 S. Exec. Rep. No. 6, 92d Cong., 1st sess. 11 (1971).

70 *Ibid.*

71 *1970 Senate Hearings, supra* note 30, at 70–71.

72 *1971 Senate Hearings, supra* note 65, at 84–85.

73 *Ibid.*, emphasis mine.

74 *Supra* notes 65–67 and accompanying text.

75 Multilateral Treaties Deposited with the Secretary-General, *supra* note 25, at 100.

76 *Ibid.*, at 101.

77 *Ibid.*, at 103.

78 S. Exec. Rep. No. 6, *supra* note 69, at 11.

79 *Ibid.*

80 *Ibid.*

81 *Ibid.*, at 20.

82 *Ibid.*

83 *Supra* note 67.

84 See understanding no. 3 in appendix C.

85 S. Exec. Rep. No. 2, 99th Cong., 1st sess. 10–11 (1985); see also comments of Senator Orrin Hatch in 132 Cong. Rec. S1274 (daily ed., Feb. 18, 1986).

86 S. Exec. Rep. No. 2, *supra* note 85, at 10.

87 Bassiouni, *Extradition Reform Legislation in the United States: 1981–1983* 17 Akron L. Rev. 508–9 (1984).

88 S. Exec. Rep. No. 2, *supra* note 85, at 10.

89 Leich, *Contemporary Practice of the United States Relating to International Law*, 81 Am. J. Int'l L. 936 (1987).

90 S. Exec. Rep. No. 2, *supra* note 85, at 10.

91 Leich, *supra* note 89, at 935–37.

92 Leich, *Contemporary Practice of the United States Relating to International Law*, 82 Am. J. Int'l L. 337–40 (1988).

93 S. Exec. Rep. No. 2, *supra* note 85, at 10.

Chapter 9 The International Court of Justice

1 J. Charney, *Compromissory Clauses and the Jurisdiction of the International Court of Justice*, 81 Am. J. Int'l L. 856 (1987).

2 See reservation no. 1 in appendix C.

3 J. K. Gamble, Jr., and D. Fischer, The International Court of Justice 97–103 (1976).
4 S. Exec. Rep. No. 50, 98th Cong., 2d sess. 37–41 (1984).
5 See discussion of survey by Fred L. Morrison in T. Franck, Judging the World Court 29–33 (1986).
6 Charney, *supra* note 1, at 855–87.
7 *Report of the Ad Hoc Committee on Genocide*, 3 UN ESCOR Supp. 6, UN Doc. E/794, at 14 (1948) [hereinafter cited as *Report of the Ad Hoc Committee on Genocide*].
8 *Ibid.*, see also 3 UN GAOR C.6 (104th mtg) at 440–41 (1948).
9 Both draft conventions are reprinted in N. Robinson, The Genocide Convention: A Commentary 122, 131 (1960).
10 3 UN GAOR C.6 (103d mtg) at 437 (1948).
11 *Ibid.*, at 437–38.
12 *Ibid.*, at 430.
13 *Ibid.*
14 *Ibid.*, at 437–38.
15 3 UN GAOR C.6 (83d mtg) at 193–206 (1948).
16 3 UN GAOR C.6 (103d mtg) at 438–40 (1948).
17 3 UN GAOR C.6 (104th mtg) at 444 (1948).
18 *Ibid.*
19 *Ibid.*, at 447.
20 3 UN GAOR C.6 (133d mtg) at 705 (1948).
21 Some portions of the 1950 Senate hearings were not released until 1976 in a compilation of documents of executive sessions of the Senate Committee on Foreign Relations. See 2 Executive Sessions of the Senate Foreign Relations Committee: Historical Series 786, 802–3 (1976) [hereinafter cited as Historical Series].
22 See Robinson, *supra* note 9, at 101–2.
23 See *India-Pakistan: Agreement on Repatriation of Prisoners of War*, 12 I.L.M. 1080–84 (1973); *Bangladesh-India-Pakistan: Agreement on the Repatriation of Prisoners of War and Civilian Internees*, 13 I.L.M. 501–5 (1974); Paust and Blaustein, *War Crimes Jurisdiction and Due Process: The Bangladesh Experience*, 11 Vand. J. Trans. L. 2–38 (1978).
24 G. Stanton, *Kampuchean Genocide and the World Court*, 2 Conn. J. Int'l L. 341–48 (1987).
25 *Ibid.*
26 H. Hannum, *International Law and Cambodian Genocide: The Sounds of Silence*, 11 Human Rights Q. 82–138 (1989).
27 *Ibid.*, at 136; and Stanton, *supra* note 24, at 343–48.
28 3 UN GAOR C.6 (94th mtg) at 327 (1948); see also *Report of the Ad Hoc Committee on Genocide*, *supra* note 7, at 12.
29 3 UN GAOR C.6 (101st mtg) at 410 (1948).

30 Hannum, *supra* note 26, at 135–36.
31 Multilateral Treaties Deposited with the Secretary-General (Status as at 31 December 1988) St/Leg/Ser. E/7 97 (1989).
32 Multilateral Treaties Deposited with the Secretary-General (Status as at 31 December 1989) St/Leg/Ser. E/8 100 (1990).
33 *Ibid.*, at 98, 101.
34 *Ibid.*, at 98, 100.
35 Gamble and Fischer, *supra* note 3, at 119–25.
36 Mikhail Gorbachev, *Address at the United Nations, December* 7, *1988*, 24 (Novosti Press Agency Publishing House, 1988).
37 UN GAOR, Doc. A/44/171, March 1989.
38 *Ibid.*, at 2.
39 *Ibid.*
40 Multilateral Treaties Deposited with the Secretary-General, *supra* note 32, at 98.
41 *Ibid.*, at 100.
42 Multilateral Treaties Deposited with the Secretary-General, *supra* note 31, at 101.
43 Multilateral Treaties Deposited with the Secretary-General, *supra* note 32, at 99, 101.
44 *Hearing on the Genocide Convention Before the Senate Comm. on Foreign Relations*, 99th Cong., 1st sess. 18 (1985) [hereinafter cited as *1985 Senate Hearings*].
45 *Ibid.*, at 103–4.
46 ICJ, Reports of Judgments, Advisory Opinions and Orders [Advisory Opinion, *Reservations to the Convention on the Prevention and Punishment of the Crime of Genocide*] 15–69 (1951) [hereinafter cited as *Reservations*].
47 See J. Koh, *Reservations to Multilateral Treaties: How International Legal Doctrine Reflects World Vision*, 71 Harv. Int'l L. J. 71–116 (1982); I. M. Sinclair, *Vienna Conference on the Law of Treaties*, 19 I.C.L.Q. 47–69 (1970); M. Coccia, *Reservations to Multilateral Treaties on Human Rights*, 15 Cal. W. Int'l L. J. 2–51 (1985).
48 For a general discussion see M. Pomerance, The Advisory Function of the International Court in the League and un Eras 117–25 (1973).
49 *Ibid.*, at 118.
50 *Ibid.*
51 ICJ, *Reservations*, *supra* note 46, at 16, 29.
52 *Ibid.*, at 31–48.
53 *Ibid.*, at 49–55.
54 *Ibid.*, at 16–30.
55 Pomerance, *supra* note 48, at 348–50.
56 Multilateral Treaties Deposited with the Secretary-General, *supra* note 32, at 101–2.

57 *Ibid.*, at 102–3.
58 *Ibid.*, at 101.
59 *Ibid.*, at 103–4.
60 See 132 CONG. REC. S1262 (daily ed., Feb. 18, 1986).
61 MULTILATERAL TREATIES DEPOSITED WITH THE SECRETARY-GENERAL, *supra* note 32, at 102.
62 *Ibid.*, at 102–3.
63 For the text of the U.S. declaration, see L. HENKIN, et al., INTERNATIONAL LAW: CASES AND MATERIALS 862 (1980).
64 FRANCK, *supra* note 5, at 20–25.
65 *Hearings on the Genocide Convention Before a Subcomm. of the Senate Comm. on Foreign Relations*, 81st Cong., 2d sess. 28–37 (1950) [hereinafter cited as *1950 Senate Hearings*]; see also HISTORICAL SERIES, *supra* note 21, at 652–53. The ABA vigorously opposed ratification of the convention from 1949 until 1976. Its representatives at hearings of the Committee on Foreign Relations argued, among other things, that ratification would be an improper exercise of the treaty-making power, and that the convention might be interpreted as applicable to race relations in the United States but not to atrocities committed by totalitarian states such as the Soviet Union. For general discussion of the role of the ABA and the human rights treaties, see V. VAN DYKE, HUMAN RIGHTS, THE UNITED STATES, AND WORLD COMMUNITY 129–51 (1970); and J. Schmidhauser, with L. Berg, *The American Bar Association and the Human Rights Conventions: The Political Significance of Private Professional Associations*, 38 SOC. RES. 362–410 (1971).
66 Ervin's 1970 testimony has been reprinted many times in Senate documents. See *Hearing on the Genocide Convention Before the Senate Comm. on Foreign Relations*, 98th Cong., 2d sess. 3–34 (1984) [hereinafter cited as *1984 Senate Hearings*].
67 *Hearing on the Genocide Convention Before a Subcomm. of the Senate Comm. on Foreign Relations*, 92d Cong., 1st sess. 88, 55–56 (1971) [hereinafter cited as *1971 Senate Hearings*].
68 *Supra* note 4, at 16.
69 *Supra* note 60, at S1252.
70 *1984 Senate Hearings*, *supra* note 66, at 67–77.
71 *Ibid.*, at 36.
72 *Ibid.*, at 37.
73 *Ibid.*, at 1.
74 *Ibid.*, at 36.
75 *Ibid.*, at 63.
76 *Ibid.*
77 *Ibid.*, at 62–63.
78 *1985 Senate Hearings*, *supra* note 44, at 2, 9.
79 Compare the Indian and Soviet reservations in MULTILATERAL TREATIES

DEPOSITED WITH THE SECRETARY-GENERAL, *supra* note 31, at 99, 101.

80 *1985 Senate Hearings*, *supra* note 44, at 21–22.

81 *Ibid.*, at 40–41.

82 *Ibid.*, at 22.

83 *Ibid.*, at 32–33.

84 *1984 Senate Hearings*, *supra* note 66, at 81.

85 *Hearings on the Genocide Convention Before the Committee on Foreign Relations*, 97th Cong., 1st sess. 8 (1981).

86 *1985 Senate Hearings*, *supra* note 44, at 22–25.

87 *Ibid.*, at 2.

88 S. EXEC. REP. NO. 2, 99th Cong., 1st sess. 4, 28 (1985).

89 *Supra* note 60, at S1274–75.

90 *Ibid.*

91 *Supra* note 88, at 15.

92 MULTILATERAL TREATIES DEPOSITED WITH THE SECRETARY-GENERAL, *supra* note 31, at 101.

93 *U.S. Terminates Acceptance of ICJ Compulsory Jurisdiction*, 86 DEPT. ST. BULL. 67–71 (Jan. 1986).

94 *Ibid.*

95 See *supra* note 63.

96 For Symms's comments, see *supra* note 60, at S1284–85.

97 131 CONG. REC. S12803–4 (daily ed., Oct. 7, 1985); S13163–64 (daily ed., Oct. 10, 1985); for the vote on the amendment, S13964–74 (daily ed., Oct. 24, 1985).

98 *1985 Senate Hearings*, *supra* note 44, at 40.

99 *Ibid.*

100 *Ibid.*, at 40–41.

101 *Supra* note 88, at 18.

102 *1985 Senate Hearings*, *supra* note 44, at 24–25.

103 *Ibid.*

104 *See* Charney, *supra* note 1, at 855–60; and FRANCK, *supra* note 5, at 29–30.

105 *1985 Senate Hearings*, *supra* note 44, at 24–25, 34–35.

106 *Supra* note 88, at 19.

107 *1985 Senate Hearings*, *supra* note 44, at 45.

108 *Ibid.*

109 132 CONG. REC. S1369 (daily ed., Feb. 19, 1986).

110 *Supra* note 60, at S1262.

Index

Lawrence J. LeBlanc, Associate Professor of Political Science at Marquette University, is the author of *The OAS and the Promotion and Protection of Human Rights*.

Library of Congress Cataloging-in-Publication Data
LeBlanc, Lawrence J.
The United States and the genocide convention / Lawrence J.
LeBlanc.
Includes index.
ISBN 0-8223-1109-7
1. Convention on the Prevention and Punishment of Genocide (1948)
2. Genocide—United States. 3. Treaties—Ratification. I. Title.
JX5418.L43 1991
341.7'78—dc20 90-45572 CIP